# Inside EA

## A Behind the Scenes Look at How Estate Agents Operate

Steve Lucas

# Acknowledgement

Thank you to my good friend and mind coach, Lakis Faconti, whose unfaltering assistance made the completion of this book an achievable task at a very difficult time in my life.

# Table of Contents

# Introduction

The information contained within this book is drawn from my career experience and that of the people I worked with over the years. Some of my directors, managers, and peers were amongst the most genuine folks I have ever met. The others, I would not recommend buying a home from and certainly wouldn't trust them with the sale of mine.

During my twelve years in the business, I worked for many different types of estate agencies in good and bad markets. I was involved in the sale of property at both extremes of the housing market, from multimillion-pound homes equipped with tennis courts and heated swimming pools, to rat-infested repossessions in areas that even the police were cautious of venturing into after dark. As you will soon see, it wasn't the life of big commissions, expensive suits, and BMWs that some have reported.

In fact, not only was it stressful work, but at times it was quite hazardous, too. In my first week as an estate agent, two memos were sent out from head office regarding staff safety. The first was about a sales negotiator (estate agent) who'd stepped on a used hypodermic needle while showing a former squat to a property developer. The second was about a member of staff who was hit over the head with a lump of wood and left unconscious in a vacant house. Both people recovered but left the business soon after.

Half of my career was spent with a corporate estate agency. This was a group of companies owned by a PLC that had offices in high street locations up and down the country. Their staff training was second to none, and the standards they demanded from their people went a long way to change the image of the industry. However, rogue elements still existed within the ranks, although they didn't last very long; the management systems soon filtered them out.

I also took jobs with independent estate agents ranging from single to multi-office partnerships. Some of the people I worked with were honourable individuals who ran well-established companies. They were respected members of their communities with an in-depth knowledge of their local markets that won them repeat business over the years. The partners of one particular firm I worked for displayed moral principles that the general public would not normally associate with estate agents. I once saw them turn away a lucrative business deal, because they felt it would tarnish their reputation amongst local folk. Shortly after I left the industry, I heard that they had sold their business and taken early retirement. Even though these people had survived several boom-bust cycles, I was told that a combination of market conditions and a new breed of competitor had forced their decision to call it a day.

I also had the displeasure of working with some really obnoxious characters who can only be described as compulsive liars. Their indifference to telling the truth was extremely frustrating and created a lot of stress for anyone who dealt with them. Interestingly, one such colleague was almost cured of his dishonesty by a first-time buyer—a former Royal Marine corporal whose patience he'd tested one too many times.

My career took me through two market slumps and a house-price boom. I learned from some of the best people in the business and noted the actions of the worst. I've written articles for leading trade magazines and assisted the researchers of property-related television programmes. There wasn't a lot that I didn't cover in my years as an estate agent. While I'll never claim to know everything, the knowledge that I share with you in this book you will find informative and in places, entertaining, too!

## Why did I write this book?

Property has always been an extremely topical subject—we are a nation fascinated with bricks and mortar. In recent years, I could not attend any type of social gathering without at least one person quizzing me about house prices or the practices of estate agents.

At one dinner party, there were several people in attendance with occupations far more interesting than mine—law enforcement, education, and the medical professions, to name a few. As soon as it was known that I sold houses for a living, I became the most popular person in the room.

Will the market crash? Do the agents buy all the investment properties themselves? How can I buy repossessions? Should I extend the lease on my flat? Is the freeholder asking too much? I've heard that estate agents instigate bidding wars to get higher commissions. Should I instruct more than one agent to sell my home?

The above were just a few of the questions I'd be asked. Some were valid, while others were nothing more than silly misconceptions. Nonetheless, this was the kind of information people were looking for. So instead of holding estate agency clinics at family barbecues, I thought I'd write this book. But that's not the only reason.

As an estate agent, your work brings you into contact with the general public on a daily basis. People from similar customer-facing occupations will tell you that it's not always an easy job. However, when you sell houses for a living, you are dealing with people who are going through what can be an extremely stressful experience: moving home.

I saw the various ways that different people coped with taxing situations like gazumping, chains breaking down, and sales falling through. Some handled it well, others didn't. It wasn't nice. The process of buying or selling a home can be difficult at the best of times; the last thing you need when doing so is the added frustration caused by the shenanigans of rogue estate agents.

For many years I wanted to provide people with a real insight into how estate agents operate. Having such information would help them avoid the bad agents, while recognising and getting the most out of the good ones. I would like to think that if the general public knew what went on behind the scenes, standards would be set, and certain companies would have no option but to alter their practices. Having said that, a professional man once told me that in selecting an estate agent to sell his home, he wanted an aggressive salesperson who was prepared to lie. Imagine being the buyer of his house.

During my career I saw many decent people upset by the tactics of the property industry's sharp operators. Some also lost money as a result. I witnessed intelligent individuals play straight into the hands of smooth-talking estate agents who'd make promises they couldn't possibly deliver. I also observed solicitors, surveyors, property developers, and other estate agents become quite irate at the mind games and trickery of some agents.

Throughout this book we'll be looking at the dark side of the industry, from the little white lies to illicit deals involving cash-filled brown envelopes.

Selling property is essentially a people business. No book can provide a balanced insight into the world of estate agency without mentioning the role of the general public. In my time I met some very nice people. They were rational individuals whose common sense made my job less stressful when dealing with dreaded property chains and the like. However, there were instances where buyers and sellers displayed some very unreasonable behaviour. In fact, some conducted themselves in a manner that the average human would call shameless. I'll tell you more in a little while.

Just some of the things we'll cover are:

## Estate agencies

We'll look at the different types and how each one operates—they're not all the same. I'll also provide an in-depth description of a typical working day in an estate agency office. I'll tell you about competition between rival firms and the impact on the customer—it can sometimes jeopardise your home move. Staff management, pay structure, commissions, and performance targets can lead to fierce infighting amongst staff. I'll also point out how the customer can win or lose from such scenarios.

## Home sellers

How do estate agents price properties for sale? How do you choose the right one to market your home? How many agents can you appoint to act for you? What are sole agency and multiple agency agreements, and how much commission should you expect to pay? When can having too many companies marketing your home hinder your chances of getting the best price for it? I'll tell you about different methods of advertising. We'll look at how enquiries from potential buyers should be dealt with, when viewings should or shouldn't be made, and the reasons why some people are unsuccessful in selling their home.

## Home buyers

I'll discuss how to register with estate agencies and the best way to contact them. What information will they require? As a buyer, how do you ensure you're notified when a new property comes to the market? How do you tell if a property is correctly priced? When do estate agents not take you seriously? When is paying the asking price necessary? We'll also look at the best way to present your offer and how it should be handled by the agent. You'll learn what gazumping means, and who instigates it.

## Investment property

Where do real investment opportunities come from? How are they sold and to whom? What profit margins are involved? Why should the estate agent contact you with an opportunity? I'll also explain how in some towns and cities it's almost impossible to get a "deal" from an estate agent, and that's not because they buy them themselves.

## Property repossessions

How do you recognise a repossession? What is the correct procedure for their marketing, how is the sale price agreed, and who are they likely to be sold to? I'll also clear up the misconception of them being bargains when they're never meant to be.

With every subject covered, I will provide you with appropriate examples based on real-life scenarios. There are stories that will bring gasps of disbelief, and one or two tales will raise an eyebrow, a smile, and a chuckle. If you've bought or sold property before, then you will relate to much of what I say, and hopefully, any questions you may have will be answered.

So, whether you're a first-time buyer or about to make your third home move, there's bound to be something in this book to inform and entertain you and perhaps make that next move a little less stressful.

# 1. Estate Agents

Estate agents, in one form or another, have been around for centuries. In fact, many years ago they were not known as "estate agents"—instead their job title was specific to the area in which they specialised. If a company's business was selling people's homes, they were "house agents," and if they were involved in the sale of land, they were "land agents." Other activities included auctioneering, surveying, and estate management; the latter is thought to be where the term "estate agent" originated.

Today the role of the estate agent is to market the client's property, negotiate the sale, and then follow the transaction through to its contractual stage. In return for this service, the agent is paid a commission, which is usually expressed as a percentage of the sale price. An estate agent must act in the interests of the client, who in the vast majority of cases is the seller and the one paying the agency fee.

An estate agent's involvement in a property transaction, from start to finish, can be broken down into four stages. Each one will be covered in detail in later chapters, but for now, here's a brief outline:

## Market appraisal

This is where the estate agent will appraise a prospective client's property for sale in the current open market. Many people, including agents, mistakenly refer to this process as a *valuation;* however, that term should only be applied to the service provided by a chartered surveyor. Estate agents carry out market appraisals of properties, and surveyors value them. More will be explained in chapter 4, "Selling."

## Advertising and promotion

When an agent is instructed to market a client's home, property sales particulars will be produced, which will include descriptive details, room dimensions, photographs, and floor plans, where suitable. All prospective buyers who are registered with the agent for homes in and around the corresponding price range will be contacted. Viewing appointments will be arranged, and the property's details emailed or posted to those people who do not immediately commit to see the house or flat.

Adverts will be placed in the local—and sometimes regional—press, as well as uploaded to one or more property websites. With the seller's permission, and provided that there are no restrictive covenants in place (common with flats), a FOR SALE board will be erected outside the property. This will generate enquiries from potential buyers, as well as the odd call from a nosy neighbour.

## Negotiating the deal

All offers to purchase the property will be handled by the agent and presented to the vendor both orally and in writing.

When the agent puts the offer forward to the client, he must also be able to provide certain information on the buyers. Do they need a mortgage, and if they do, what arrangements have been made? Will their prospective purchase be dependent on the sale of another property, and if so, is that property on the market? Is it under offer? How long is the chain? The last few questions will require a call to the buyers' estate agent for verification. This is a routine procedure and should be done prior to speaking to the seller.

## Progressing the sale

The price has been agreed, buyer and seller have instructed solicitors to act for them, and the estate agent has written to all parties confirming the sale. How much involvement the agent has with this part of the transaction is a debated subject within the industry. While much of what happens at this stage of the sale is outside of the agent's remit, they still have a role to play. The term "sales progressing" refers to the process of an agent keeping their file up to date with events in a running sale. They should do whatever is in their power to keep the sale moving as smoothly as possible and provide clients with regular updates along the way. This will involve regular communication with buyer, seller, solicitors, and other agents in the property chain.

## Qualifications

In the United States, a person wishing to be a real estate broker must have a license to do so. Eligibility to apply for a license requires the candidate to pass a written exam. In turn, the prerequisite for sitting that exam is the completion of several (eight in the state of California) college-level courses in subjects such as real estate practice, real estate law, mortgage, and finance.

In England and Wales, no academic or professional qualifications are required for an individual to practice estate agency, and there is no licensing procedure in place. Some firms will accept applications for employment from people with GCSEs, while others boast of only recruiting university graduates. Incidentally, both have had staff featured in television documentaries about rogue estate agents.

The closest we have to an industry qualification are the diploma courses provided by the National Association of Estate Agents (NAEA). The NAEA is the United Kingdom's leading body for professional estate agency. The organisation was set up in 1962 with the objective to uphold good practice and provide high standards of estate agency.

At the time of my membership, I had to provide two referees and obtain a technical award in the sale of residential property by passing an exam. Members are also required to continue their professional development by completing a number of hours of study on a yearly basis.

Some estate agencies insist on their senior staff being members of the NAEA. One particular firm, a well-established industry name, makes membership a condition of granting a franchise. Unfortunately, membership to the organisation and attainment of their qualifications is not a requirement for practicing estate agency.

While estate agents in England and Wales do not have to be licensed to practice, they must belong to an Office of Fair Trading-approved redress scheme. The schemes provide a free and independent service for dealing with disputes between estate agents and actual or potential buyers or sellers of residential property. Their purpose is to resolve disputes and, where appropriate, make an award of financial compensation or other action, such as an apology. If the scheme identifies serious misconduct, they have a duty to report it to the relevant enforcers. Membership to a redress scheme is obligatory for all estate agencies. Failure to join a scheme will result in a £1,000 fine, which can be repeated. The Office of Fair Trading can ban a company from carrying out estate agency work if they persistently fail to join an approved scheme.

We'll be looking at the various acts that govern the practice of estate agency in a later chapter.

## Opening hours

The estate agent's working week can be a long one. Many will work nine to six, Monday through to Saturday and have a day off during the week. Typical working hours for some agencies would be an eleven-day fortnight; once again Monday through to Saturday, although staff have the option of a half day off weekly, or a whole day every two weeks.

I have had jobs with companies where the sales negotiators worked until seven every evening, the late finish being in order to facilitate viewings or market appraisals for people after they'd finished work. In the eighties and nineties, certain offices would also be open on Sundays for several hours. During the week there were two shifts—nine to six and midday until nine.

In estate agency, the pace of business can be so fast that being out of the office, sometimes even for a few hours, can cost you a sale. I lost count of how many properties I saw come onto the market and go under offer the same day, the same morning, or even the same hour. If that's the day that you're away from the office, you're going to lose out. This is why negotiators work a lot of unpaid overtime—staying late or even coming in on their day off. Tough hours perhaps, but being available when your colleagues or competitors aren't can make a significant difference to your wages.

## Earnings

The salary of an estate agent can vary considerably, depending on the area they work in, its housing stock, and local market conditions. It's difficult to say which is the more lucrative—selling penthouses and loft conversions in big cities, or detached country homes in rural areas. In saying that, I know agents who are quite content selling three-bedroom semis in trendy suburbs. Such locations can be quite busy, and an instruction to sell a house within a popular school's catchment is usually a sale in the bag.

Most companies will pay their negotiators a basic salary along with commission, expressed as a percentage of what they earn for the company. As a very rough guide, and at the time of writing, an estate agent working in a city suburb could expect a basic salary of £15,000 with 10 per cent commission. So, if an estate agency sells a property at £300,000, and the fee payable by the client is 1.5 per cent, the company earns £4,500. If the negotiator accredited with the sale is on 10 per cent commission, their share of the deal would be £450.

With the example figures given above, in a good market, the target earnings of this person would be £30–35,000. Once again, I must stress that this is a very general guide; I've known people in similar scenarios who earn considerably more while others, a lot less.

Some negotiators work on a commission-only basis, earning as much as 50 per cent of the estate agency fee. Once more, if we use the example above, three or four sales a month would generate a pretty decent income. The downside to this is that a bad month could mean going home with no money at all.

Generally, an estate agency's commission will become due at exchange of contracts and payable on, or before, completion. Exchange of contracts is the point at which the property transaction becomes legally binding. It is also the time when the agent will invoice the seller's solicitor for payment of the commission account. The estate agency will normally receive payment of the fee from the seller's solicitor at the time of completion. This is when ownership of the property is transferred to the buyer, and the seller's solicitor authorises the estate agent to release the keys to the new homeowner, thus completing the transaction. The time period between exchange and completion is normally around twenty-eight days, but it can be less if agreed by buyer and seller.

In most estate agencies, the individual negotiator's commission becomes due when a sale completes, and it is paid in arrears the month following completion. As an example, if number 35 The Grove completes in March, the negotiator will be paid the commission in April's salary.

Even though the industry norm for estate agencies is to pay staff commission once a sale has completed, I've seen a few variations in my time. In some companies, staff commission only became due once the client's cheque had been banked and the funds cleared. So, if the house sale completed in March, but the fee was not paid until April, the negotiator would have to wait until the end of May for the money. If, for whatever reason, the seller didn't pay the agency fee, many companies wouldn't pay their staff. I even heard of an estate agency that had a minimum threshold for commission payments, and if its negotiators didn't meet that threshold, they didn't get paid. Needless to say, this company had a higher than average turnover of staff.

On a more positive note, I worked for a company that paid its staff commission the month following contracts being exchanged. They did this regardless of whether or not the sale completed, or if the client paid the fee. There are also estate agencies that pay bonuses to members of staff who exceed their performance targets. Doubled commissions, weekend breaks, or the use of a high-performance sports car for a week are just some of the incentives offered.

Exactly how much money an estate agent takes home every month will depend on the individual, whom they work for, the area they work in, and the state of the housing market at the time. Another factor that can influence an estate agent's earning potential is integrity, or lack of it. In a later chapter, we'll look at the underhand methods used by the industry's rogues to boost their salaries.

## Stressful work

Any job selling goods or services in today's competitive business world will have some degree of stress. Whether selling cars, replacement windows, or life assurance, there will be targets to meet, managers to answer to, rivals to contend with, and difficult customers to deal with. The world of estate agency is no different, although there are a few things that distinguish it from other sales careers.

Firstly, estate agents market property and land—both of which are in scarce supply. Unlike other products, you can't send an order to the factory to meet the extra demand, so competition is fierce. Secondly, if an estate agent agrees a house sale today, it could be weeks or months before they get paid, and that's only if the deal goes through. Lastly, if moving home is considered to be one of life's more stressful activities, then as an estate agent, you're dealing with stressed people on a daily basis.

There are several stages of a house sale and to make it all possible requires the involvement of numerous parties: solicitors, surveyors, banks, local authorities, and insurance companies. However, it's the estate agents who are on the front line.

When a buyer asks to renegotiate the agreed price after the survey has been carried out, someone gets gazumped, or there's a disagreement on moving dates, it's the agent's job to sort it out. Over the years, when trying to resolve such matters, I saw people react in different ways. Some were calm, composed, and logical; others would cry, scream, shout, swear, and even threaten violence.

In my role as a property sales negotiator, there were often times when I felt like a counsellor. On one occasion, I found myself in the middle of a blazing row between a married couple. A man had telephoned our office to arrange an appraisal of his home. He said he and his wife were getting divorced, and the house would have to be sold.

At the property later that afternoon, he appeared very anxious, and I soon found out why. He hadn't told his wife about the divorce. The first she knew of the matter was when she got home and found me measuring her lounge. It was then that he decided to break the news and the point at which I thought it best to leave.

In one transaction, just days before contracts were due to be exchanged, the seller accepted a higher offer through another agent. They did this even though they'd agreed to take the property off the market once the survey had been carried out. When my colleague phoned the buyer to give him the bad news, the man developed difficulty breathing and struggled to talk. We later learned that the poor fellow, on hearing he'd lost the property, had suffered a severe panic attack. Luckily it wasn't worse, as we initially thought.

One man, when outbid on a property by another buyer, was so upset that he reported the estate agency to the Office of Fair Trading, accusing them of favouring the other buyer on the grounds of racism. This claim sparked an investigation, which was immediately halted when officials discovered that the other buyer was of the same ethnic origin as the man who had raised the complaint.

A woman sat sobbing at my desk after her third attempt to buy a flat had gone wrong (only one was through me, by the way). Structural issues, a chain breakdown, and sellers changing their mind had caused this lady considerable heartache. It also left her with a bill of nearly £2,000 for survey and legal costs.

Buying or selling a home can be a testing time for many. It's often a long, drawn-out process, with no guarantee that the transaction will proceed and very little protection for those involved when it doesn't. I met many people, through my work and outside of it, who like the lady mentioned above, had several prospective purchases go wrong before they finally got the keys to their new home. For them, it was a stressful and rather expensive experience.

It's not just the public who lose money when a property deal collapses; estate agents are also left short-changed. One of my employers, a corporate agency, had calculated that each property placed on the register would cost the company £400. This was prior to commencing any form of advertising or marketing. There were times when a lot of effort and expense went into promoting a property, only to find the owner had either changed their mind about selling or sold it through another agent.

Estate agency is a job where your efforts and hard work are not always rewarded. One typical example I can remember was being called in to appraise a three-bedroom semi-detached house for both sale and rental. The property was vacant, and the owner had left it to deteriorate. In fact, its condition was so poor that getting it to a suitable state for tenants would have required considerable refurbishment.

I told the owner what sort of rent I thought he could expect once certain areas of the property were improved. I explained that although the house required some attention, it had a lot going for it. The rooms were spacious, it had a decent-size south-facing garden, and the location was excellent for schools, transport, and local shops. We discussed marketing the property for sale, and I suggested an asking price to reflect the present condition of the house but also to take into account its positive points—size and location. The owner was very pleased, although he felt I was a bit optimistic with my appraisal. He gave me a set of keys so that we could start showing the property and asked that I keep him updated on our progress.

Back at the office, we got to work immediately. Property particulars were produced, and details were uploaded to the three property websites we used, including our own. An advert was prepared for the local newspaper, and we arranged for our For Sale board to be placed in the front garden of the house. We began telephoning all prospective buyers who'd registered with us for three-bedroom, semi-detached houses in and around the price range of the one we'd just taken on.

As mentioned, the property was located in a popular turning and that, combined with our proactive marketing attempts, resulted in twenty-seven viewings in the first week. I remember devoting the entire Saturday to showing just that house. My colleagues and I attended the property in shifts in order to cover the appointments. Spending hours in a dilapidated house, which lacked central heating, and in the middle of February—it was cold! Nonetheless, we received six offers, two of which were at the asking price.

We kept our client updated and presented all offers to him both orally and in writing. As agents, it was our job to obtain the best price for the property and from the strongest buyer. With the amount of interest we'd generated, we were confident that we'd achieve our task. It was now time to bring the matter to a close. We planned to continue showing the property until the end of the week. This would allow people to see it more than once and give them the opportunity to bring their trades people along to provide quotes for refurbishment. During this time, all interested parties would be advised to submit their best offer to us in writing by midday the following Monday. The offers would then be put forward to the seller, along with information such as the prospective purchasers' ability to proceed, their financial arrangements, and chain details, where applicable.

I telephoned the seller to bring him up to date with events and to recommend that we proceed with the deadline for offers in writing—sometimes referred to as sealed bids. He was delighted with the level of interest and suitably impressed with our efforts, and so we put our plan into action.

On that Monday morning, just a couple of hours before the proposed deadline, our client came into the office to collect the keys to the house. In a very concise manner he told us that he would not be proceeding with the sale, as he intended moving into the property himself. He apologised for the inconvenience and said he wouldn't hesitate to recommend us, as we were very good at what we did. He smiled ruefully, and then left the office as quickly as his legs would take him—probably because he was embarrassed. I looked at one of my colleagues, who appeared as stunned as me. Both of us were left wondering what on earth had just happened.

And it wasn't just our own time that this chap had wasted. There were at least six people on their way to us with written offers to buy the property. One person had seen the house several times and even brought his builder along to provide guidance. We set about calling everyone who'd expressed interest in the property to advise them that the deal was off. All the people we spoke to were disappointed. Some even asked if the owner could actually do that to us without penalty. One person implied that there was foul play on our part, and another remarked that we were probably buying the property ourselves.

After all the time and money we'd invested trying to sell that man's house and after achieving offers far in excess of his expectations, we had nothing to show for it. The owner had changed his mind at the eleventh hour, and there wasn't anything we could do about it. Such was the nature of the business.

## The dreaded chain

Being in a property chain can be an incredibly frustrating experience for anyone. As the agent, you could put together what appears to be the perfect sale. The buyer and seller are motivated to move, there are no problems with the survey, the mortgage is being processed, and the legal work is moving along quite smoothly. It looks like you've done your job well, but that may not be enough. If you're in a property chain, you may only be able to move as quickly or as slowly as the rest of the chain dictates.

Imagine the following scenario. You are selling a property for your clients, a charming young family who have outgrown their two-bedroom flat and are hoping to move up the ladder to a house with an extra room and a garden. You introduce to them a very pleasant couple, first-time buyers, who love the flat and agree to buy it. Both parties are motivated, committed to the move, and apply common sense throughout. They get on so well that they've exchanged telephone numbers, so if the buyers want to measure their new home for curtains, they arrange this directly with the sellers. They even negotiate the fixtures and fittings list over a bottle of wine. Everyone is happy so far, and they think you're doing a good job—great!

Your clients find a three-bedroom, semi-detached house to buy, in their preferred location a few miles farther out from where they presently live. The agent handling the sale is efficient, polite, and always returns your calls. He advises you that his client is buying a property through another agent, and the seller, a Mr Jones, is moving into rented accommodation and not buying another home. This is the end of the chain, which is not a very long one, as it only consists of three properties: your clients', their seller's, and Mr Jones's home. Solicitors and surveyors have been instructed, and people have begun to discuss moving dates. It all looks very good.

Several weeks later, you routinely call the estate agent above you to see how things are progressing at their end. He tells you that he's waiting for an update from Mr Jones's agent and has left messages for him as well as for Mr Jones's solicitor. The next day, the estate agent calls you to say that he's just got off the phone from Mr Jones's solicitor. It now appears that Mr Jones has decided to buy another home and will not be moving out of his house and into a rented flat. What's more, there are now a further three properties in the chain, with two more estate agents, three sellers, and their solicitors. On a positive note, the person at the top is emigrating to Spain, so the chain ends there. However, the downside is that while the sale you were handling was nearing an exchange of contracts, the new transactions at the top of the chain have yet to get going. Neither your seller nor the first-time buyers are happy with the news. Any experienced estate agent will tell you that they've lost count of how many times they've encountered such situations.

There are many variations on how a scenario like the above can conclude. It could all go through quite smoothly and with minimal delay—rare, but I have seen it happen. The chain may drag on for another ten weeks before contracts are exchanged. Eventually everyone moves into their new homes, bringing a stressful experience to a close. Either way, the estate agent will get paid the commission.

A more negative outcome can be someone pulling out of the purchase and breaking the chain. This can happen for a variety of reasons, including a bad survey, redundancy from work, or people simply changing their minds.

When a property transaction fails to reach an exchange of contracts, it is known in the industry as an abortive sale—the jargon being "abo." During my time, I saw such ill-fated deals run at a rate of extremes between 18–50 per cent. In other words, as many as half of the sales agreed would fall through—a shocking statistic!

If a break in the chain causes your sale to abort, all your hard work and the excellent service you provided to your clients would amount to nothing. You can be three months into the deal, but if someone at the top of the chain pulls out, you have to start all over again. You're not likely to ever speak to or meet this person; they may be across the other side of the country, but their actions can affect your clients' home move and your commission. I've seen it happen countless times.

I remember a similar case where a family were selling their Edwardian semi in North London and going to a rented house before moving to New Zealand. Their buyers were expecting their first baby and decided to sell their flat, which was under offer to a first-time buyer, via an estate agent in a different area.

There were three sets of people and two properties in this chain, yet it dragged on longer than a chain three times the length. The parties holding everyone up were the first-time buyer and his solicitor. As for the estate agent dealing with the sale, he just didn't seem motivated to push his buyer forward. Some twelve weeks later, we were finally looking at an exchange of contracts, when our clients stopped telephoning us or returning our calls. Several days after, the husband told us that they'd found a buyer through another agent, and for more money.

While the first-time buyer in the above example was wasting time, house prices were increasing on a monthly basis. A rival estate agent saw their chance, knocked on our client's door, gave a pitch, and found themselves in the right place at the right time. Annoyingly, we'd twice warned our buyer that there was a very real danger the seller would look elsewhere. At one point we even suggested to our client that we start showing the property again as a precaution. They declined. When we phoned to tell our buyer that our client, the seller, had found a buyer through another agent, we met with verbal abuse.

The longer that a property sale in a chain drags on, the more chance there is for the deal to fall through. I've known the exchange of contracts to be held up for some very bizarre reasons, and I've described two below.

The first was the sale of a middle-aged couple's house which, for reasons I would rather not mention, was very time-sensitive indeed. We found them a buyer who was chain-free (did not need to sell another property) and was happy to move quickly. We were ready for an exchange of contracts to effect within the allotted timescale, when things suddenly ground to a halt. The delay was with the seller's solicitor, a large firm of conveyancers, who were normally very forthcoming with updates. We put in call after call and left countless messages. We chased them up for nearly two weeks, being told the person dealing with the sale was off sick, out of the office, on another call, or with clients. The buyer's solicitor experienced the same when she also tried to contact them. Eventually, contracts were exchanged.

Why was there a delay? We found out from an insider that a member of the administrative team had gone to the office stationery cupboard for supplies, taking the property file with her. She placed it on top of the cupboard in order to pick up a box of envelopes and some A4 paper. Back at her desk, she answered the phone, got busy with other work, and forgot the file. She was then off sick for the rest of the week and didn't tell any of her colleagues where the file was. Basically, we'd rushed our buyer along only to delay them because the seller's solicitors had mislaid the file.

In another case, we were involved in a chain of five properties; the one we were selling was second from the bottom. At the top of the chain was a vacant bungalow somewhere in Devon. We were near to exchanging contracts, and a completion date was agreed by all parties in the chain (solicitors cannot exchange contracts without setting a completion date).

Once again, everything stopped, and we were trying to find out why. News had filtered down the chain that the woman buying the bungalow had changed her mind about the completion date. Apparently, she owned several dogs and wanted to get her pets acquainted with the sights, sounds, and scent of the area around the bungalow prior to her moving in. The problem was that she was now unable to visit the property before the day of completion, which was the date originally suggested by her. Furthermore, we were told by the estate agents farther up the chain that unless everyone agreed to the new completion date, the woman threatened to withdraw from her sale and her purchase.

To this day, I don't know if the above story was true, or if it was a ploy by the estate agents at the top to get the rest of the chain to fall in line. Eventually, and not without reluctance, everyone agreed to the new completion date, and contracts were exchanged.

This chapter has provided a brief insight into the world of estate agency. Much of what has been discussed will be covered again in later chapters and detailed in real-life scenarios throughout the book.

Next, we look at the different types of estate agencies, their staff, and how they're structured.

# 2. Not All Estate Agencies Are the Same

Some years ago at a social gathering, a family friend asked for my advice regarding estate agents. This man's business was doing well, so he decided to sell his house and move to a larger property. He called in two local estate agents to appraise his home and instructed one of them on a sole agency basis. Sole agency generally means only one estate agency is given the property to sell. I'll explain how this works in a later chapter.

When the businessman told me which agent he'd entrusted with the sale of his home, I almost rolled my eyes in disapproval. So dubious was the reputation of this estate agency that on numerous occasions, I heard other agents refer to them as "cowboys"! In fact on hearing their name, a common reaction from local housing market insiders was, "Oh no, not them!" Luckily I didn't react that way, as doing so may have embarrassed my family friend.

As the conversation went on, I thought I'd ask what made him choose one agent over the other. His response was, "Well, estate agents are all pretty much the same, so I went with the one who recommended the highest asking price."

There was some accuracy in this man's logic; all estate agents want to sell people's homes for commission and fundamentally, they all go about it in a similar way—advertising, FOR SALE boards, websites, and so on. But that's also like saying all bricklayers are the same, because they'll all use bricks, mortar, and a trowel to build you a wall. What we're going to look at in this chapter are the different estate agencies and the different methods they use to reach a common objective: selling property.

In England and Wales, the three main types of estate agency are corporate, independent and franchised. There may be variations on each, especially so with the independent agencies, but those are the main three types.

## Corporate

These are estate agencies that are generally owned by PLCs, financial institutions, or insurance companies. Your local high-street branch may form part of a group which consists of hundreds of offices up and down the country. Sometimes the group may be made up of different estate agencies, which even though owned by the same parent company, may still be in competition with one another, especially at branch level.

The hierarchical structure of the corporate estate agency will differ depending on the scale of its operation. Below I have given an example based on my experience of working within such an organisation.

At the very top will be the board of directors at the PLC. These people may not be estate agents at all. Next, you will have the regional directors or managing directors of the subsidiary estate agencies within the group, who may also be board members. Quite often, these ladies and gentleman will have built long careers in the property industry.

In our example, the managing director will be responsible for forty offices in a particular region, assisted in their running by a team of area managers, which on this scale is likely to be four or five people.

Typically, an area manager will be a member of staff who has worked their way up through the company to this position. They will be assigned a group of offices within the region and allocated an annual budget with which to operate. The area manager will be responsible for things like the profit or loss of each branch, health and safety issues, advertising expenses, and the recruitment of personnel, to name a few. Generally, the resolution of customer complaints should not have to go beyond this level of management, and only very serious matters are escalated higher.

Area managers earn a basic salary and commission based on the profitability of their allocated offices. This may also come in the form of bonuses or profit sharing. At this level of management, the benefits include share options, pension schemes, health care, an allowance for personal expenses, and a company car. They get to choose the latter from within an agreed budget or by class of vehicle, although all the area managers I knew drove prestige cars.

The offices within an area manager's group may differ from one another, as will the structure of teams that work in them. Here is an example of how a busy high-street branch might be set up and a description of the individual staff member roles.

## The office manager

This person should be competent and have a proven track record in all aspects of estate agency work. They will have also received training in human resource issues, as well as how to correctly supervise and motivate staff. Corporate estate agencies focus heavily on management being proficient in delegation, and there are several reasons for this.

Firstly, one of the office manager's tasks is to report weekly and monthly statistics to the area manager. This includes figures such as how many properties (new instructions) the office listed on their books against the number of market appraisals carried out; how many prospective buyers (applicants) registered with the company and, of those people, what number had property to sell in the agency's area; the total figure for viewing appointments made; how many sales were agreed; and how many sales were aborted. These are just some of the figures that are collected, and the responsibility for doing so lies with the office manager.

Also, many companies have operational procedures in place to ensure that they are in compliance with the various acts that govern the practice of estate agency. Once again, it is the office manager's job to ensure his team conform to the rules.

To give you an example, the Property Misdescriptions Act 1991 was passed to prohibit the making of false or misleading statements about property matters in the course of estate agency and property development business. One estate agent described this act as having taken away his poetic license! Basically, this meant that anything said or written about a property had to be accurate. An estate agent's defence under the act is to prove that they took reasonable steps and exercised all due diligence to avoid committing the offence.

When a property is measured and described, it is standard procedure for the promotional material to be checked at several stages during production. I've known occasions where as many as four people endorsed the accuracy of a house's particulars of sale: the negotiator who measured the property; the administrator who produced them; the office manager who checked them, and finally, the homeowner who approved them. As you can see, a key part of the office manager's workload is ensuring his branch complies with the Property Misdescriptions Act.

Generally, office managers are paid a basic salary and a commission, which is expressed as a percentage of the office's turnover. Of the corporate estate agencies I knew and worked for, managers did not earn commission for any sales they made personally. Also, they did not get paid until a month after the company had received the cheque from the seller's solicitor in settlement of the account. On the rare occasion when the home-owner failed to pay the estate agency fee, the managers would not get paid either. Other benefits enjoyed by office managers are company cars, share options, and a private pension.

Effective delegation of tasks allows the office managers to take a step back from front-line estate agency work. This, in turn, enables them to carry out their own role, plus supervise, train, and motivate their staff. Interestingly, a couple of guys with whom I worked took delegation a bit too far, to the point where we were all wondering what it was they actually did for their salary!

One last point before we move on—an estate agency manager can be quite influential on who gets what property. I've seen clever psychological manoeuvring deployed by some cunning individuals to steer people in and out of property transactions. Nobody was any the wiser, and it was all perfectly legal. I've included real-world stories in later chapters that will provide examples of such scheming.

## Senior negotiators

Dedicated and well-organised senior negotiators can be an extremely valuable asset to their manager. I've known many senior negotiators who competently run the office while their managers were out improving their golfing handicap.

Often thought of as assistant managers, senior negotiators carry out many of the same tasks as their bosses: market appraisals, sales progressing, assisting with paperwork, and even staff training. However, the senior negotiator is assigned targets for achieving sales, which requires their involvement in arranging and carrying out viewing appointments. They are also expected to introduce prospective buyers and sellers to the other services offered by corporate estate agencies—mortgage and finance, as well as conveyancing—which we'll talk about in a while.

In the context of their company's career progression model, senior negotiators should be aspiring office managers. They are involved in managerial tasks and maintaining their own performance-related goals. They do not have the decision-making power of their team leader, but they also don't have the responsibilities.

In a busy high-street branch, there could be two or more senior negotiators who either divide the role's duties between them or are assigned specific tasks. One may carry out all the market appraisals for the office, the listing or inspecting negotiator, while their colleague may be responsible for progressing the running sales files, the sales progressor.

Senior negotiators are paid a basic salary plus commission on personally achieved sales. There are also bonuses payable for introducing customers who take up any other services that the estate agency has to offer. A listing negotiator may be paid commission on properties that they get onto their agency's books once those properties have been sold. The agent responsible for progressing the running sales may be paid a commission for every property that proceeds to the legally binding stage of contracts being exchanged. The benefits enjoyed by a senior negotiator include a company car, and they may also qualify for share options and the company pension scheme.

## Negotiators

The primary role of the negotiator is to agree property sales and provide customer leads and introductions to the mortgage consultant based in their office. Just like their senior colleagues, they are given monthly performance targets to work towards.

Negotiators are responsible for registering prospective buyers' details for the mailing list and alerting them, as well as those already registered, of properties new to the market. They arrange and carrying out viewings, and they handle all offers to purchase, negotiate, and close the deals. Occasionally the office manager may ask the negotiator to check on the progress of a sale and update the file. Negotiators may also attend market appraisals with their office manager or a senior negotiator. Such tasks can be looked at as training for the negotiator.

When an enquiry comes in, be it from the Internet, newspaper, magazine, leaflet, or the estate agency's FOR SALE board outside a property, the negotiators, and sometimes seniors, are the first point of contact for the public. Sales staff are required to answer the phones quickly—usually within three rings—and any visitors to the office are to be greeted as soon as they walk through the door. Being the first negotiator to pick up the phone or acknowledge the potential buyer entering the office can get you a sale, and with it, the commission. I lost count of how many times I saw a person walk into an estate agency, register their details, ask to view a property, and the deal was agreed within the hour.

I once answered the phone to a housing group who told me they needed to find six flats in as many weeks. I ended up selling them five. Three were already on our books, whereas the other two came from my efforts in leafleting various roads. My colleagues were extremely envious; one of them even tried to get in on the action and resorted to underhand tactics, which I'll talk about a bit later in chapter 12, "Infighting."

The pay structure of a negotiator is very similar to that of their senior colleagues: basic salary (lower than that of a senior) plus commission on personally achieved sales. There may also be incentives for negotiators who assist in bringing properties to the market, and bonuses are also payable for providing customer leads to the estate agency's other departments—lettings, conveyancing, and mortgage.

## Mortgage consultant

Estate agency can be an excellent outlet for selling mortgages and their related insurance products. In fact, there have been instances where agents have seen more profit from arranging home loans than from selling people's properties.

There have even been months where, as a result of estate agency introductions, more loans were agreed on a particular mortgage product than the lender was able to do directly on their own.

In order to provide a quality mortgage service, one capable of achieving the volume of business mentioned above, corporate estate agencies use a simple but effective system. A mortgage consultant is based in each branch, and the estate agency teams are tasked with obtaining as many customer leads for that consultant as they can. This is incorporated into the sales negotiators' monthly performance targets, and corporate bosses place great emphasis on achievement in this area.

This means that almost all prospective buyers who make contact with the estate agency must be offered the company's mortgage services. When a person visits the office to register their property requirements, the negotiator will suggest suitable homes, arrange viewings, and try to get them in front of the mortgage consultant. When someone telephones the estate agency to enquire about a property they've seen advertised, they too are a mortgage appointment prospect. Sellers, if moving up the property chain and requiring a loan to do so, are also offered the service.

The aim is to get the mortgage prepared to the point that the loan becomes subject to the survey being satisfactory. This means that the credit checks and any documents or references associated with the mortgage application are dealt with before the client finds a property to buy. Both the customer and the estate agent benefit from things being done this way.

The mortgage departments of large estate agencies have strong links with certain lenders. Sometimes, these banks or building societies may offer the estate agencies exclusive packages with incentives for their customers—a free survey, paid legal fees. So going through the estate agency may save money on certain mortgage products.

When the customer finds a suitable home, and their mortgage is ready, they will be in a position to proceed quickly if required to do so by the seller. Also, if there is more than one buyer interested in the same property (a very common scenario today), the people who have bothered to get their finances in place may be favoured by the seller, providing there isn't a great difference in the offers, of course.

Lastly, if the property is being sold by the same agents who arranged the mortgage, they will have more to lose if the transaction goes wrong; so it's in their best interests for the deal to go through. The benefit to the agent, other than the extra commission, is that they are working with a buyer whose financial position has been pre-approved. Agreeing a house sale to someone who can't get a mortgage is bad PR for the agents. Not only is it a waste of time and money, but it also makes the agent look bad to their client, the seller.

Having a list of buyers whose finances are already in place can assist the agent in taking properties onto the market. When appraising a home for sale, the estate agent is likely to be up against several competitors. Being able to offer the property owner quality buyers who are ready to move, can put the agent at an advantage over their rivals. This worked for me many times during my career, and both buyer and seller were happy on each occasion.

If the prospective purchaser is happy with the mortgage service, yet finds a property through another agent, all is not lost. The estate agency will still earn revenue from the mortgage and any related insurance product taken by the customer.

Mortgage consultants work longer hours than their estate agency colleagues, typically because they schedule their appointments to suit their clients' working hours. When the sales negotiators are packing up to go home, the mortgage consultant may be just starting the final client meeting of the day, and these can last over an hour. They work Monday to Saturday, but have a day off during the week.

Unlike estate agents, mortgage consultants must pass several exams before they can practice. Once they are qualified, they must operate within the guidelines set by the industry's regulators.

## Office administrator

In all the years I worked as an estate agent, in every location at which I was based and every sales team that I was a member of, the office administrator was female. These women would also refer to themselves as the office secretary, and they played a vital role within the team.

The office administrator's many duties include preparing property brochures and uploading the details to the company website, typing letters, answering phones, updating the customer database, maintaining the office window display, and archiving and indexing records. Some managed all the above tasks and more, as well as spoiling their colleagues with frequent cups of tea or coffee.

All administrative personnel are trained in and expected to be fully conversant about matters relating to the Property Misdescriptions Act 1991. They are an extra line of defence against possible infringements of the act by the estate agency.

When a property is taken onto the market, the office administrator prepares the brochures using the dictated or written notes provided by the listing negotiator. This is the first checkpoint against errors in the property's description that could leave the agency exposed under the Property Misdescriptions Act. Several of the office administrators with whom I worked never failed to pinpoint mistakes in their estate agency colleagues' written depiction of buildings, including spelling and grammar.

Some of the women I worked with would assist with registering prospective buyers and arranging viewing appointments, even though they were not required to do so. Occasionally the viewings would convert to sales, but very rarely was the transaction attributed to the office administrator. If any commission was paid, it was at the discretion of area managers or directors. Typical working hours for the office administrator are nine to five Monday to Friday.

## Staff training

Anyone involved in the business of estate agency needs to be familiar with the acts that govern the industry. Estate agents must follow certain procedures in order to conform to the legislation, and staff training in this area alone is crucial. Also, in a competitive business like estate agency, the better your staff are at what they do, the longer your company will be around.

There are several options available for estate agencies wanting to train their people. Organisations such as the National Association of Estate Agents (NAEA) run courses that are hosted by experts in the field. There are also many companies that specialise in providing bespoke training for estate agency personnel. In saying that, the corporate estate agencies that I knew of did not outsource their staff training. These companies would provide in-house tuition for their people at their own dedicated training centres. These buildings had classrooms that were specially set up to record telephone role plays between staff in different rooms. Mock customer appointments would be videotaped, and the results analysed by the trainers. Here, too, exams were taken, ensuring staff were up-to-date on legislative requirements. It was all quality stuff.

## Operational procedures

Estate agency is a very competitive industry. Being able to recognise an opportunity and capitalise on its earning potential is essential for survival in the business. One estate agency had a system in place that, when followed by staff, made sure such opportunities were not missed. The system was not specific to local markets, so it was replicated in every office throughout the country. I'll explain exactly how it works in forthcoming chapters, but for now, here's a brief outline.

A person makes contact with the estate agency. If they are a first-time buyer, or they are simply looking to buy a home without having to sell one, the negotiator will try to find them a suitable property. If the person requires a mortgage, then this is a lead for the financial services department of the estate agency. This buyer can also be a potential client of the estate agency's conveyancing arm.

If the prospective buyer has a property to sell, and it's located in the area that the estate agency covers, it's the negotiator's job to try to get that property onto their register. This is perhaps considered the number one opportunity that the negotiator should always go for. Failing to do so, especially when the area manager is around, will cast doubt on your career progression. So potentially, this estate agency office could earn from selling a person's property for them, selling one to them, arranging the mortgage, and handling the legal work for the sale and purchase.

What if the prospective buyer's property is located outside of the estate agency's catchment? This is where the corporate office network and referral system comes into play. Here's how that scenario should work.

A person registers as a buyer with an estate agency in North London. That person has a flat in South London to sell. The negotiator working in the North London office should still offer the company's services for selling, but they will pass the referral on to their colleagues south of the river, who in turn will contact the homeowner to offer their services. However, the North

London agent should, if applicable, offer the prospective buyer an introduction to the mortgage consultant based at that office. If they don't, the South London team will.

The same thing can work the other way around. A Hertfordshire-based estate agent appraises a house, the owners of which would like to move to Cambridge. The Hertfordshire agent can pass his prospective clients' details (with their permission) to his counterparts in Cambridge. The Cambridge agents will register the Hertfordshire homeowners as prospective buyers and notify them as and when new properties come to the market. Once again, if the Hertfordshire agent has not offered the company's mortgage services to his prospective clients, the guys and girls in the Cambridge office should.

This referral system, when used correctly, is an excellent way of obtaining customer leads. Also, the leads are not cold; they are people who have expressed interest in buying or selling property. They are also people who have given consent for their details to be passed to the relevant estate agency branch within the group.

Business being referred through a large network of offices is a unique selling point for corporate estate agencies. However, in my experience, the referral system worked best between offices in neighbouring areas. I say this because during my time with a large corporate firm, the vast majority of our customer leads came from offices based in adjoining postcodes to ours. So on a local scale, the interoffice referral system also worked well for small independent estate agents, and I'll give examples in a short while.

All estate agencies, regardless of their size or type, must follow certain operational procedures in accordance with the acts that govern their industry. We'll be taking a look at such procedures in forthcoming chapters.

## Office catchments

Each branch within a corporate estate agency operates within its own geographical areas, which are usually defined by postcode. Sometimes two offices will share a postcode, but in doing so, they must stay within their designated boundary and cannot take on properties that fall outside of their catchment. I'll explain what this means and how it works.

A prospective seller takes note of a SOLD board outside a property in the road next to theirs. As this person is thinking of selling their own home, quite naturally, they decide to call in the agents whose number is on the board. They telephone the estate agency to arrange an appraisal but are told their details will be passed to another office that deals with their street. Basically, their property is right on the border of two offices, but it falls just within the boundary of one. This is not to say that both offices cannot market the property at the same time; in fact, many estate agencies operate this way.

In certain locations, property prices can vary considerably from one end of the postcode to another. Quite often, some parts of a town are considered trendier than others. Where this is the case and the postcode or town is split between two offices, prospective sellers tend to approach the one based in the more upmarket of the two areas. The rationale is that that estate agency office will achieve a higher sale price than the other. Once again, if a person has contacted the wrong office, the negotiators must refer them to the right one, although not everyone follows the rules!

I remember working for a corporate estate agency where the boundaries and catchments for each branch were clearly defined by head office. There were no grey areas, and everyone knew exactly where their territory ended and the other offices' began. One particular branch was located in a very popular part of town, and the rascals who worked there exploited this to the full. Whenever they were approached by someone wishing to sell a property, and that property was situated just outside of their territory, they'd take the instruction and not refer it to the relevant office. This was a sneaky tactic that not only impacted their colleagues' earnings and performance figures, but also affected the public. I'll explain exactly how in a later chapter, but now, let's look at the other types of estate agents.

## Independents

This type of estate agency can vary considerably from one company to the next. Some have branches nationwide and employ hundreds of people. At the other extreme, I've known single-office estate agencies that were successfully run by two people. I even knew someone who single-handedly ran a letting agency from his home, using his garage as an office.

I've also known of independent estate agencies that were owned by solicitors, surveyors, property developers, accountants, stockbrokers, and plumbers, to name a few. In saying that, during my time in the business, most of the estate agency owners whom I met had worked for a corporate at some time during their career.

A number of the larger independent companies are set up and operated much in the same way as corporate estate agencies. They also have a hierarchical structure similar to that of their corporate counterparts, with managing and regional directors, office managers, senior negotiators, and so on. Other similarities are the additional services they offer: financial, legal, and surveying.

As already mentioned, some firms have branches up and down the country, while others are more localised, operating on a regional level. I knew of one company that had six offices across two neighbouring boroughs. All their offices were located within the catchments of the most popular schools within those boroughs. Furthermore, the predominant properties in these locations were semi-detached family homes.

Another key point in this company's geographical setup was that most of the buyers they dealt with would consider living in several of the locations they covered. Many people also chose to stay within these areas when moving up or down the housing ladder. This meant that the estate agency often had two or more property sales in the chain—selling for their clients and to them. Also, each office would market the other offices' properties.

This was a very successful setup. Whether it was strategically built this way, or it evolved with the market, I'm not sure. What I will say is that locally, this firm could rival the marketing of any of its competitors, large or small, corporate or independent.

Even small, single-branch estate agencies can extend the marketing of properties beyond their own efforts. They can enlist the help of other local agents, striking up agreements to share the sales commission, known in the industry as a "half-comm." Another, more formal, way of sharing property instructions is through an estate agency network.

Such networks bring together independent estate agents from around the country and combine their property registers into one. Each member agent uploads their property listings via an Internet portal to a centralised database. That database is visible to other agents in the network, who contact the listing agent for viewing arrangements on the relevant properties. If one member sells another's property, the commission is shared; how it is divided differs between networks.

Membership to an estate agency network allows the small independent estate agent to multi-list their clients' homes in a similar way to that of their larger competitors. The network's Internet portal and referral system puts the smaller agent in partnership with other member agents across the country. I must point out, though, that during my time in the business, the referral systems of both the independent and corporate networks saw more success on a local rather than national scale. We did receive enquiries from different parts of the country, but these were quite rare.

## Niche markets

In my experience, where a specialist area of the property market existed, whether it was country homes or city loft flats, an independent estate agent was always the dominant player. Corporate firms still had a piece of the market, either through departments set up specifically for that niche, or by the acquisition of firms already established in the field. However, during my years in the business, the most successful niche specialist I saw was an independent estate agency.

This company was hugely successful in the marketing of high-end detached homes in affluent London suburbs. They were firmly established in the different locations they covered as the estate agent to celebrities, sports personalities, and the business and professional elite. A real measure of their accomplishment was that their FOR SALE boards were like status symbols. Having one of their boards outside your property meant that you were successful enough to deal with the same agent that the rich and famous did. Whilst no single estate agency will ever totally dominate their area or niche, this firm held a very large percentage of the business wherever they were based.

## An independent setup

We're now going to look at an example of how an independent estate agency is structured and the way business is conducted. In order to best illustrate the differences between them and their corporate counterparts, I've chosen to depict the smaller independent agency. This is a one- or two-office setup, typically owned by one person or a partnership.

## The directors

The majority of independent estate agency owners whom I met had worked in the industry for several years before deciding to set up on their own. Most of them had learnt the business while working for corporate agencies or multi-office independents. In contrast, I met two estate agency owners who'd never worked as agents prior to opening up their own businesses; although they both had experience in property development.

Directors of small estate agency firms tend to be very hands-on with their business. They will carry out market appraisals, register prospective buyers, make viewing appointments, and negotiate the sales. Where there is a partnership, the directors may divide the workload between them. Sometimes, one may be more adept than the other in a particular area of estate agency. They may be set up so that one partner deals with the sellers, and the other handles all the buyer enquiries, and so on.

Many of the independent estate agency directors I knew happened to live and work in the same area for most of their careers. People would buy their first home from them, then years later, when it was time to move on, they'd use the same agent to sell it for them. One such estate agent told me that his firm had been instrumental in one man's home move three times in twelve years. They'd sold the chap a flat when he was a first-time buyer, then moved him and his new wife into a house, and finally sold him another flat when he and his wife got divorced.

In my experience, the people who own independent estate agencies tend to be closer to their local community than their corporate counterparts. I've known these men and women to sponsor school fetes, organise neighbourhood watch schemes, and head up their town's chambers of commerce or business groups. One was even a governor of a secondary school.

My former employers turned away a lucrative contract to sell several flats, as they felt it would damage their reputation amongst local residents. It was a controversial building development, the planning permission for which was heavily opposed. The people who built it were very difficult to deal with and were known to treat prospective buyers very badly. For example, someone proceeding to buy one of their flats would have to put up with the property remaining on the market and fully available for viewing, right up until an exchange of contracts. It didn't matter how quickly a buyer would move or how much money that buyer had spent on surveys and legal fees, this company would readily accept a higher offer through any one of the many agents they used. My bosses didn't want to be involved in such messy scenarios, and they didn't want to represent unscrupulous sellers, as they felt it was bad for future business. Unfortunately, not all local estate agents displayed the same integrity.

Directors of small independent estate agencies do not have the same security as their corporate counterparts; if their business has a bad month, they may not get paid. One estate agency owner told me that during a difficult run in the housing market, she and her partner did not take a salary for three months, ensuring staff were paid first. In another partnership, the directors earned what they described as a "living" wage and would supplement this with quarterly bonuses, but only if the business had done well during that period. In saying this, all of the estate agency owners whom I knew were also property investors and benefitted from a secondary income. Some were buy-to-let landlords, and others dabbled with development and refurbishment projects.

I remember a chap who owned a successful single-office estate agency. His firm's SOLD and LET BY boards were dominant over those of other agents in the local area. He drove a £30,000 car and had a fondness for fine Italian suits; he boasted of owning a dozen of them. One day, during conversation, he claimed to have never taken a salary from his business in the three years since setting up. However, within the same time frame he'd built a portfolio of nine rental properties, which he said came as a direct result of owning the estate agency. This agent also mentioned that he'd bought, refurbished, and sold "a few" other flats; the profit from one of them paid for his car.

Directors of independent estate agencies are less restricted than their corporate counterparts when it comes to buying property that's listed on their books. As long as the independent estate agent informs the seller that it is they who intend to purchase the property, and they haven't purposely undervalued its worth, then they are acting within the rules. In one particular case that I remember, the estate agent waived the agency fee as a sweetener for the homeowner to agree to the sale. It is not as easy for corporate estate agency directors to do the same, as there are very strict rules on staff purchasing their clients' properties. There are systems in place to ensure the agent is paying the correct price for the property, and should they wish to resell it within twelve months from the purchase, they must inform another director.

Estate agents buying property from their clients is a practice open to abuse by the industry's rogues. This is why many agencies have procedures in place to ensure that an employee's purchase of such a property is conducted in an ethical manner.

## The staff

As mentioned earlier, some single-office partnerships will have little or no staff at all. A typical setup may be the two directors, an office administrator, and perhaps a negotiator. In some smaller independent agencies, administrative personnel may only work on a part-time basis.

One particular company that I worked for had two offices, each headed by one of the partners. The staff of this estate agency consisted of three negotiators, an office administrator, and a part-time negotiator who assisted with weekend viewing appoint-ments. The offices were located within a mile of each other and were identical in their setup—same property listings, client database, and so on. The staff had access to all the information they required to carry out their work, regardless of which office they were based at. This allowed for people to alternate between the two branches as and when business volumes would dictate.

## Office managers

Some estate agency directors, especially those involved in property development, may not want to be directly involved in core estate agency work. Where this is the case, an office manager will be tasked with the day-to-day running of the business.

The office manager may be an individual who gained their experience while working for a large estate agency chain. It is also possible that their present employer trained them on a one-to-one basis before giving them the responsibility of running the office.

Generally, the office manager should be accomplished in all areas of estate agency. What tasks they carry out on a daily basis will depend on how the office is set up and the team they have around them. Most managers will focus their efforts on market appraisals and obtaining property instructions, sales progress-ing, and supervising staff. One chap I knew only ever got involved in the latter two tasks, and he did them very well.

The pay structure of an office manager within a small indepen-dent estate agency differs widely from one company to another. Typically, managers are paid a basic salary plus a percentage of their office's turnover as commission. Some managers receive additional bonuses, which I've known to include a share of the company profits. One agent told me that he was quite happy working on a commission-only basis, which he claimed to be at 40 per cent of what his office earned.

During my years in the business, I never knew a small independent estate agency to provide its employees with perks such as pensions or private health care. However, in saying that, one estate agent told me his director paid for him to see a consultant surgeon after a health scare. The directors of another firm, after a successful year, rewarded their manager's efforts by upgrading his company car to a prestige model.

On the subject of company vehicles, nowadays, more and more of the smaller estate agencies opt to provide their employees with a car allowance rather than a company car itself. This way staff are paid a monthly allowance to use their own vehicle for work purposes; they may also invoice their employer for fuel costs, but any increase in the insurance premium will be the employee's responsibility.

## Negotiators

Within a small firm of estate agents, the negotiator role may vary, depending on the office setup. If the director is very hands-on, or an office manager is employed, the negotiator's duties may be purely to sell property. They contact buyers, send out property particulars, arrange and carry out viewings, and maybe negotiate offers to purchase. If the director is less involved with front office activities and not customer facing, then the negotiator may play a more senior role. Along with selling properties, they may carry out market appraisals, prepare particulars, negotiate sales, and progress those sales through to exchange of contracts.

Negotiators are paid a basic salary plus commission, either expressed as a percentage of what they've earned for the company (personal commission), or a percentage of the office turnover (pooled commission). As mentioned, some negotiators will work on a commission-only basis.

## Mortgage consultant

Many smaller estate agencies do not offer a mortgage advisory service to their customers. Often this is because business volumes do not warrant the costs of employing a full-time mortgage consultant. Also, some agents prefer to focus solely on property sales and simply don't want to get involved in the mortgage side of things. Those that offer the service usually do so by having a business agreement with an independent financial advisor to whom they introduce clients. The financial advisor will arrange to meet the clients either at the estate agency, his office, or their home.

## Office administrator

The role of the office administrator within a single office estate agency is very similar to that of the larger independent or multi-branch corporate. The only notable difference that I recall was with the working hours. Some smaller firms would only employ office administrators on a part-time basis as opposed to the nine-to-five, five-day week of the larger estate agencies.

## Staff training

As mentioned earlier, the people who own small estate agencies, in most cases, are experienced estate agents who've spent several years in the business. Such individuals do not need ongoing training and generally only return to the classroom when a new piece of legislation is introduced to the industry.

Employees of small independent estate agencies usually get on-the-job training from their directors or managers. Managers and senior staff may belong to trade organisations such as the NAEA, which provide regular training courses to their members. There are also companies that provide bespoke courses for small and medium-sized estate agencies.

## Operational procedures

Many small estate agencies use the same work systems as their larger independent and corporate counterparts. Perhaps this is so because a lot of the people who own and run small estate agencies once worked for the big firms, and so they adopted the same business systems. When I was recruited to assist in starting up a new estate agency office, most of what I implemented I'd learnt through my years of working for a corporate. These were tried and tested systems that worked for the multi-branch national estate agencies and could easily be adapted for the single-office agency, too.

Smaller estate agencies have more flexibility in how they operate. If a particular procedure becomes cumbersome, or a more effective way of doing things is found, the smaller independent agent can apply changes quickly. With a larger firm, new ideas must be approved by several layers of management, which may include compliance officers, too. Sometimes, if a new procedure is not deemed suitable company-wide, it may be scrapped regardless of whether it would improve business in selected offices. This was my personal experience.

## Office catchments

In the example of corporate estate agencies, I mentioned that they can only operate within the geographical areas defined by their head office. A single-office estate agency does not have the same restriction; they are free to choose what properties they take onto the books and where.

I have seen estate agencies take on and sell property located several miles from the office—a practice made easier by the use of the Internet. In contrast, I knew of a small independent firm that refused to take on flats in a block that was located across the road from its office. The building's managing agents were notoriously difficult to deal with and as such, caused a string of property sales to abort, hence the estate agent's reluctance to get involved.

Generally, home sellers prefer to instruct an estate agent who is based locally to them. It's common sense, really; if a buyer wants a garden flat in any one of a particular group of roads just off the high street, they're likely to visit the agent(s) located in that immediate vicinity. Good estate agencies will usually have a strong board presence in the roads immediately surrounding their office.

There are exceptions to the above, assisted more by the introduction of the Internet, but also having occurred long before the use of any website.

Some years ago, while working for a small firm of estate agents, I was called to a property situated in an area we didn't normally deal with. In fact, between the property and our office, there could've been half a dozen or so other agents to choose from. However, I was familiar with the location and its properties. People I knew lived in an adjacent road, and I'd been involved in selling houses around there while working for another firm years before.

On this occasion, we'd been recommended to the owner by their relative. We were instructed as sole agents and began marketing immediately. We had lots of interest in the property and achieved the asking price within ten days of it going onto the market. The owner was delighted.

A few days later, one of the neighbours asked if we could have a look at their home. I visited the property, provided an appraisal, and told them that I had a list of people who were interested in the other property, but had lost out. Once again, we were instructed as sole agents. I called all the people who'd seen the other property on that road and had an offer on it before the first advert hit the local newspaper.

Amazingly, the above scenario was repeated once again, two weeks later. And the owner of that property bought a house, through us, just minutes from our office. It must be said, though, I never did anything again on that road for the duration of my time in estate agency in that area.

In summary, a single-office independent estate agency will, within reason, list properties anywhere they feel they'll be successful—they have that flexibility. Obviously, they will focus their efforts first and foremost on the area immediately surrounding their office.

Now, we move on to the last type of estate agency.

## The franchise

Anyone wishing to start their own estate agency business can do so by setting up as an independent or by buying a franchise.

Like any other franchised business, an estate agency franchise allows an individual or partnership to trade under an established name using a tried and tested system. Also, the franchisor will provide support and guidance on various aspects of running an estate agency. In return, the franchisee will pay the franchisor a percentage of their turnover on an ongoing basis. This is in addition to any initial outlay and setup costs.

In essence, the owner of a franchise is still an independent estate agent, but there will be certain terms and conditions that must be adhered to. For example, all advertising must follow a specific format, and any special promotions or marketing must have the prior approval of the franchisor.

Also, not just anyone will be granted a franchise, and there are many conditions that must be met. For example, some franchisors insist on all franchisees and their senior staff being members of the NAEA. The purpose of such a condition is to ensure that a high standard of estate agency practice is upheld, as membership to the NAEA requires taking the association's technical award or diploma course.

In general, the people who own and run franchises come from an estate agency background. And having worked for this type of estate agency, I would describe their individual offices as being somewhere between those of the corporate and independent firms.

## Staff

The staffing structure of a franchised estate agency is often the same as that of an independent firm. The various examples I have given of how small independent estate agents are set up could easily be applied to franchises.

Franchisees have several options available to them for training their staff. Firstly, they can train them themselves in the form of on-the-job training. The franchisor will provide regular training courses, usually outsourced to specialist companies. The NAEA is also a valuable resource for staff training in all aspects of estate agency work. Training courses hosted by the franchisor or the NAEA will be at an additional cost to the franchisee.

## Operational procedures

All estate agents must follow certain procedures if they are to operate in accordance with the acts that govern their industry. Beyond that, how an agent runs their business is pretty much up to them. This is more true for the independent estate agent rather than the other types.

As mentioned, the corporate estate agency branch will work to a system as set out by their head office. Where the franchisee is concerned, as long as they adhere to the conditions of their franchise, then the day-to-day running of the office is their concern; however, they do not have the same freedom of the independents.

When I worked for a franchise, all our business stationery, advertising, and promotional material had to state that we were a franchise. We may have had the franchisor's name over the door, but on our letterheads, cards, and inside the office, we were required to display that we were trading as an independent company.

Our newspaper advertising had to follow a certain format; any changes required the franchisor's prior approval. On one occasion, we ran a feature advert for a specific property. It was a three-bedroom house that belonged to a family. The woman was studying interior design and made a project of her home—very successfully, I might add.

We fought off fierce competition to win the instruction. The house was stunning, and I knew that neither we nor any other agent would have trouble selling it. Also, I could see that the owner was very proud of what she'd achieved with her home, so I told her I'd run a special advert—centre page, featuring both internal and external photos. My idea worked, and the property went under offer very quickly. The franchisor, on the other hand, expressed displeasure that we had not notified them before altering the advert (an advert we were paying for) and asked that we didn't repeat the oversight.

Another time, shortly after setting up the new franchise, we decided to run a promotional campaign. Anyone who instructed us to sell their home within a specified time period would be given a discounted fee, subject to certain conditions. One condition was that they instruct us on a sole agency basis (no other agents involved), and the other was that they allow us to put our FOR SALE board outside the property.

The purpose of our campaign was to get our cash flow moving but also to gain a board presence in the area. Having a strong board presence leads to more enquiries from both buyers and sellers and in turn, more business.

Our plan started to work. We provided people with a good service, and they got their homes sold for a discounted fee; meanwhile, our FOR SALE and SOLD boards began springing up everywhere. Local residents we knew commented on how well we seemed to be doing and slowly, referrals came in. We must've been doing something right, because our competitors started complaining. Unfortunately, amongst those who disapproved of our strategy was another franchisee, who reported us to the franchisor. We were contacted by head office and asked, nicely, to halt the campaign. It was felt that our discounts were having a negative impact on franchisees in surrounding locations.

I like to think that in the above scenarios, we were both resourceful and creative in an extremely competitive arena. We did nothing that was illegal, deemed unethical, or that breached the guidelines of the trade associations of which we were members. However, we were a franchise and had to abide by the franchisor's terms and conditions; besides, the brand name above our door alone brought us many enquiries.

## Office catchments

Just like the corporate and multi-branch independent estate agencies, the catchments of franchised firms are determined by their head office.

Where a property is located on the border of two franchised offices, and its owner approaches the wrong one, the enquiry must be referred to the correct franchisee. It's regarded as a very serious breach of the rules to take instructions to sell a property in another franchisee's catchment.

If a house or flat is to be marketed by more than one office, this will be by agreement between the franchisees and at the discretion of the one within whose area the property falls.

This chapter and the last have provided a brief insight into the different types of estate agencies and how they operate. In the next chapter, we'll examine the good and bad points of the three types of estate agencies we've mentioned.

# 3. The Pros and Cons

## The corporate

The most obvious benefit for the larger estate agencies is the marketing strength they have through their network of offices. The referral systems mentioned earlier are very effective. There's also power in the brand name and inspired confidence in dealing with a well-known company that's been around for a while.

Staff training is taken very seriously and is ongoing. Considerable investment is made in this area, from new employee induction through to senior management programmes. Additional courses are run to ensure staff are up to date on subjects such as new legislation and changes in market conditions.

Customer complaints are dealt with through the hierarchical management structure. If a negotiator has done something wrong, you can speak to their manager. If the issue is not resolved at this level, there will likely be an area manager or managing director whom you can contact, although involving the latter usually means a serious offence has been committed.

From my own experience and through customer feedback, the fees of larger estate agencies were usually higher than those of their smaller competitors. There were times when rates were matched, but generally the bigger firms charged more.

Members of the public would often tell me that they felt the larger estate agencies lacked the personal touch of the smaller independents. One of the reasons given for this was that the bigger firms have a higher turnover of staff, especially when compared to a local partnership operated by just the two directors.

Below is a typical scenario given by people when they explained how high staff turnover could hinder that personal touch.

A person is looking to buy a flat and registers with all the estate agents in their area of choice. They build a rapport with a negotiator and the staff of an agency on the high street. The negotiator gets to know the buyer's requirements and works to find them the right property. The buyer is happy and proceeds to purchase a flat.

Three years later, that person is looking to sell their flat in order to buy a house. They contact the same estate agency they bought through, only to find that neither the negotiator or the rest of the staff work there anymore; some have left the company, others have been moved to different branches.

This is a common scenario, and while there are exceptions—like the senior members of one corporate office living and working in the same area for over ten years—they're quite rare.

The larger estate agencies can be quite rigid in their approach to advertising. For example, if a branch manager wanted to run a special marketing campaign, they'd need the approval of their regional manager or head office. And in my experience of such circumstances, the answer was always a resounding no. I'm sure there were reasons for this; however, it got to the point where we stopped suggesting or even thinking about ways to improve how we did things. Any special promotions were the brainchild of head office, and they were applied regionally, not to any specific area or property.

So as a negotiator, imagine you've just taken a house onto the market, the garden of which looks like it's been designed by Alan Titchmarsh and built by Tommy Walsh. Your head office is unlikely to sanction an extra photo of that garden in the weekly advert, no matter how much enthusiasm you try to rub off on them.

Another point regarding advertising is that people tend to think that the larger estate agencies spend more on their newspaper ads than the smaller agents. Obviously, a company with twenty branch offices will have a greater advertising budget than a company with only one. However, next time you look at an estate agency's double-page advert, check how many different offices that ad lists.

I've seen as many as eight different branches located in different parts of a borough advertise in the same edition of a newspaper at once. The company's advert covered the centre spread, but each branch only got to advertise four of their own properties. So while this large, two-page advert appeared quite grand, the cost would've been taken from the budget of the eight offices it featured.

In the above example, if you're listing your home for sale with one of the eight featured branches, your property may not get advertised in the newspaper every week. Obviously, which property is advertised, and when, is at the branch manager's discretion. Also, if a prospective buyer calls from an advert to enquire about a particular property, it is the negotiator's job to present that caller with other similar properties that the agency has on their books. So an advert for one property can help to sell another.

While the larger estate agency companies have bigger marketing budgets, they may not spend more on advertising per office than some smaller independents, as we'll see in a moment.

## Independents

Once again, we'll be basing our examples on the smaller independent estate agency, the type owned and operated by a sole trader or partnership. As mentioned earlier, a good independent estate agent can provide their customers with the personal touch. Let me give you an example.

Years ago, I worked for a small independent estate agency that was based in a North London suburb. The company had two offices that were located a couple of miles apart, with each one headed up by one of the two partners. I was the senior negotiator in one of the offices.

One morning, not long after joining the company, I arrived for work at exactly the same time as my boss. We parked our cars and made our way to the office. Several local residents, one after the other, greeted us good morning as we walked along. My boss explained who each person was and that they'd bought their home through our company. He then gave a brief summary of the transaction—the type of property, its price, location, and when the sale went through.

Former customers, both buyers and sellers, had kept in touch with the company and were always waving hello as they passed by. On occasion, some of these people would stop into the office for a chat, asking how the market was doing and what we thought their house was worth today.

One particular family had purchased a property that required complete refurbishment. Both husband and wife were DIY enthusiasts and rather adept, too, because they did an excellent job remodelling the house. Three years later, they were looking for their next project, but as my director explained, it wasn't purely a commercial venture. The couple was moving up the property ladder and needed a bigger home. What they wanted to do was buy a rundown property, renovate it themselves, and complete it to their exact preference. He told me that they'd probably live in the house for a few years and then repeat the process again once they'd outgrown their home. They weren't looking for the same profit margins that the professional developers worked to, either. All they wanted to do was to have a newly refurbished home, to their specifications, and not lose money on their investment.

The couple did not want to put their house onto the market until they'd found a suitable property to buy. Generally, this is not the best way of doing things, and I'll provide the reasons why in a later chapter; however, they'd built a rapport with my boss and he, knowing how saleable their home was, said we should persevere with the situation.

Just over a year later, we found the couple the perfect property. We agreed the sale to them and less than a week later, received an asking price offer on their house. On the day that contracts were exchanged, our company's fees for the two transactions became due and were in excess of £15,000.

Such a scenario was possible because the estate agent knew his local market well, got to know his customers, and understood their requirements. Now, you might say that any good estate agent should do that—regardless of the size or type of their company— and you would be right. However, when the director of a small independent estate agency hands a buyer the keys to their new home, they're thinking of the future and repeat business. That buyer then becomes a potential seller and furthermore, a seller that the agent may have already built a relationship with.

In the example I gave above, the couple came to our company as prospective buyers and returned a few years later as both sellers and buyers. During those years, they got to know and trust the agent they bought through, who in turn, gave them his time and advice—the personal touch.

I'm not saying that such a level of service isn't provided by the larger companies. There are examples of senior staff with the bigger estate agencies who have been at the same branch for well over ten years. In that time, they've got to know local residents and have seen countless buyers and sellers come and go. What I will say is that the high staff turnover of the estate agency industry as a whole means it's rare to see staff working in the same branch for many years.

Another point worth mentioning is that the men and women employed by the bigger agencies usually have monthly sales targets, which are reviewed by managers. So, if we apply the old adage "time is money," a negotiator will probably not want to visit a property he sold to a previous buyer just to see what they've done with the place and let them know if its value has increased. This is especially so when they've already told him that they've no immediate plans to sell, and also when his regional manager wants to know why he didn't personally sell eight properties last month.

The small local estate agency owner doesn't have a manager to answer to. So if she decides to spend thirty minutes of her day looking at a previous buyer's refurbished flat whilst chatting about market conditions over a cup of tea, it's her business and her decision. Furthermore, if the homeowner is not selling just yet, the agent will still view them as a prospective client, because she plans to be around when they do decide to sell.

Another area in which the small independent estate agent has more freedom than their corporate counterparts is fees. The owner of a small estate agency can charge whatever fee works for them—they will not have an area manager to scrutinise the minimum fee level. Here's an example of what I mean.

While working for a large estate agency, I was invited to appraise a house that was situated on a very popular road. We'd sold a similar property in the same location just a few days before. I explained to the prospective seller that we had a lot of interest in the neighbouring property and received several offers as a result. We now had a list of "hot" buyers who would be keen to see his house; therefore we would not need to spend as much on advertising, so I could offer him a discounted fee. I also told him that I'd have his property under offer within a week.

Now chances were that some, if not all, of those hot buyers were also on the registers of the other agents who were called in to provide appraisals. However, the seller liked what we had to offer and gave me the instruction. We received an asking price offer within twenty-four hours of taking the property onto the market. The buyers were a couple who missed out on the previous house we sold on the same road.

Our estate agency fee for selling the above property was £6,250; however, several weeks later, after checking the monthly figures, my area manager questioned why I'd given the seller a 0.25 per cent discount from our minimum fee.

As mentioned earlier, high staff turnover is an industry-wide issue that affects large and small estate agencies. However, this shouldn't really be a problem when the business is run by its owners or directors. If less senior staff come and go, this will not impact the company as much if the bosses are customer facing and play an active role in the day-to-day running of their firm.

With regard to advertising, I've known small independent firms that run far more extensive marketing campaigns than their corporate competitors. Obviously, I don't mean that a single-office estate agency spent more money on advertising than a corporate giant. I'm referring to the marketing done at branch level. Let me explain.

I worked for an independent estate agency in a small town centre. Their immediate competition was the office of a large corporate (where I was based some years before) and several independent estate agencies, one of which had branches nationwide.

Where the larger estate agencies took double-page adverts in the local newspaper, these would be shared by at least four of their branches. The single-office independent took a whole page to itself every week.

Where online advertising was concerned, the bigger firms would use their own websites along with one or two well-known property portals. The smaller company was on six different websites, or at least that was the number at which I lost count.

Whether advertising on half a dozen different websites was worth the investment or not, we certainly got the buyer enquiries coming in. So at branch level, the smaller firm spent more money on advertising than its much larger competitors.

Staff training is perhaps an area of the business where the small estate agent loses out to the bigger independent and corporate rivals. There are specialist firms that provide estate agency training, and their courses cater for smaller companies; however, costs are high, and throughout my career, I never worked with a firm who sent their staff on such courses.

As mentioned in a previous chapter, owners of small estate agencies generally tend to be very experienced in their trade. If they do have staff, they will train them themselves. However, such training will not be as structured as that of the bigger companies.

If the director of a small independent estate agency has upset you, what recourse do you have? Well, if they've breached any of the rules that govern their industry, you can report them to the relevant authorities, such as the Office of Fair Trading, or any trade association they may belong to, like the NAEA. However, if your complaint is that you don't care much for their attitude, or you dislike the tone of their voice, there's not a lot you can do about it.

In a larger company, if a negotiator has been discourteous, you can speak to his manager. If you feel the manager has been impolite, then you can contact his area manager, and so on. Obviously, no company owner inside or outside of estate agency should want to gain a reputation for bad customer service, but humans are not infallible, and personalities do clash.

Whenever I discuss this subject, I'm reminded of a story told to me by a very experienced estate agent, in which he confessed to being less than tolerant with a difficult customer. A member of the public walked into the agent's office to register as a prospective buyer. The middle-aged woman was very specific in her property requirements and told the agent, in a very direct way, not to send her properties that differed in the slightest to her requests. The agent agreed and began to take her contact details. When he asked if she needed to sell her home in order to buy another property, the woman erupted.

"I don't see why that's any of your business," she said rather sharply.

"Madam, I have a duty to provide my clients with at least an outline of a prospective buyer's position and their ability to proceed with a purchase. I'm sure you would expect the same service from your estate agent," he replied. The agent then attempted to explain that most sellers would not remove a property from the market if their buyer's own property was not under offer. The sharp-tongued woman wasn't interested in what he had to say and interjected, "Well, if we ever get to the position where you find me a suitable house—and judging by your attitude I think that's most unlikely—then you can pry into my finances. Until then, whether or not I need to sell my home is not your concern. Now, if you persist with this manner, I will want to see your manager!"

"I am the manager, madam," was the agent's reply.

"Well, your director, then. Your treatment of customers is appalling!" she snapped.

"I own this estate agency and do not want you as a customer, so please leave!"

The lady persisted. "What association do you belong to? I will be making a complaint."

"Madam, the only association that I belong to is the local angling association. So, unless you'll be reporting me for fishing trout without a rod license, then I don't think they'll be interested. Now get out of my office!"

Under normal circumstances, the estate agent would've have dealt with such a thorny customer in a different way. He would have been pleasant and agreed with everything she said. Then he would have waited for her to leave the office before throwing their details in the bin. However, on this occasion, the estate agent admitted to having an argument with his ex-wife thirty minutes or so before that rather difficult woman walked into his office.

## The franchise

As mentioned in the previous chapter, a franchised estate agency may be viewed as being somewhere between the corporate estate agency and the small independent. That was my view when working for such a company, and my director at the time often complimented my pragmatism.

We operated under a branded name and followed the rules and guidelines as set out by head office; however, our company director was based in our office every day. Our customers would get the marketing strength of a large estate agency but also the personal attention of the company director, who worked in the branch.

In terms of customer service, or indeed complaints, dealing with the owner of a franchised estate agency is similar to dealing with the owner of a single-office independent. The only difference is that a customer who feels their complaint has not been correctly addressed by the franchise owner can take that complaint to the head franchisor. It's worth pointing out that while the franchisor may speak to the franchisee about the customer's grievance, they can only enforce action if a serious offence has been committed.

I remember a real-life scenario that perfectly illustrates the above. A prospective seller disagreed with our appraisal of his property. The chap had told us that he owned a four-bedroom terraced house. When we got there, we found that it had three bedrooms on the first floor and two receptions on the ground floor, one of which was being used as the fourth bedroom.

We explained to the home owner that we could not appraise his house as a four-bedroom property simply because there was a bed and wardrobe in the second reception room. The gentleman did not share our views and after arguing with our director, he complained to our head office that we'd been rude. Our director received a call from the franchisor who suggested that we call the prospective seller and apologise. Our director refused, and that's where the situation ended.

Franchised estate agencies can spend as much money on their advertising as they can afford. As long as their marketing material meets with the approval of the franchisor, then it's really up to the franchisee how many pages they take out in the local paper or how many websites they advertise with.

During my time with such an estate agency, the owners of neighbouring franchises would group their adverts together in the local press. Four offices would take half a page each, allowing the franchisees to have a two-page spread between them. My boss would alternate his weekly advertising between a whole page in the busy months and half a page at quieter times. In fact, during weeks when there was a bank holiday, we wouldn't advertise in the local press at all. Response was very poor and hence not worth the cost.

A condition of one estate agency franchise was that each office paid a sum into a central advertising fund on a monthly or yearly basis. That money would then be used to run campaigns in the national and regional press, property supplements, and glossy magazines. Not all offices would be included in every advertising run; instead, the adverts would alternate between the different offices. Eventually everyone would get to take part in the campaign, but it was rare that any one office was allowed to submit more than a couple of properties at a time for advertising.

The franchisees would also contribute to the production of a quarterly magazine featuring a larger selection of each participating office's properties. This was a good-quality publication that included information on housing market conditions as well as articles on other property-related subjects. My opinion of such marketing campaigns was that they were more effective in creating brand awareness than actually selling properties off the page.

Franchised estate agencies will have staff training made available to them through their franchisor. The company that I worked for had dedicated classrooms where courses were taught by in-house tutors. On occasion, external consultants were brought in to lecture on their particular area of expertise in estate agency. I remember attending an important seminar, the subject of which was the proposed introduction of home information packs (HIPs). The event was held at a plush venue in London, and the guest speaker was a very prominent figure within the property industry. The purpose of the event was to help us understand HIPs and how they would change estate agency work.

After the seminar, when talking about HIPs with other estate agents, I found that I was far more knowledgeable on the subject than they were. In fact, a significant number of those agents knew nothing at all about HIPs. This wasn't altogether strange, because at the time the law had only just received royal assent, and many companies didn't ever expect HIPs to be launched anyway. So the point I'm making is that the franchisor's proactive approach ensured the franchisees had up-to-the-minute information on changes to their industry.

The only drawback to such seminars and training courses was that they were not cheap, and as a result, franchisees were reluctant to send their staff on these courses too frequently, especially when business was tough. In my personal experience, where the corporate and large independents were concerned, staff training was not optional; it was compulsory. Courses were held in-house and were paid for by head office, which meant everyone had to attend.

Franchised estate agencies, like the small independent agents, can pretty much charge whatever they like, or so you would think. As mentioned in a previous chapter, we ran a promotion to mark the opening of our new franchise. Our special offer was a 50 per cent discount on our standard selling fees. While this was a generous offer, at the time there were estate agencies that were advertising zero commission for selling people's homes (we'll be discussing this in more detail later). Nevertheless, the franchisor frowned on our methods and suggested we withdraw our promotional offer immediately. It was felt that our discounted fee offer was having a negative impact on other franchisees in the area.

Basically, we were not free to set our estate agency fees at a level we wanted. Then again, if you were running a fast food franchise, you'd be expected to charge standard prices.

In ending this chapter, I will say that during my entire career in the property industry, the most sincere agents I ever met were from all three types of estate agencies, as were the most devious and dishonest ones.

# 4. Selling

Sellers are the lifeblood of any estate agency. Buyers are important, too, but it is the property vendor that provides the business with its stock, which in turn attracts the property purchaser.

Sellers pay the agent's fee; so good or bad market, they are king. This sentiment is reflected perfectly in the different ways estate agents treat buyers and sellers.

A good friend of mine is a tradesman with a long line of satisfied customers, all more than willing to give recommendation. A more honest and sincere chap you couldn't hope to meet. Dressed in his work clothes, he walked into a local estate agency, a reputable firm, and in his Cockney accent announced that he wanted to buy a house in the area. The negotiators didn't even look up from their desks. As soon as my friend mentioned that he needed to sell his home, which was also situated locally, both negotiators stood up and immediately ushered him to a seat. My friend chuckles every time he recounts this story.

One of the key factors for the house price boom of recent years has been the scarcity of property. As a seller, you hold a product that is in short supply. Estate agents need your home and will compete fiercely with one another to win your business. So if you have a dozen local agents covering the area you live in, how do you go about selecting the right one to sell your home?

In my experience, many people will instruct an estate agent based on which one suggests the highest asking price for their property or quotes the lowest fee for selling it. Some people's choice of agent will depend on whether or not they liked the negotiator who carried out the market appraisal. I've also known people to instruct the agent whose office is nearest their home.

Another common selection criterion, and in my opinion a sensible one, is calling in the agent who's most active in the locality—the one displaying the most For Sale and Sold boards. A rare variance on this was the woman who instructed a particular estate agent to sell her flat because she liked the colour scheme of their boards.

Common dilemmas for prospective sellers include: must they market their property before finding one to buy, or should they make an offer on one and then put theirs up for sale? And lastly, is it best to instruct one agent (sole agency) or several (multiple agency)?

To answer these questions and many more, we'll look at what estate agents do from the point of the prospective seller's enquiry through to when the property is sold.

## Market appraisal

When planning a home move, the first thing you'll need to do is find out how much your own home is worth. Today, anyone with access to the Internet can get a pretty good idea of how property prices are performing in their area. There are websites that provide data on what houses actually sold for, along with the many sites that advertise properties currently for sale. Even before the Internet's advent, checking local newspapers and estate agents' window displays could provide a homeowner with a guideline on their property's value.

Even after carrying out their own research, the vast majority of prospective sellers will call on a local estate agent to recommend an asking price and market their home. And the start of this process is the market appraisal.

Many people, including some agents, refer to a market appraisal as the "valuing" of a property. This is incorrect. So before we move on, let me explain the difference between the two.

When carrying out a market appraisal, the estate agent provides the homeowner with a figure of what their property is likely to achieve in the current market. The agent is stating that if the property is put up for sale now, it is likely to sell for X, or thereabouts. They are not saying this is a definite outcome, and many will have disclaimers saying so in their small print. Also, an estate agent's market appraisal figure cannot necessarily be used in legal or financial matters relating to the property.

Market appraisals are almost always carried out free of charge and obligation.

In contrast, a valuation is carried out by a surveyor. It is chargeable and can be relied on in a court of law where circumstances require a statement of a property's value—divorce, probate, bankruptcy, and so on.

Estate agents providing free market appraisals is something that I remember certain members of the public exploiting. One particular occasion springs to mind when, after looking around a prospective seller's home, the owner was given a suggested asking price, presented with the company's services, and quoted the agency's fee. At the end of the appraisal, the gentleman was asked when he'd be likely to put the property on the market. He replied, "Oh, I'm not giving my house to an estate agent; I'm selling it to my brother. I just wanted you lot to let me know how much I should ask for it!"

OK, back to how the process begins. A person contacts an estate agency with a view to finding out how much their home is worth. Once the negotiator has the prospective seller's contact details, they need to establish how serious the enquiry is. This they can do by asking simple questions like: How soon does the person need to move? Where are they hoping to move to? Have they found another property?

The negotiator who handles the enquiry records all relevant information on a market appraisal (MA) form. Along with the seller's contact details, they need to know a little bit about the property. Is it a house or a flat? Is it terraced or semi-detached? Is it a purpose-built flat or a converted one? How many bedrooms/reception rooms does the property have? Does it have parking? What's the general condition? Has it been extended? An experienced negotiator should ask these questions and record the answers without sounding like they're reading from and filling in the MA form. They should be just having a chat with their prospective client.

Once all the relevant details are obtained, the date and time of the appraisal are agreed with the homeowner. When making this appointment, the negotiator should allow some time to carry out a bit of research; however, this is not always possible. I lost count of how many times people would call or walk into the office and demand we carry out a market appraisal immediately. And if we didn't do it, there wasn't a shortage of competitors who would.

There are several things an estate agent does in preparation for a market appraisal. To provide an accurate asking price to the seller, the agents should look at comparable properties that have sold recently. They should check their own records, look at what their competitors have done, and carry out research on websites that hold house price data.

If they have established that the seller is likely to market the property imminently, the agents should prepare a short-list of their strongest buyers. These are people who are ready and able to buy, whom the agents feel the property may be suitable for.

I once heard of an estate agent taking a prospective purchaser along to a market appraisal. Whether or not this was planned—and with the homeowner's permission—I never knew. However, such a practice, while showing initiative and willingness on the agent's part, also reeks of desperation on both the agent's and the buyer's. Anyway, back to the preparation for the appraisal.

The estate agents should also know what type of property their prospective client would like to move to and where. If this happens to be in the area they cover, the negotiator should have also registered them as potential buyers and taken details of any suitable properties along to the appraisal. Scenarios such as this are common when people move home within the same area, like from a flat to a house.

Amongst the kit that the agent takes along to the MA are a folio (or presenter) containing sample property particulars, and brochures and other marketing materials. Details of comparable properties recently sold or currently on the market are very important items, as are a clipboard, a measuring device, and a camera. As more and more industries begin to embrace the technology available to them, some agents are using laptops for their presentations. One tech-savvy negotiator whom I know has replaced his folio presenter with a tablet computer device.

## At the property

There is no set format for carrying out a market appraisal. Most agents introduce themselves to the seller and then have a quick chat with them about their moving plans. They then have a look around the property and maybe take a few notes along the way. After that, they sit back down with the seller, present their company's services, and discuss asking prices and agency fees.

Some agents greet the seller and then get on with inspecting the property right away, even taking measurements and photos. Such an approach can convey an agent's enthusiasm in selling a prospective client's home; however, most do not write up a detailed description of a property unless they've already been instructed to sell it.

Experienced negotiators know one thing: before going to the effort of measuring and photographing the property, first tell the sellers what you think it is worth, and what your fees will be for selling it.

## Asking price

On a good day, my market appraisal presentations would rival the best in the business. I had a very pragmatic approach to marketing my clients' properties, which came from possessing a thorough knowledge of the local market and an awareness of its conditions. I wouldn't just turn up at the property and blurt a sales pitch; I offered people a common-sense plan to marketing their property and achieving the best possible price for it. And at the end of the market appraisal, no matter how eloquently it was delivered, it all came down to one thing: asking price.

There were occasions when I had the prospective seller's undivided attention. They would listen attentively, some hanging on my every word without breaking eye contact, until they heard an asking price that fell short of their expectations. After that, they couldn't look in my direction, let alone at my face. Conversely, there were people who appeared to be indifferent to anything I said. Nothing about market conditions, specialist reports, or comparable properties could spark their interest until the suggested marketing price of their home was mentioned.

Here's an outline of how I'd conduct a market appraisal:

- Once the introductions were out of the way, and the seller and I had a brief chat about their moving plans, I'd take a look around the property, maybe jotting a few notes along the way, but not listing a full description at this stage.

- Next, I would explain to the seller the process of how estate agents appraise properties and how we arrive at the suggested asking price. I would show them details of comparable properties recently sold, including those listed on various house price data websites.

- Then I'd describe current conditions in the local house market and points such as seasonal factors and buyer sentiment.

- Marketing was a key subject, and when discussing it, I'd provide sample adverts from the various publications and websites that we used to promote our clients' properties.

- All that remained now was to suggest an asking price, and at this point, some agents would, rather cunningly, ask prospective sellers what they thought their property was worth. Or another way the question was asked: Did they have a figure in mind of what they wanted to achieve for their home? Occasionally, this approach would solicit the required information, and the negotiator would know the seller's expectations. Now aware of what the seller wanted for their home, the negotiator would adjust his appraisal accordingly.

Here's a real-life scenario where this happened. We were called to appraise a luxury apartment in an affluent North London suburb. The flat was part of a modern development that had not long been completed. The owner was one of the first buyers to move in, but almost a year later, a change in her personal circumstances led to her putting the flat back on the market.

We knew that she had paid £265,000 for the property eleven months prior, when it was new. It was a tricky one to appraise because it was a new development, and we had hardly any comparables to base it against. Nonetheless, after some research and a bit of guesswork, we thought £300,000 would be a liberal asking price.

Arriving at the property, we were greeted by the owner, who explained that she had an urgent phone call to make and asked if we didn't mind showing ourselves around. Then, with hand signals rather like an air hostess's safety presentation, the lady pointed to which rooms were where before lighting a cigarette and excusing herself to the kitchen.

We looked around the property, which was immaculately presented. Both bedrooms were doubles and had en-suite bathrooms. The lounge was spacious and bright, having windows and a patio door to the balcony. The kitchen was in two parts: fitted units, worktops, and appliances at one end, and an ample dining area at the other, which also had a door and windows to the balcony. It was a lovely apartment.

While we were waiting for the seller to finish her phone call, my colleague, without saying a word, pointed to the figure of £300,000 that was written on the appraisal form held by her clipboard. She raised a thumb to signal that she felt we were spot-on with our estimated asking price.

Back in the lounge, we sat down with the owner. She lit another cigarette, and in a concise manner, explained that work relocation was driving the home move. The plan was to buy another property from the proceeds of the sale of her present flat, so renting it was not an option. Also, the owner hadn't liked some of the fixtures and fittings in the builder's original specification, so she had paid extra to have her own fitted—now knowing she'd overspent. Marble flooring throughout the flat, granite worktops, and top-of-the-range appliances in the kitchen were probably a little overboard for a rented flat; another reason why she preferred to sell it.

My colleague, listening intently to what the owner was saying, said, "You have a lovely flat. The finish is of a very high standard, and you've obviously spent a lot of money. How much were you hoping to get for it?"

"Well, I can tell you right now, I won't take a penny less than £320,000," replied the owner rather assertively.

"Yes, that's what we were thinking. An asking price of £329,950 to achieve around £320 to £325,000," said my colleague, looking in my direction for acknowledgement.

We were? Of course she was lying through her teeth, but nonetheless, I nodded in agreement. A few minutes later, we were measuring and photographing the property, and the owner was signing our sole-agency contract.

If we appraised that property at £300,000 when the owner was expecting at least £320,000, we would probably have lost that instruction. However, by asking a straightforward question, we got the property onto our books and eventually sold it, although it took time, and the owner had to revise her expectations a little.

It must be said that sellers are not always forthcoming with what they want for their property. In fact, when asked the question, more often than not, their response is that they want to hear what the agent has to say first.

Getting the marketing price right isn't always an easy task. I remember one particular period of uncertainty in the housing market. The country's two biggest mortgage lenders were issuing conflicting reports on house prices. One claimed they'd increased on the month, the other said they'd fallen. Industry specialists were reporting the market to be slowing in some areas but buoyant in others, while acclaimed economists were forecasting an all-round crash. We'd put a property onto the market and get a record price for it within the hour, yet a similar house would be up for sale for weeks without any interest at all. With such confusing information, how could I ensure I would get the right price for my clients' properties?

At the market appraisal, when it came to suggesting an asking price for the prospective seller's home, in the first instance, I would draw on comparable properties sold. Occasionally, people would question such an approach saying that no two properties were exactly the same. To some extent, these people were right, but what they didn't know was that surveyors would include comparables within the process of valuing a property for mortgage purposes. Also, if there were two similar houses, but one needed refurbishment and the other had a brand-new £10,000 kitchen, obviously, this would be taken into account. So comparables were always a good base to start from.

A further point to remember is that the average property transaction can take between eight and twelve weeks to complete. So if a sale completes at the end of May, it is possible that the actual offer was made in March. If you're looking at this comparable in June, then you're five months behind. And if you're in a fast-moving market, the figures may already be slightly out of date.

At another market appraisal, I was showing the prospective seller comparable properties that sold at £350,000 a couple of months prior. The market had moved on slightly since then, so I thought the property should be appraised around £365,000 to £370,000. On that basis, I suggested a marketing price of £375,000.

Now, I was fairly confident that I'd carried out my research correctly, and the asking price I'd quoted was reasonably accurate. However, we were in an erratic market and saw sharp price increases, month on month, that were fuelled by a shortage of property, especially that type of property. Also, my prospective clients had other agents visiting, so there was every chance one of my competitors would suggest a higher asking price, and I'd lose the instruction. What was I to do?

Well, I could've overpriced the property, gained the seller's confidence and then hoped that the market caught up with the property's inflated price. Either that, or I could have asked them to reduce the price at a later stage once they were locked in to an agreement with me—not my style.

Instead, I would tell people what I thought their property would achieve in the current market, and then I'd listen. If they wanted me to try marketing at a higher asking price, then I would, within reason, of course. What I'd say to people was that if after six weeks of the property being up for sale there hadn't been any offers, then they'd have to question whether it was overpriced. This was especially so if the property had been correctly promoted, and they weren't trying to sell during a seasonally quiet time in the market, like Christmas or the summer holidays.

So in our pricing example above, I told a prospective seller that their asking price should be £375,000; however, I might consider marketing at £385,000 if they asked me to. Most agents would've done the same.

More often than not, having such a flexible approach worked well for all involved. My clients knew that we did everything we could to get the best possible price for their property, and we won instructions, which we converted to sales.

Sometimes, however flexible we were, it wasn't enough. Telling a seller you'd be happy to "test" the market at £385,000 would be futile if a competitor told them £420,000 could easily be achieved for their house without needing to test anything.

## Overpricing

A few years ago, I was at a dinner party where once again, house prices became the focus of the evening's conversation. My fellow guests were commenting on how property prices seemed to be spiralling out of control. A friend, who was also at the party that evening, was looking for a flat in the local area. She was quite specific about the type of property and location she wanted and so limited her search to a small pocket of the area—about six to eight roads.

After just a few weeks of flat hunting and a bit of Internet research, she got to know the area and its property prices quite well. My friend said she'd noticed a significant increase in prices over a short period of time. "I saw a maisonette, in a road that I like, listed on a house price website as having sold for £190,000 two months ago. Yesterday, an estate agent called to offer me a similar property, on the same road, for £250,000. Have properties really gone up that much in just two months, or are they overpriced?" she asked.

Before I could answer, another guest said, "I've heard that competition amongst estate agents has led to them overpricing properties. Do you think this has helped push prices up?"

Firstly, I explained that data on house price websites, while helpful, was slightly out of date; especially in a fast-moving market. The date that the property was listed as sold was likely to be the date the transaction completed. The sale itself would have commenced when the buyer's offer was agreed, and that could've been three months before the completion or sold date.

So in my friend's case, the data she was looking at could've been five months and not two months old. Even so, the figures she pointed out amounted to a price increase of over 30 per cent, which on the face of it was extremely high. However, what the house price websites won't tell you is whether the flat at £190,000 was dilapidated and the one at £250,000 refurbished, which in our example might have been the case. We'll talk a bit more about property and the Internet in a moment.

Does competition amongst agents lead to overpricing? Does it ever!

Imagine you're the owner of the property in our earlier example. One agent's appraisal is £375,000, with the suggestion that you could test the market at an asking price of £385,000. The other agent is confident that the property will sell for £420,000. Both agents' terms are "no sale, no fee," so you only pay them the agreed fee once they've sold your property. If you go with the £420,000, and it's overpriced, you'll lose a bit of time. If you go with the £385,000, and it's underpriced, you might lose £35,000. Which estate agent will you instruct to sell your home?

I remember a sales manager at one of the large corporate estate agencies offering advice to his negotiators as they left for their market appraisals. "Be bullish on price," he used to say.

The director of a well-established independent estate agency once attributed his success to only taking properties onto his books if they were correctly priced. He knew that overpriced properties were hard to sell (often not selling at all) and as such, increased advertising costs. Competition became so fierce that towards the end of this man's thirty-five-year career, he would be heard saying, "Nowadays, you've got to price as high as you dare!"

It is rare for a seller not to favour the agent who quoted them the highest asking price. Estate agents know this, and that's one of the reasons why they overprice properties. Another reason is that they simply don't know the property and haven't done their research. Below is a classic example.

In a part of North London where I worked, there was a road that stretched across two postcodes. It had an interesting mix of housing. On one side of the road there were Victorian and Edwardian properties, while the opposite side comprised mostly sixties purpose-built flats.

One such block consisted of nine flats over three floors— ground, first, and second. This building didn't have too much "kerb appeal." The front appeared run down and always seemed to be strewn with litter where residents' refuse sacks had been torn open by foxes and cats. The block was not within reasonable walking distance to a train or tube station, and the nearest bus stop was several hundred metres away. However, the major setback for these flats was that they had bad leases. They were low in unexpired years and deemed to be defective by lenders, who in those days were not keen on granting mortgages on such terms. It was possible to renew the leases, but the freeholders were quoting £10,000 plus legal costs, and let's just say, they weren't the easiest of people to deal with.

While they may not have been the most desirable of properties, these flats did have a few positive points. They had generous room sizes, and even though they weren't situated close to transport or shopping facilities, they still managed to rent well.

Their lease problems made them cheap, and this appealed to professional property investors with cash. One landlord owned several similar flats on that road, which he'd let to housing associations on fixed terms of two years or more. This chap told me that he'd bought a one-bedroom flat in this particular block at an auction in 1994 where he paid £26,000. He then rented the flat for a three-year term at £110 per week—a gross return of 22 per cent.

In 2007, I was asked to appraise another one-bedroom flat in the same building. We hadn't sold anything in the block recently, and neither had any of our competitors. We did, however, just rent a one bedroom on the first floor for £157 a week which, according to the house price websites, was the last flat sold in the block— eighteen months prior—for £142,500.

The flat we were looking at on this day had been rented for years and was coming to the end of its most recent tenancy. The property needed attention in some areas, but on the whole it was in fair condition.

We thought the property would likely achieve around £155,000 and recommended an asking price of £159,950. Two other local estate agents appraised at the same level, with one recommending a slightly higher asking price of £165,000.

A fourth agent, one from outside the area, was also asked to provide an appraisal. They were an independent firm, very strong in central London, but they only had a couple of offices in the north of the capital, the closest one to the property being three miles away. What was their suggested asking price? Wait for it…£225,000!

When the owner told me, I did well to maintain my composure and asked her if she'd questioned their appraisal. The owner had indeed asked this agent how they arrived at an asking price that was around 40 per cent higher than three other estate agents. The answer they provided was that their firm was able to achieve higher prices than other agencies. Why? Because they dealt primarily with city workers, who would pay record prices for property using their hefty bonuses.

An interesting selling point, but one more appropriate when discussing penthouse apartments in Canary Wharf rather than buy-to-let flats in Wood Green. The real reason for this agent pricing higher than their competitors was that on this occasion, they simply didn't know what they were doing. And this particular seller wasn't falling for it.

## When overpricing goes wrong

Let us look at the scenario of flat owners wanting to sell their home and move up the property ladder to a house. By browsing the Internet and checking the property supplements in their local newspapers, the prospective sellers have a rough idea of their property's value. They also know what their new home is likely to cost.

With savings and a mortgage increase, they can raise £100,000. So if they sell their flat for £200,000, they can look at houses of up to £300,000. For the purpose of simplifying this example, I have excluded other costs associated with moving home like estate agency commission, legal fees, and stamp duty.

The sellers now need to invite local estate agents in to provide current market appraisals and hopefully confirm what their own research has shown. After that, they need to register as buyers with the agents covering the area they'd like to move to.

Four estate agents have provided appraisals. Three of them seem to think £200,000 is an achievable figure in the current market and have suggested asking prices of £205,000 to £209,950. However, the fourth agent has recommended the owners market their home for £230,000 with a view to taking offers of around £225,000. As this figure is £25,000 higher than the other quotes, and this chap seems confident in getting it, the sellers decide to instruct him as their estate agent.

So now that their property's on the market for £230,000, perhaps the sellers can increase their purchase budget. Maybe they can start looking at houses up to £330,000. Maybe now they'll only need to raise £70,000 instead of the £100,000 they initially thought. This will only apply if their property is indeed worth £225,000–£230,000 and not overpriced.

Problems begin when the owners of the flat find a house that they like and offer £325,000, only to find that they can't sell their flat for more than £200,000. In reality, they are unlikely to get their offer on the house accepted if they have yet to secure a buyer for their flat.

What if a buyer came along who absolutely loved the flat and paid the full asking price? Surely this would mean the property wasn't overpriced, right? Not necessarily so. If the buyer offering the asking price needs a mortgage, then the lender's surveyor has to justify the agreed sale price. If that surveyor thinks the property is overpriced, then he or she may "down value" it.

## What's a down valuation?

When a property purchase requires a mortgage, as most do, a surveyor will be instructed to carry out a valuation on behalf of the lender. The mortgage valuation (paid for by the borrower) is not a survey as such but more a basic report listing the type of property and its age. The surveyor will comment on the condition of the property and may recommend further inspection in areas which may have caused concern—structural, electrical, damp, and so on.

The main purpose of the mortgage valuation is so that the lender can establish the property's true value and assess whether it is worth lending the money against. The surveyor will submit the valuation report to the bank or building society and when doing so, provide evidence of comparable properties sold recently at similar prices.

If, after all his research, the surveyor cannot justify the agreed sale price, he will value the property at a lower figure. This is what is meant when a property is said to have been down valued. This is also when problems can arise, as in the following example.

We were called to look at a property that was located on a road predominant with terraced houses. The properties, built just after World War II, were quite small. In their original state, the houses had kitchens measuring nine by six and third bedrooms of six by six. The latter could really only be used as a study or a child's bedroom. The gardens were forty to fifty feet in length. Most had garages to the rear, which were accessed via a service road that ran across the back of the properties.

This particular house was an end of terrace, so there was access to the rear garden from the side of the building, a bit like a semi-detached. It also had a full-width single-story extension to the rear, which provided a spacious kitchen diner and utility room.

Low interest rates and a shortage of family homes had pushed prices up. In a matter of a few months, houses like this one, as well as similar ones in the surrounding roads, had gone from £250,000 to £285,000. As this property had been extended, we were thinking that an asking price of £300,000 might be spot-on. The owner, on the other hand, told us that they wanted to put the house on the market for £310,000. We didn't have any other properties available at this price, so we agreed. Besides, had we not taken it onto our books, one of our competitors would have.

We put the property on the market and got lots of viewings in the first two weeks, but no offers. We were starting to think that perhaps we'd been a bit too optimistic with the asking price, when one of the negotiators got an offer of £300,000. My colleague telephoned our clients to report the good news and to put the offer forward. It was rejected. The husband said that they'd seen a property they really liked and wanted to put in an offer. However, the property was slightly above their initial budget, so their finances would be a little stretched. This meant that they needed to achieve the asking price of £310,000 on their present home. My colleague explained the situation to the prospective buyers, another young couple, who agreed to go at the asking price.

This particular sale formed part of a small property chain. Our buyers were selling their flat to first-time buyers, and our sellers were buying a house from someone who, in turn, was buying a brand-new home. This was the end of the chain, which consisted of four properties. On the face of it, things looked good, but we were all waiting to see what our buyers' surveyor would have to say about the sale price of £310,000.

The mortgage valuation was booked, and the surveyor visited the property. A week later, the buyers called our office with a copy of the valuation report. The surveyor valued the property at £300,000; it had been down valued by £10,000.

This meant that the buyers' bank was still prepared to lend on the property, but they didn't think it was worth £310,000. As a result, the amount of mortgage they were giving the buyers was revised by £10,000. So, if our buyers had a £100,000 deposit and were originally borrowing £210,000, they would now only be given £200,000.

With a shortfall of £10,000 to their mortgage, our buyers might not have been able to proceed with the purchase. If this was the case, then three other property transactions could have also gone wrong.

What happens in such scenarios?

The buyers can try and renegotiate the price, using their valuation report as a negotiating tool. Whether this works depends on many factors. Estate agents and sellers, up and down the chain, may adjust their fees and sale prices to help make up the shortfall. This is a very rare occurrence, but when people cooperate with each other, things get moving.

The estate agent can try to get the surveyor to revise his valuation. This is done by supplying the surveyor with evidence of comparable properties sold at the relevant price. This is also a rare occurrence, as getting a surveyor to U-turn on his valuation isn't easy.

Lastly, the buyers can make up the mortgage shortfall using their own money. In our scenario, the buyers presented the valuation report and asked if the sellers would consider amending their asking price by £10,000. The sellers were quite stretched financially, so there was no room for further negotiation. The other options listed above were not explored, as our buyers managed to get the £10,000 from their parents, and the sale went through at the originally agreed price. A precedent had been set, and there was now a comparable of £310,000 that future property sales on that road could use as evidence.

In this example, we were fortunate that the buyers were able to find the required additional funds. If they hadn't, not only would this sale have gone wrong, but the whole chain could've collapsed with it.

Overpricing a property, whether instigated by an optimistic seller or an over enthused estate agent, can cost time and money for all those involved, both directly and indirectly.

## When overpricing works

I was once asked to provide an appraisal for a thirties semi-detached house. We knew the type of property well and had been involved in several recent sales on that road at the time. All our experience, comparables, and research pointed to figures of £110,000–£120,000.

As usual, we were not the only estate agents called in. Two of the other agents agreed with our appraisal and also suggested asking prices within the same price range that we did. We all lost out. Another agent told the sellers that £140,000 was a realistic asking price, and unsurprisingly, the sellers chose to instruct them. Was the house overpriced at that figure? Yes, at that time, it was.

Our competitor had signed up the sellers to a twelve-week sole-agency contract. This meant that for three months, they could not instruct any other estate agents to sell their home. During this time, demand for property continued to outstrip supply, and prices began to rise. So while the house may have been overpriced when it first went up for sale, the market eventually caught up, and the property went under offer.

I very much doubt that our competitor set out to price the property at what he thought it might be worth twelve weeks later and then commit the seller to a contract of the same duration. More likely, this agent wanted to get the property on the market before his rivals did, and a good way of doing so was to price higher than they did. Also, experienced estate agents know that when demand outstrips supply, they just need to get properties on their books, overpriced or not. You stand a better chance of selling an overpriced property if it's on your books, then if it isn't.

A longer sole-agency agreement gives the estate agent more time to work with the property. The extra few weeks allow the agent to adapt to any fluctuations in the market or changes to their clients' circumstances. We'll be looking at sole-agency and multiple-agency agreements in more detail shortly.

## When sellers overprice

Estate agents may recommend an asking price; however, it is the homeowner who has the final say on what the property is marketed for. Countless times, customers would ask us to set the price a bit higher than we'd appraised. On occasion it worked for them, but in most cases, it didn't. Years ago, there were even times when we walked away from a potential property instruction, because the seller's expectations were just too unrealistic.

I remember looking at a flat that belonged to a successful legal executive. The woman's motivation for moving was work related. Several agents provided appraisals and at £200,000, ours was one of the lowest. The owner called me to ask if I'd be prepared to take the flat onto our books at £225,000. Another agent had quoted this figure, but if I'd consider marketing at that price, she preferred to give me the instruction.

I told my prospective client that I thought an asking price of £225,000 was a little optimistic. We struck up an informal agreement: I would take the property on at her price, and if after a month of marketing, there were no offers; she'd reduce the asking price, bringing it closer to my recommendation.

We marketed the property using every means at our disposal. We updated our client with feedback on every viewing appointment and informed her of every newspaper advert, website, and leaflet we used to promote her property. Six weeks into our sole-agency agreement, she accepted an offer of £195,000.

Why did she accept the lower offer?

Firstly, she found a property that she really liked, and for less money than originally anticipated, so she made a saving. She tried to hold out for the higher price on her own sale, but the longer she did so, the greater the risk of losing the property she wanted to buy. *Remember:* estate agents and sellers will rarely withdraw a property from the market if the buyer's end of the chain is incomplete.

Secondly, with the amount of marketing that we carried out, if £225,000 was the right asking price for the flat, we'd have got it, or at least very close to it.

And because we kept our client updated every step of the way, when she accepted £195,000, she did so without any doubts in her mind as to whether she could have got more money for it. Not all homeowners apply such common sense, however.

One gentleman had his house on the market for two months. He was asking £239,950 for his three-bedroom end of terrace, which was a bit higher than we'd recommended, but not overly optimistic.

Eight weeks of marketing got him quite a few viewings, but there were no offers. The property was reasonably well presented, although areas of it were starting to appear a little worn and dated. On a positive note, the house was situated within the catchments of several popular schools. This provided us with a lot of interest from families, but none of them made an offer.

Clearly, the asking price was wrong; however, we were cautious about how we'd communicate this to our seller. There was a significant shortage of homes for sale, and our property instruction levels were falling. At the time, the media were reporting that, on average, there were fourteen buyers for every property for sale in London. There were also reports of properties going under offer within an hour of being put on the market, which we'd seen first-hand. For sellers like the man in our example, this proved quite frustrating. His house had a lot more than fourteen viewings but still hadn't sold after eight weeks. Also, while he was looking for a property to buy, whatever was available was selling fast and at record prices.

In our office morning meeting, one of the properties being discussed belonged to this seller. We were looking at how long the house had been on the market, how many times it had been advertised, the number of viewings, and the general feedback from prospective buyers. We were debating whether or not it was time to suggest the seller reduce the asking price, when the office door opened, and in he walked. We were in regular contact with this client, but he obviously felt the need to pay us a visit.

My colleague stood up to greet him and said, "I was going to call you in a few minutes, but you've beaten me to it. How can I help?"

"I have it on good authority that my property has increased in value by £5,278, so I'd like to amend the asking price, please," replied the seller in a very matter-of-fact way.

Overhearing this, I immediately thought that seller had been talking to one of our competitors who would, quite naturally, be touting for business while trying to scupper ours. However, after chatting with this gentleman, my colleague learned that the good authority he was referring to was the Nationwide Building Society's monthly report on house prices. That morning, the mortgage lender reported an average monthly increase of 2.2 per cent. Our client applied this percentage increase to his property and came up with the figure of £5,278.

My colleague explained that the figure of 2.2 per cent was a national average. It did not mean that every property had increased in value by that exact amount. She then provided the seller with a summary of all the marketing that had been carried out on his property. "After eight weeks of advertising and several dozen viewings, we're concerned as to why we haven't had any offers. In fact, I was going to phone you this morning and suggest that we actually lower the asking price."

The seller didn't reduce the asking price; however, he didn't increase it either, which was his intention to do that day. We received two offers on his property, but he rejected both of them. After our twelve-week sole-agency contract had expired, the seller took the property off our books and gave it to one of our competitors. We saw the house advertised at £249,950, but we never found out if it eventually sold, or for how much.

Some homeowners would overprice their property but never accept that as the reason why it wasn't selling. They'd blame everything from market conditions to their estate agent not photographing or describing the property correctly. Rather than lower their expectations on price, they'd switch from agent to agent, hoping that one of them would do something different to find that special buyer.

Other homeowners, who failed to acknowledge that an inflated asking price was hindering their chances of securing a sale, felt the best remedy was to instruct every estate agent they could. If your property is overpriced, having six estate agents market it simultaneously isn't necessarily going to help. In fact, such a plan can adversely affect your chances of getting a good offer; exactly how, I'll be explaining in the forthcoming chapter on estate agency agreements.

## Pricing correctly

Getting the asking price right is important. If you set your sights too high, your property may stay on the market without getting much interest from prospective buyers. If it lingers long enough, it may even become what the industry refers to as "stale." Buyers will wonder what is wrong with the property and question why it hasn't sold. They will not want to be the ones to commit to it, when no one else has.

In contrast, what happens if you price your home realistically, and the first viewer through the door offers the full asking price? Have you underpriced your property, could you have got a bit more money for it, or have you found the right buyer straight away?

I remember when I first started out as an estate agent and really got into the swing of things. My manager was called to appraise a house, and I told him that I had the perfect buyer in mind for it. The property came onto the market; my buyer viewed within the hour and offered the full asking price. Quite proud of my achievement, I went to my manager with the good news. After a brief wince in his facial expression, he said, "Hmm, that's too quick. They'll think we've gone in low on the price."

I'd been working with that buyer for several weeks, trying to find the right property for her and got to know exactly what she was after. When that particular house came onto the market, I knew immediately that she'd like it. When I presented the offer to the seller, their initial reaction was exactly as my manager said it would be; however, a week later, they decided to accept the offer.

So, when selling, how can you ensure you haven't overpriced your property and hindered your chances of a timely sale, or worse, underpriced it and lost money on the deal? In some market conditions, this is not always an easy one to call, so here are some notes that can help in setting the correct asking price.

*Get the asking price right.* Do your own research before calling in the estate agents. The property pages or supplements in local newspapers, house price websites; estate agents' websites, and their window displays are all good resources for house prices data.

*Select the right estate agent.* Look around your local area. Which estate agents appear to be active? Which ones are displaying the most FOR SALE, or even better, SOLD boards? Invite at least three local agents to provide you with a market appraisal. If one agent quotes a much higher asking price than the others, don't be afraid to ask why. They may have just achieved a record price on a comparable property and have a list of buyers who lost out on it and are eager to find a similar home.

Alternatively, the agent may have suggested a higher asking price than his competitors just to gain your confidence and obtain your instruction. A seller once told me that he gave his instruction to an estate agent even though he knew she was overpricing. He said she gave such a convincing presentation and was so enthusiastic that he felt she was the best person to sell his home, even if she was too bullish with the asking price.

What if you've had several appraisals of your property and want to go with the highest, but you haven't taken to the estate agent who suggested it? What do you do? If you have a preference for one of the agents, either because of an instant rapport, or you instinctively feel they're right for the job, ask them if they'll market your property at a higher price. As long as your suggested asking price is not outrageously high, most estate agents will not turn down the instruction.

## Best months to sell

Historically, spring through to early summer has always been the best time to sell property in England and Wales. More precisely, I recall our busiest periods to have always been from the end of the Easter Bank Holiday up until when schools broke up for summer holiday. Autumn can also be a good time to put your property on the market. In my opinion, buyers searching for their home at this time of year generally wanted to be moved in by Christmas. Maybe this is why for most of the years I was an estate agent, my busiest sales month, year in, year out, was always October.

August and December are very quiet periods in estate agency. In all my time as an estate agent, I never knew a negotiator to hit their sales target in either of these two months. In August, people are away on holiday and in December, their attention is drawn to the festivities. Having said that, of the very few buyers who did walk through our doors in August or December, most of them were highly motivated to move. After all, anyone whose attention is focused on buying a property at a time when most of us are preparing for Christmas has got to be serious.

## Testing the market

Let's say that you've decided to sell your property and have invited three local estate agents to provide appraisals. The asking price suggested by one of them is higher than those quoted by his competitors and a lot more than you expected to achieve. This agent seems to know what he's talking about and is confident that he'll get your property under offer quickly to one of the buyers on his waiting list. His optimism and positive attitude is winning you over.

It has crossed your mind that the agent's appraisal might be a tad unrealistic, but if it does prove too high, you can always reduce the asking price later. As the agent will be bearing the marketing costs, you have nothing to lose (except for a few weeks of your time) by trying the price he's recommended. You're not in a chain and not in any particular hurry to sell, so you decide to give him the instruction.

Such scenarios are very common. All sellers would like to get the best possible price for their property, and there's nothing wrong with that. However, if you're going to test the market at the higher end, you must keep a close eye on things and be prepared to review and adapt as the situation requires. Let me elaborate further.

In my experience, a property that's on the market at the right time of year and promoted correctly should go under offer in four weeks or less. If it doesn't, then something is wrong. Now, there are several reasons why buyers may be deterred from making an offer on a property, but probably the most common one is the price being too high.

So if it's July, and your house has been on the market since the end of March, and you've not had any offers, then you need to ask yourself and your agent why. In saying that, if your agent hasn't already provided feedback and voiced their concern at this stage, then they're doing you both a disservice.

I once saw a house advertised for sale in my local newspaper. The picture used for the advert showed the property with snow on its roof. The last bit of snow we had that year was at the end of January, yet his particular advert appeared in the local paper twice in May. Anyone looking at the advert would immediately know that the property had been on the market for nearly four months.

Now, there may well have been a genuine reason why the property hadn't sold. Perhaps another part of the chain had broken down, causing the sale to fall through; regardless, a new photograph should have been taken. This is a typical example of sloppy marketing on the agent's part and apathy on the seller's. It gives a poor first impression, which may discourage buyers from making an offer, or it may attract low offers from people "taking a chance."

If you want to price your property high and test the market, then by all means do so, but don't get into a situation like those mentioned above. Monitor progress, obtain feedback, and communicate with your agent, or agents. This brings us to the topic of our next chapter: Is it better to instruct one estate agent or several to sell your property? Should you sign up to a sole-or multiple-agency agreement? Let's take a look.

# 5. Agency Agreements

So you've had several local estate agents around to appraise your property. There's very little difference between them in what asking price they've suggested, and they've all quoted the same percentage rate for their fees. You're a bit unsure as to which one you should instruct. They all seem to talk a great game, and they all have told you about the list of buyers they have waiting. You can't separate them. What do you do?

One of them has slightly more estate agency boards up in the area than the others, but he's a little smarmy. Maybe you'll give the instruction to the woman whose pleasant manner you liked. She was very positive and even suggested you might try a slightly higher asking price. Perhaps you should appoint all of them to sell your property and let them scrap it out—let the best agent win. That way you should get the best price for your property and the quickest sale, right? Maybe, maybe not. Let's now take a look at the different estate agency agreements and their pros and cons.

Generally, the two main types of estate agency agreements are sole-agency and multi-agency agreements. We will discuss these in detail and also look at variants of the former. However, please note, estate agency agreements are legally binding contracts. If you are unsure of the terms and conditions of any such agreement, please seek the advice of a suitably qualified person before putting your signature to any document.

## Sole agency

A sole-agency agreement is where only one estate agency is instructed in the sale of a property for a set period of time. If a seller enters into a sole-agency agreement, they will not be permitted to appoint additional estate agents for the duration of that agreement.

Should the seller wish to terminate the sole agency prematurely, they can do so; however, the conditions of that agreement may prevent them from instructing any other agents until the expiry of the originally agreed term. For example, if a seller signs up to an eight-week sole agency and cancels halfway through, they may not be permitted to instruct other agents for a further four weeks. Also, on terminating a sole agency, the seller may be required to provide notice—usually one or two weeks.

The length of a sole-agency contract can differ, and there isn't a set timescale. During my years in the business, anything from six to twelve weeks was pretty much the norm, but there were extremes at either end.

I once signed up a seller to a sole-agency agreement, the length of which was stated on the contract as "for one viewing only." The property was a first-floor flat which had two double bedrooms, a lounge, a kitchen/diner, and a roof patio with steps down to its own section of the rear garden. The flat was converted from a detached Edwardian house and occupied the entire first floor of the building. It boasted many period features, including high ceilings with ornate mouldings, cornicing, and a lovely fireplace in the lounge. The property's location was also a strong selling point. It was less than three hundred metres from the tube station and local shops but sufficiently tucked away from the noise of the high road.

Basically, this type of flat was very sought after, and I had the perfect buyer for it. Just a few days before, I'd registered a first-time buyer whose property requirements would be met precisely by this flat. I knew that if I could get her a viewing appointment—get her through the front door—she'd make an offer. But first I had to win the instruction, and that wasn't an easy task.

I was up against a very strong competitor who was also invited to appraise the property. This agent was a successful independent who seemed to have an estate agency board in almost every road in the catchment, including a SOLD board directly opposite the flat I was appraising. Also, that agent's office was located less than 150 metres from the flat, whereas our office was nearly two miles away. If that wasn't enough of a challenge for me, the independent was far more flexible on their fees than we were. I was up against it here and had to think creatively and pretty quickly.

I asked the seller to let me show his property to the first-time buyer that same evening. If, after that one viewing appointment,

I didn't get him an offer that would cover the difference in fees between ours and the local agent's, our agreement would end, and he could walk away. The seller agreed, and the first-time buyer saw the flat and offered £118,000 for it. The seller accepted the offer, which stood at £3,000 more than the asking price suggested by competitor.

Looking back, I think that in that particular case, if I'd tried for a sole agency term of six, eight, or twelve weeks, it may have cost me the instruction and a sale. There was every chance that the first-time buyer would've registered with the independent agent and purchased the flat through them. After all, she wanted a flat in that area, and the other agent was very well established there.

The seller really didn't have anything to lose by accepting the one-off viewing appointment. Even if it proved to be a complete waste of time, it would've cost him ten minutes of his life to find out. As for me, I got a sale, and my competitors, including the "sharks" who worked in my office, didn't even get a look in.

In contrast, while working for an estate agency franchise, I accompanied my director to a market appraisal, where the seller gave us a sixteen-week sole agency.

This property was a seven-bedroom detached house occupying several acres of greenbelt land. It had everything you would expect for its £4.5 million price tag; indoor heated pool, sauna, gymnasium, tennis court, stables, paddock, and orchard.

There was no way that my boss was going to accept anything less than a four-month sole agency on that house, and I'll explain why.

Firstly, we had to accompany all viewing appointments. The sheer size of the property and its grounds meant that showing buyers around took much longer. The average viewing was about thirty to forty minutes in duration. In fact, on the first few appointments, the owner opted to show me and the prospects around, and when they did so, the viewings took over an hour each time. It really was a big property, and there were times when I felt like a tour guide showing visitors around a museum or gallery.

It took us nearly two hours to measure the property and prepare its particulars. At that time, the software used for creating floor-plans of buildings was not as widely available as it is today, so we had to call in a specialist company to assist. We also brought in a professional to photograph the property inside and out.

Our advertising extended from the weekly local and regional newspapers into the national monthly glossies. We also included a two-page editorial piece in the company's quarterly magazine. My boss had planned this promotional campaign from day one; something that would not have been possible if we only had a six-week sole agency, for example.

Now, had we managed to find a buyer in the first few weeks, our marketing expenses would have been much lower. What happened was that we actually found a buyer several weeks after our sixteen-week sole agency had lapsed. The owners of the property, having seen the effort and expense we'd gone to in order to find them the right buyer, were happy to keep us on.

For estate agents, it is in their interests to sign up sellers to the longest term they can. The longer the sole agency, the more control the agent has. They can budget their advertising without the worry of losing money should another agent sell the property before them. Also, the longer an agent has a sole agency on a property, the greater the period their competitors haven't.

## Multiple agency

Also known as multi-agency—or in the industry, referred to as "multi"—this type of agreement allows the seller to instruct more than one estate agent to sell their home. There are no restrictions; a seller can instruct as many agents as they like and whenever they like. In terms of duration, all the multi-agency agreements I've known have been open-ended—no set term for the agent and no lock-in period for the seller.

I once heard of an independent estate agency that tried to apply a two-week notice period for clients wishing to terminate their multi-agency agreement. This never made sense to me. If a seller has three agents marketing their property and decides to let one of them go, it is pointless for that agent to insist on a notice period. The seller will simply refuse any further viewing appointments from that agent during that time and accept only those made by the other two.

Estate agents' approach to multi-agency agreements is considerably different to that of sole agencies, and here too, I've seen extremes. Agents either become ultra-competitive, doing whatever it takes to beat their rivals to the sale; or as I've seen on numerous occasions, turn down the multi-agency and walk away. I'll explain this all in more detail in moment, but for now here are a couple of real-life scenarios to provide a brief insight.

In the summer of 1999, I was working for a corporate estate agency selling homes in a leafy suburb of North London. At the time, the market was very tough. There was a shortage of property, and our instruction levels were down to half of what they normally were.

A telephone call came through from a seller who needed their property sold yesterday. A previous sale had gone wrong and rather than lose the house they were buying, they obtained a bridging loan enabling them to buy independently of selling. They'd moved into their new home, and the old one was now empty. We were told that the original agent was holding keys. We could borrow them and get a set cut for us.

We met with inevitable delays, no doubt created by our competitor to give themselves a head start. When we finally got to show the property, there were several other estate agents and buyers already there. Parking on this road was never a problem, but on this occasion there weren't any free spaces near the house.

I was to show the property to a woman who told me that if she liked the house, she'd want to see it again with her husband, either later that day or the following morning. Unfortunately, such a luxury didn't exist. As we approached the garden path, through the window we could see an estate agent showing people around the front room. Another agent walked out of the house and was talking to the couple he'd just shown the property to. I'll never forget what happened next.

As the three of them were chatting, they noticed a car slowing down outside the property. It looked like yet another prospective buyer. The couple outside the house glanced in our direction, then back at the agent, nodded at him, and then all three darted towards their cars. The scene was hilarious and yet quite sad. The estate agent ran to his vehicle, his tie blown over his shoulder by the breeze. The couple, who looked to be in their late thirties, scurried back to their car, the woman lifting her flowing skirt to aid her pace. The man, a portly chap, almost didn't stop himself in time, soles slapping the pavement as he passed the door of his car. Their haste was so that they could present their offer to the seller before the other agents and prospective buyers could.

Why did I think the above to also be sad? Well, people should not have to buy a house (probably the biggest financial commitment of their life), the same way that they'd buy a much-publicised, heavily discounted item at the January sales.

My client, accurately reading the scenario, was quite taken aback. She looked at me and said, "I really don't want to get involved in that sort of situation, and neither will my husband. It doesn't happen a lot, does it?" Unfortunately, in such circumstances and in such market conditions, it did happen a lot.

Four years later, in a slightly improved market, I was working for a franchised estate agency, located about a mile away from the area in our previous story. We were called, at very short notice, to appraise a ground floor flat—a one bedroom that was being sold by a property investment company.

Once again, several estate agents were there at the same time. Only on this occasion, the assembly was premeditated by the seller and didn't happen by chance.

Basically, we were pitted against each other by the representative of a hard-nosed seller. We were told what the asking price was to be and what fee the winning agent would be paid; done so in a take-it-or-leave-it manner. All the agents present, corporate, independent, mature, young, experienced, and new agreed to the terms without question.

Everyone went off in different directions around the property to start measuring and taking notes. Some started in the kitchen, others in the lounge, all watching one another's movements in their peripheral vision as their paths crossed. One chap seemed to have one eye on his clipboard and the other on me as he scribbled frantically with his pen. He, just like the rest of us, wanted to get out of there as quickly as possible and back to the office to start calling prospective buyers.

This property suited either the first-time buyer or novice buy-to-let investor, the latter being more common than the former at the time, I found one who was willing to pay cash. The very next morning, I presented the offer to the seller. I was promptly told that they'd received an identical cash offer from a buyer introduced by one of the other agents. What were the odds? A bidding war ensued, which we eventually won, but only after we were made to jump through numerous hoops first.

As I mentioned earlier, I have known estate agents to turn away certain multi-agency instructions and in doing so, reject a possible commission. They did this because they felt too many agents were involved; such a situation would become messy.

An example of such a situation was the property developer who, when selling a completed refurbishment, would instruct almost every estate agent in the area. The developer did this to appease the agents, because he relied on them all to contact him whenever an investment opportunity came their way. This business arrangement meant there would always be at least six agents involved in the sale of the developer's properties. Furthermore, the agreement was that once a buyer was found, the property would remain on the market until contracts were exchanged. As a result, the estate agents involved were always trying to outdo one another and scupper the others' sales.

Some years ago, a first-time buyer was proceeding with the purchase of a flat belonging to this same developer. The survey had been carried out, and solicitors had been instructed. An exchange of contracts was only days away. The buyer asked if they could go back to the flat and measure up for the new curtains they wanted to order. A colleague greeted the buyer outside the flat and as they walked in, they found a rival estate agent showing the flat to a prospective buyer.

The next morning we received news of a higher offer being made through the other agent. Our first-time buyer was very upset. We then had a phone call from her irate father, who offered to match the other buyer's price and also realign the property developer's nose!

The sale went through, and the first-time buyer got the flat, but at the higher price. And even though we were not at fault, the buyer's feelings towards us had cooled. Our directors refused to do business with that property developer again. In fact, they were quite cynical about most property developers. As for multi-agency instructions, they were quite happy to take them on, but they judged each one individually. If a seller had instructed more than three agents, they'd reserve the right to walk away, and quite often they did.

## Joint sole agency

This type of estate agency agreement usually means that two agents are instructed to sell the property. The agents will share the commission regardless of which one introduced the buyer.

I've heard several definitions of this type of estate agency agreement, many of which didn't make sense. One such explanation was that two agents are instructed, but only the one who introduces the buyer gets the commission. To me, this is a multi-agency agreement.

Sometimes, estate agents will collaborate and subcontract one another to assist with selling a property. In this scenario, the seller still has a sole agency agreement with one estate agency and will only pay a fee to that agent. The agents then share the commission however they agree to. This is not a joint sole agency.

## Sole selling rights

Throughout my years as an estate agent, I never used this type of agreement. In fact, I only ever knew of one residential estate agent that did. Nonetheless, sole selling rights are still being employed, so here's a brief description of how they work.

Whether a seller is in a sole- or multiple-agency agreement, if they were to find a buyer themselves, generally, they would not be liable to pay an estate agent's fee. In other words, if they sold their property to a friend or relative, as long as that friend or relative was not introduced by an estate agent, then no fee should be due. Please note: this may not apply to all sole- or multi-agency agreements, so if you are unsure of the terms of your agreement, please seek the advice of a suitably qualified individual.

Now, with sole selling rights, the seller may be liable to pay a fee regardless of who introduces the buyer during the agency term. For example: if the owner sells the property to their brother, cousin, or long-lost school friend, the agent will be owed their fee.

Sole selling rights may not be as commonly used as other estate agency agreements, but they do exist. As mentioned, please ensure that you understand the terms of your agreement before signing it.

## Sole- and multi-agency fees

Estate agents usually quote their fees as a percentage of the property sale price. There isn't a standard rate and fees can vary between different companies, the geographical area, its inhabitants, and the type of property.

In one town, sellers may be reluctant to pay more than 1 per cent for sole agency and yet, two miles away, property owners will sign up for twice that amount without question. Someone selling a one-bedroom flat may happily use an agent quoting 1.5 per cent but the owner of a four-bedroom house located three streets away will buck at paying more than 1 per cent to sell his property.

I once worked for a company that replaced percentage commission rates with fixed-fee amounts. They did this for a trial period, which was short-lived. Whenever we quoted a fixed fee, people would always ask us what the figure would work out to as a percentage.

Another point often raised by sellers was that if they were to negotiate an offer, or lower their asking price, the fixed fee would remain the same. For example, if a property went on the market for £100,000, a fixed fee of £1,500 would be equal to 1.5 per cent. If the property then sold for £95,000, the fixed fee would remain at £1,500. If the fee was quoted as a percentage, the amount would be £1,425.

The difference may not sound like a lot of money, but to an estate agency group selling ten thousand properties a year, this works out to be a considerable amount. Perhaps this was why my employers trialled the fixed fee. However, they quickly found that most sellers preferred to be quoted in percentages.

When examining estate agency fees, the one thing that remains constant is that agents will always quote a lower fee for sole agency than for multiple.

## Which is better, sole or multi?

Some sellers prefer to instruct a sole agent. The fees are lower, and there is a single point of contact. Other property owners will go with a multi-agency agreement, believing the more estate agents involved, the quicker the sale and the higher the price achieved. Let's now take a look at the plus and minus points of both sole and multi-agency agreements, and you can decide which is best for you.

As already mentioned, the first benefit of sole agency over multi is that the fees are lower. As a general example, sole agency could be 1.5 per cent and multi-agency 2 per cent. In some areas the fees may be lower and the difference between the two types of agreement smaller—0.25 per cent instead of 0.5 per cent.

Also, in any given town, there will be at least one agent whose fees are much lower than that of their competitors, so much so that their multi-agency fee equals everyone else's sole-agency fees. There are also special promotional rates, usually offered by new estate agency start-ups; however, even in these scenarios, sole agency will be cheaper than multi.

Another reason people prefer sole agency is that they'd rather deal with one company instead of the several that multi-agency may entail. If too many estate agents are instructed, sometimes things can get a little messy. As rival firms compete for the commission, the information provided to the seller may not be the most accurate. Here's an example of what I mean.

A sole agent introduces a buyer to a property, and that buyer makes an offer. Before putting the offer forward to the seller, the agent checks the property chain in order to confirm the buyer's position and their ability to proceed with the purchase. After making a few phone calls, the agent finds that the bottom of the chain is incomplete. The chain has another two levels below, and the buyer's buyer has yet to secure a sale on their property.

The agent puts the offer forward to the seller and provides details of the chain.

He suggests that they continue to show the property until the bottom of the chain comes together, or a stronger buyer is found. This is pretty much what any agent would advise their client—it's routine procedure and a common-sense approach.

Now, take the exact same scenario, but this time the estate agent is up against four competitors in a multi-agency agreement.

In an attempt to get the edge over his rivals, he might tell the seller that the buyer is in a stronger position than they really are. For example, the agent might report that the chain is complete. He may even neglect to mention the incomplete part of the chain altogether, thus making the property chain appear shorter.

The seller may then be persuaded to withdraw the property from the market to allow the buyer to proceed. That being the case, the other estate agents will be asked to hold off from marketing the property any further. This will provide the less than truthful agent with exclusivity on the sale of the property. During this time, a genuine buyer may be found, completing the chain, and no one will be any the wiser.

If a buyer isn't found, and time passes without the sale advancing, the seller, quite naturally, will query the delay. The agent, buying himself time, will appear to be chasing up the bottom of the chain to find out what is going on. To cover his tracks, he may fabricate a story about the buyer at the bottom of the chain pulling out of the purchase. Furthermore, he will blame the estate agents below for not updating him, or for misinforming him about the extra level in the chain to begin with. Appearing to have his client's best interests at heart, he will suggest to them that their property go back onto the market immediately. By this time, the agent will have lined up a number of new buyers, giving himself a head start over his competitors.

I am not saying that all estate agents who find themselves in the competitive arena of multi-agency will lie to their clients in order to beat their rivals to the sale. What I am saying is that the greater the number of agents involved, the more likely that one will resort to underhand methods to succeed over the others.

The example that I have provided above was typical of the tactics employed by one sales negotiator, not only in competing with rival firms, but also to triumph over his colleagues. This chap once told a seller that a buyer he'd introduced to their property was chain-free, when in fact he knew they had a flat to sell. He then convinced the seller to take the house off the market, saying the buyer would not proceed otherwise—the buyer had said no such thing.

When buyer and seller eventually met up, the truth came out, and all hell broke loose. The seller removed his property from the estate agency's register and sold it through one of the other agents. The buyer made a complaint to senior managers and then asked to be taken off the mailing list. It was rumoured that this incident (amongst others) led to the eventual dismissal of the negotiator.

Sometimes instructing too many estate agents can have an adverse effect when marketing your home. I'll explain what I mean.

When a buyer decides to look for property in a specific area, they are likely to register with as many of that area's estate agents as possible. They may do this online, by telephone, or in person by visiting the estate agents' offices. Whatever method the buyer chooses, when they register, if they are given details of the same property by six different agents, how do you think this reflects on that property? Does the owner appear keen to sell, or are they desperate?

I worked for a company that had an office on a busy high street where we were one of five estate agents within a hundred-metre stretch.

One day, a woman walked into the office and asked if she could register for three-bedroom houses. I noted her requirements and gave her details of all suitable properties in and around her price range. She shuffled through the sheets of A4 that I'd given her and singled out one of the properties. "All the agents seem to have this one," she said, showing me the particulars given to her by three of our competitors. "Is there anything wrong with it? Are the owners desperate to sell or something?" Not waiting for my answer, the woman handed me back the property particulars and said, "I think I'll leave this one." To my knowledge, she didn't view the property through our competitors either.

The Internet has become an invaluable tool for estate agents in marketing their clients' properties. However, the adverse effects that may arise from instructing too many estate agents will apply to online advertising as well as traditional methods. In fact with the Internet, it's sometimes worse. Below is an example.

Two first-time property developers had completed a project of refurbishing a house they'd bought at auction. They instructed several estate agents to market the property at a rather optimistic asking price. From there on, pretty much any estate agent who approached the sellers and offered their services was instructed. At one point, there were eleven estate agents trying to sell the property.

What the novice property developers didn't know was that all eleven estate agents subscribed to the same property portal; therefore, they all advertised the house on the same website at the same time. This meant that when buyers searched for houses in the area at that price, they got an entire web page of the same property. And because each estate agent took their own photos and measurements, there were now eleven adverts listing slightly different specifications for the same house. It all looked a bit messy and certainly didn't give the right impression. I remember a buyer commenting on how the property was the one everybody had, but nobody could sell.

After several months of marketing, a few offers, and a sale that fell through, the owners of the house decided to withdraw it from sale and rent it out.

Now, I must say that during my career I saw many multi-agency scenarios, involving four or more estate agents, that did work for the sellers. However, many of those sellers were experienced property developers whose approach to selling property is totally different to that of the average homeowner. Such people deal with estate agents on a daily basis and understand how they operate. In fact, many were once estate agents themselves.

Taking all of the above into account, some sellers prefer to instruct more than one estate agent to sell their property. Perhaps in the past they appointed a sole agent who proved to be less than proactive, leaving them tied to the agent for the duration of the agreement. If that agent was up against a competitor, he'd be less likely to adopt a relaxed attitude for fear of losing the sale to his rival. Both estate agents would be kept on their toes, so to speak.

As a seller, if you prefer to go for a multi rather than sole agency, then here's my advice as to the best way to go about it.

Aim to instruct two or three agents at maximum. Look for the more active ones in your local area. As mentioned in the previous chapter, a good indicator of a busy estate agent is their "board presence." This is the number of FOR SALE and, more important, SOLD boards they're displaying in the vicinity. Once you've short-listed four or five companies, invite them to carry out market appraisals.

When ready to instruct, perhaps go for one corporate and one independent agent—get the best of both worlds. If possible, appoint estate agents who are located in different parts of town and not next door to or opposite each other. This way you'll reach more buyers and won't limit yourself to only those visiting the high-street estate agents to register for property. You'll also avoid situations like the one mentioned earlier, where the buyer was given details of the same property from consecutive agents she visited, thereby creating the impression of a desperate seller.

On the other hand, if you prefer the exclusivity, single point of contact, and lower fees of sole agency, once again, board presence is a good place to start the selection process. Whether you go for a corporate or independent estate agent will be your choice. Don't be afraid to negotiate fees and don't commit yourself to lengthy contracts. By all means give your estate agent enough time to fully market your property, but they don't need three or four months to do so. Besides, if the sole agency expires, and you're quite happy to stay with that agent, you can always renew the agreement.

# 6. Estate Agency Boards

In recent years, advances in technology have greatly increased the number of marketing tools available to the estate agent. Yet with all the different property websites, automated updates, and email and text alerts, the estate agent's board (a 0.5 m² corrugated plastic sheet on a two-by-two wooden post) remains one of the most effective forms of advertising for the industry.

An estate agent's flag, or signpost, displayed outside a property not only promotes the item being sold but also creates brand awareness for the company selling it. A FOR SALE board tells its intended audience who the agent is and what they have to offer, and the SOLD board says they're good at what they do. As mentioned in previous chapters, a strong board presence is a good indicator of how successful the estate agent is, and it is a key factor in selecting an agent.

When a prospective buyer enquires about a property after having seen a FOR SALE board, it generally means they like the property's location and its exterior. If the asking price is within the buyer's budget, then all that remains for the agent to do at this time is to arrange a viewing appointment for them. I've lost count of how many property sales started from by a board enquiry.

Some properties benefit greatly from having boards placed outside them, and others don't. A FOR SALE board in a bustling location will obviously generate more enquiries than one in a cul-de-sac. With certain properties, no sooner had a board gone up outside than our phones would start ringing off the hook with enquiries. The significant increase in call volumes would make us realise just how popular that particular property and its location were.

Then again, there were some properties where the FOR SALE board produced a great deal of interest, but once people asked what the price was, alarmingly few committed to viewing appointments. In such scenarios, the board served as an early indicator that we'd been optimistic in our appraisal of the property—people didn't expect the asking price to be that high. It was either that, or as I learned on a few occasions, there were a lot of nosy neighbours wanting to know what local house prices were doing.

Sometimes, board enquiries will come from surveyors and valuers looking for comparable evidence. As mentioned in an earlier chapter, when a surveyor carries out a mortgage valuation, he will need to supply the lender he is acting for with details of similar properties that have sold locally. One of the ways in which a surveyor can obtain this information is by checking the surrounding roads for properties displaying SOLD boards. If the surveyor finds such boards, he will call the relevant estate agents for further details such as the sale price and what the internal condition of the property was.

A point worth mentioning here is that surveyors researching for comparable evidence will use their discretion in applying the information given to them by estate agents. The reason for this is that the property being valued by the surveyor may have been sold by a competitor to whom the agent lost the instruction. That being the case, the agent might then give misleading information to the surveyor in an attempt to scupper the competitor's sale. Exactly how this is done I'll explain in chapter 11, "A Competitive Business," where we'll take a closer look at the gamesmanship and skulduggery that goes on between rival agencies.

Some estate agents will discount their fees for sellers who allow a For Sale board to be placed at their property. I've also known of companies that ran special promotions (often to mark the opening of a new branch) where for a limited period, no fee would be charged for selling the property. One of the main conditions of this offer would be that the seller must agree to the agent's board being erected at the property.

When correctly utilised, an estate agency board can create additional business for the agent. Even in a cul-de-sac, or a quiet road with few passersby, a single Sold board could lead to further instructions and sales for the agent.

A marketing strategy we employed, combining boards and leaflets, proved quite successful for us. As soon as a For Sale board went up on a new instruction, we'd leaflet drop that and the surrounding roads. The leaflets put through people's letterboxes would announce that we had a new instruction and a strong demand for more.

When the property went under offer, we'd repeat the process. This time the leaflet would state that a sale had just been agreed. Then, once contracts had exchanged, and the board changed from FOR SALE to SOLD, we'd go out and drop leaflets again, saying that the sale had gone through and that we needed similar properties. It worked well.

Boards have been the source of many conflicts between rival estate agencies. A typical example is where a company instructed in a multi-agency puts up a FOR SALE board but takes down their competitor's one in the process. The competitor then instructs their board contractor to do the same—take down the other agent's board and replace it with their own. Meanwhile, each agent will be paying their respective board contractor every time a board is put up, taken down, or replaced. And if a board goes missing altogether, the agent will incur additional costs to replace it.

It has been known for the rivalry between estate agents to descend into what the media described as a "board war." This is where competing agents embark on a campaign to purposely remove each other's boards from outside properties. They may not necessarily go out of their way to do so, but whenever they pass a competitor's board, it will mysteriously disappear, or "accidentally" get knocked down. Fortunately, this sort of thing is quite rare.

Estate agents' boards can also be a point of contention for people outside of the business. Council planning enforcement teams, freeholder management companies, and homeowners, to name a few, have all had run-ins with agents over boards being placed where they shouldn't.

A friend told me an interesting story about a brief stint she had in estate agency during the eighties. Staff training at this firm was carried out by managers or directors. My friend said that in her first week she was shown how to answer the phones, register prospective buyers, and deal with board enquiries. Her manager also mentioned "fly boards."

Years ago, before the introduction of legislation banning the practice, some estate agents would place boards outside properties that weren't on the market. Such boards, known as fly boards, were routinely used by estate agents to boost their board presence in the area. Below is what my friend's manager told her to do about fly board complaints.

"If a member of the public calls to say that one of our boards has been put up outside their home that shouldn't be there, this is how you deal with it. Get the address of the property, apologise profusely, and ask if they don't mind holding while you get the board contractor on the other line. Place the call on hold while you pretend to call the board contractor. Then, go back to the caller, apologise again for the mistake, blame the board contractor, and say that you've arranged for the board to be removed. Then call the board contractor and ask him to collect the board a day later."

My friend didn't enjoy working as an estate agent and left very soon after receiving the above training. However, she remained in the role just long enough to be able to recount a story about how that company's fly boarding activities had worked out for them.

A man had called the office to say that on returning home from work he found a SOLD board had been erected in the front garden of his ground floor flat. He went on to say that he'd spoken to the owners of the other two flats in the building and neither knew anything about the board. My friend, being new to the role and therefore a little nervous, sought the assistance of a more experienced colleague. She transferred the call to a brash young negotiator who was dubbed the office hot shot. The young man dealt with the fly board complaint in the way his manager had requested; however, his manner was rather condescending. My friend felt her colleague's tone was rather dismissive, almost as if he was doing the man a favour by arranging removal of the fly board. The call ended and my friend, grateful for her colleague's support, asked if he wanted her to order the board's removal with the contractor. "No, I'll do it later," he replied, handing her some property particulars to send out to a prospective buyer he'd registered earlier.

As the day progressed, the negotiator, racing around trying to get his next sale, forgot to call the board contractor. Two days later, the flat owner called to say the board still hadn't been removed. He wasn't very pleased. He decided to take the board down himself and left it lying behind the wall in the front garden, ready for collection. Unfortunately, once again the negotiator forgot to call the board contractor.

That Saturday afternoon, the front door of the estate agency opened, and in walked a man carrying one of company's boards. It was the flat owner. He laid the board and its post down on the floor in the middle of the busy office and in a firm voice said, "I know what a fly board is, and I don't want one outside my home. My flat's not for sale and if it was, it certainly wouldn't be with you lot."

The man walked out of the office leaving behind him the now embarrassed estate agents and several of their customers, all in an uncomfortable silence. The manager raised his eyebrows to mimic a surprised look and then rather sheepishly moved the board out of the office and into the back yard. The young negotiator, whose forgetfulness contributed to the incident, was out of the office showing a property at the time.

Much has been done to improve estate agents' standards of practice since those unruly days of the eighties. Ask anyone who worked in the business back then who is still doing so today, and they'll tell you of the vast differences. However, even with all the legislation introduced since, and the much-publicised prosecution and hefty fining of offenders, unfortunately, fly boarding still goes on today. It may not be as widespread as it was in the past and certainly not as obtrusive as our example from the eighties, but it's still happening. And the type of property outside of which you're most likely to see a fly board is a purpose-built block of flats.

If an estate agent places a fly board outside a building of single dwelling, it's unlikely to be there very long. The property owner will instantly notice it, and the board will need to be taken down immediately. If placed outside a house that's been converted to three flats (as in our example), the residents will speak to each other, and once again the agent will be found out quite quickly. Also, if a For Sale board relates to a building in multiple occupation, the agent should state, where reasonable, which part of the building the board relates to. So in our example of the conversion, if it is the ground-floor flat that's for sale, the agent can add a slip to the For Sale board's post indicating: ground-floor flat, or G/F/F, and so on.

Now, in a block consisting of four floors with eight flats on each, a fly board becomes much harder to detect. Even if a board slip indicated which floor the flat was on, in this example it could be any one of eight. This means it will take longer for the rogue estate agent to be found out (if at all they do), which in turn leaves the fly board in place for an extended time, serving its purpose.

I remember one such building, a Victorian school conversion, which consisted of thirty-two flats. The property became known amongst local estate agents as "board heaven." At one point, the estate agents' boards had almost completely covered the ornate wrought iron gates that surrounded the building's grounds. It was very unsightly. Eventually, the residents, who were also the freeholders, prohibited the display of estate agents' boards throughout the development. All agents were informed of the changes in writing and asked to remove existing boards. They were also warned that, from that point on, any agent placing a board at the property would be reported to the relevant authority.

One management company didn't waste time warning estate agents and wouldn't bother reporting them either. Instead, they would immediately take down and destroy any boards placed outside their developments. Even new estate agents quickly learnt that putting a board up outside one of this management company's blocks was a waste of time and money.

Some local authorities have banned the displaying of estate agents' boards in certain conservation areas. Entire groups of roads have been declared as board-free zones.

It's not just outside blocks of flats where estate agents flout the rules on displaying boards. When selling a corner property where front and side aspects of the building face different roads, some estate agents will erect two For Sale boards. Typically, they'll place one board in the front garden and the other on the property's side boundary—a garden wall or fence. This is a more subtle way to boost their board presence, but it's not legal. Regulations state that only one estate agency board is permitted to be placed outside a property.

If a property is being marketed by multiple estate agencies, two boards may be displayed, but they must be joined (back to back) and attached to a single post.

In other words: one flag post with a different agent's board showing in each direction. If a third agent was instructed, they would only be allowed a board if it was to replace one of those already on the post. Should more than one flag be placed at the property, the first one displayed will be deemed the lawful advertisement.

Even in scenarios as that just mentioned, where the competitive element is rife, estate agents will still attempt to outdo one another. And the one-upmanship may start with their boards.

I remember a house being marketed by only two agents, yet they were embroiled in a board war. The property was located on a small, quiet road, the last part of which ended at a field. It wasn't quite a cul-de-sac, because halfway up the road, there was a right turn into another road, which then led to a slightly busier avenue.

The house sat just after the T-junction opposite the other road. Unless you drove right to the end of the smaller road, turned around and then came back, only one side of the For Sale board would be visible. Whether you drove past the road or entered or exited from the T-junction, you only saw one side of the board. The agent whose advert was facing the field may as well have taken their board down, as few people saw it. In fact, to passing traffic, it wasn't at all visible.

Almost every week, one agent would change the boards so that their own would face the road and their rival's, the field. Then a few days later, the other agent would switch them back again. This carried on until a third agent was instructed who, quite resourcefully, fixed their board to the post, facing the road, but under the other two agents'. In the end, the seller asked all the three agents to remove their boards, and as the property wasn't selling, he took it off the market shortly after.

For estate agents, boards can be an excellent aid to marketing. However, there are also times when a For Sale board outside a property can have a negative impact for both the agent and their seller. This is especially so if a property is not selling and has been on the market for a prolonged period of time. The board then becomes a visual indicator that a problem exists. Where the intention of the board was to draw enquiries from prospective buyers, those people will now be questioning why it is taking so long for "for sale" to turn into "sold."

A For Sale board outside a property can also attract unwanted attention. Unfortunately, some members of the public will see a board outside a property they'd like to view and instead of contacting the estate agent, they'll approach the owner directly. Many estate agencies will have a small placard attached to the board stating "viewing by appointment only," but not everyone will abide by that request.

One chap knocked on the door of a house we were marketing and told the seller that we'd sent him along for a viewing— something we would never do. Fortunately, the seller, a young mother whose husband was at work at the time, sensed something wasn't quite right and refused to let the man into her home. We never did find out if that man was a cheeky buyer trying to bypass the estate agent or someone with more sinister intentions.

On the subject of circumventing the estate agent, another man approached a seller directly after seeing the For Sale board displayed on the gatepost. He rang the door-bell and asked if the seller was interested in doing a "private deal."

Some years ago, there was a spate of burglaries across the borough, where the police found that the houses targeted were all on the market for sale. Furthermore, all the properties had For Sale boards outside them. It was thought that the perpetrators would first note the boards, then posing as prospective buyers, approach the agents to arrange viewing appointments. This allowed them to see the inside of the property, casing the joint for entry and exit points, as well as to check what was worth stealing.

Fortunately, incidents like those I've just mentioned did not occur very often, and none of the properties we had on our register at the time were affected. Nonetheless, security is a concern for many people when deciding on whether or not to display a For Sale board outside their home.

Another group from whom For Sale boards draw a great deal of attention are other estate agents. You see, one of the methods used by estate agents to gain instructions is to poach them from their competitors. And the easiest way to identify a property on another agent's books is from the board sitting outside it. This leads to activities known in the industry as board counting, board spotting, or the more broad term that agents use—canvassing.

I'll be explaining exactly what estate agents do when canvassing in chapter 11 "A Competitive Business." However, as the subject bears considerable relevance to the focus of this chapter on estate agency boards, here's a brief outline.

Some estate agencies will go to considerable time and effort to find out which properties their competitors have on their registers. Once they identify a rival's instruction, estate agents will target it with promotional material. They will send letters, post their business cards through the letterbox, or even knock on the door, all with the intention of persuading the owner to instruct them on the sale of the property.

A former colleague was selling his garden flat, which was located on a popular road in a sought-after part of our catchment. To say that the For Sale board outside his home attracted the attention of local estate agents would be putting it mildly.

Within the first week of the property going onto the market, my colleague received a sales letter and a couple of leaflets. In fact, only hours after the board was erected, a compliment slip was posted through the letterbox by an agent; written on it was, "Please contact me urgently regarding the sale of your home." This was a tactic used by some estate agents with the aim of intriguing the seller enough to want to get in touch with them. If the seller called, the agent would then push for a market appraisal and instruction.

Targeting properties this way is very much frowned on by the various bodies that govern the business of estate agency. In fact, it is a direct breach of the code of conduct as laid out by the NAEA for its members. However, if the agent in question is not a member, the code of conduct will not apply to them.

As mentioned, aggressive canvassing is just one of the subjects we'll look at in chapter 11.

Some sellers refused to have any boards displayed outside their home and there were a few reasons for this, security concerns being one. However, over the years, the most common objection I received from sellers not wanting a For Sale board was: "I don't want my neighbours to know that I'm selling."

Any seasoned estate agent would have heard the above board rejection countless times. Now, the way we were trained to respond was to say that the neighbours would likely get to know that the property was for sale, with or without a board being present. For example, they might see the property advertised in the local paper or the agent's window. And if the neighbours are "curtain twitchers," they'll definitely notice prospective buyers turning up for viewings.

When it was put to a seller that way, objecting to a board on the grounds that the people next door would find out the property was for sale seemed silly. Even so, many sellers would remain steadfast in their refusal of a For Sale board. And as for one man, he gave an interesting counter to our response: "Perhaps my neighbours won't see the property advertised. They may not even notice people coming round to view, but if they do, they might then *guess* that I'm selling. However, they'll definitely notice a For Sale board outside, and there won't be any guessing then."

Even the hard-nosed veteran negotiators in our office admitted defeat on that one.

As you can see, boards are very important to estate agencies. Some companies incorporate the attainment of boards into their staffs' monthly performance targets. Other agencies will pay bonuses or offer incentives to staff who achieve the most For Sale and Sold boards in a month.

Boards are extremely effective marketing tools for estate agents and can greatly assist sellers in the sale of their property. Countless times, a prospective buyer would call us after seeing a board; arrange to view the property, and we'd then agree the sale—all within the same hour.

Having said that, boards are a matter of choice, and not every seller will want a For Sale flag outside their home. And countless times, too, we sold properties the same day that they came onto the market that *didn't* have estate agency boards.

So that's all about boards. In the next chapter, titled "Viewings," we're going to look at what happens after the board has done its job.

# 7. Viewings

Once a person has seen a house or flat they like the look of, whether from an estate agent's board, website, or brochure, the next step is to arrange a viewing of the property.

The appointment to view will be organised by the estate agent, and either they or the seller will show the property. Generally, the more viewings an agent makes, the more offers they'll receive, which in turn, should lead to a greater number of sales agreed.

Estate agents will carry out viewings and accompany buyers when a property is not occupied, and the agent has the key. Such properties can be repossessions, probate sales, a previously rented property that is now vacant, or simply where the seller has already moved out.

Some sellers, even though living at the property, will still provide their estate agent with a set of keys. This way the agent can carry out viewings during the day when the seller is at work. The sellers can then show the property when they return home in the evening, thus maximising the potential for a sale.

There are sellers who prefer not to get involved with meeting buyers and carrying out viewings at all, so giving their agent a set of keys helps them avoid this. The drawback here is that viewings will be limited to office hours only and many prospective buyers, due to work commitments, prefer to view in the evenings and at weekends.

Sometimes where the seller lives at the property and will be home at the time of the viewing, the agent will still attend and accompany the buyer. One scenario where this may be required is when the seller is a single female who feels nervous of showing males around her flat on her own. Similarly the seller may be an elderly or infirm person. In both cases, the agent's presence provides some security.

On some occasions, the seller may be home but is just too busy to show the property. This could be someone who works from home, or is a busy mum (or dad) who has young children to attend to. The agent can show the property to prospective buyers without causing too much disruption to the seller. Also, accompanying the viewings allows the estate agency staff to see the property themselves, which enables them to describe it first-hand when dealing with enquiries from buyers.

I have also encountered situations where sellers just did not want to interact with prospective buyers at all but also didn't want to provide us with keys to their property. Here, I saw some rather unusual personalities, like the couple who would agree a time for the viewing appointment, open the door to us and the prospective buyers—not greeting or even acknowledging them—then disappear upstairs. Once the viewing of their property progressed to the first floor, they'd wait for us to enter one of the bedrooms, and then they'd quickly dart out of another bedroom and down the stairs.

Another peculiar pair of vendors were the couple who would also be home for every viewing but wouldn't show the property unless we were present. In fact on one occasion, someone turned up to a viewing appointment ten minutes early, and the couple refused to open the door until the negotiator arrived. And this wasn't due to security concerns, for Mr and Mrs were both built like rugby players. Unlike the other couple, these guys were far from shy of prospective buyers. They'd follow the negotiator around the property to ensure he said all the correct things to the people viewing, like which fixtures still had warranties on them. During one viewing appointment, they let everyone know that they were serious sellers and would not take kindly to any time wasting. Needless to say, this didn't help them in selling their home.

I remember being instructed in the sale of a property, the owner of which was a car salesman. This gentleman didn't provide keys, as he was nearly always available for viewings and was quite willing to show the property himself. Yet, strangely, he insisted on a negotiator being present at all viewing appointments.

Now, even more bizarre was that whenever we accompanied buyers to the property, the owner would greet everyone, and then discreetly wink to us in a gesture that indicated, "I've got this," or "Leave this to me." He'd then lead the buyers off around his home, selling it as if it were a used Toyota. We'll come back to this chap in a moment.

## Out-of-hours viewings

What if a buyer's work commitments make it difficult for them to view properties between nine o'clock in the morning and six in the evening?

Well, most estate agencies are open six days a week, sometimes seven. Also, many will be open for business before and after what may be deemed normal office hours. For example, an estate agency that is open from eight in the morning till eight at night allows house hunters to enquire about and register for properties before they go to work and then view them on their way home after work.

Back in the eighties, one estate agency that I knew of would have their staff work a rota of two shifts – the standard nine to six and a noon to nine. The later shift enabled sales negotiators to accompany buyers in viewing properties outside of usual office hours. This helped buyers and sellers with busy schedules and also gave the estate agent an advantage over competitors whose hours of operation were more traditional.

In recent years, I was employed by a firm whose negotiators worked a five-day week, with the office closing two hours earlier on a Saturday. During the week, however, we were open until seven o'clock at night. And the last hour of the day was usually spent showing properties to people after they'd finished work.

Even where an estate agency's hours are nine to six Monday to Saturday, some staff will work beyond those times in order to carry out viewings or market appraisals. More often than not, such work ended up as unpaid overtime, but that was the chance those negotiators took.

Some of the best buyers I ever dealt with bought their respective homes through me after I showed them properties outside of normal office hours.

One was a schoolteacher who lived and worked outside of the area but had just accepted the position of deputy headmaster at a local school. I'd shown this man several properties, a couple of which he liked, but not quite enough to want to buy. He began to trust my judgement; so when I telephoned to say that a flat had just come onto the market that I thought would be perfect for him, he asked to view it as soon as possible.

My working day finished at six, but I agreed to show this buyer the property at seven thirty, which I did for two reasons. Firstly, he was a strong buyer, whose prospective purchase was motivated by a job move. When I notified him of the new instruction, he immediately altered his plans for that evening and travelled halfway across London to see the property. Secondly, the flat in question was very much in demand. Had I not shown it to my buyer that evening, my colleagues would have sold it to one of the many other buyers lined up to view the next day. Fortunately for me, the schoolteacher walked around the flat once then offered the full asking price.

While working at the same estate agency, I sold a house to a family after showing it to them at eight o'clock in the morning. The couple were moving back to the United Kingdom after living abroad for several years. The wife had returned to London with the two children, ahead of her husband, who was completing his work contract shortly after. She had seen several properties through me but had short-listed this particular house so that her husband, who was in London for that day, could also view the property.

The couple made an offer, which was agreed just over an hour after the viewing. They instructed their solicitor and made the financial arrangements for the purchase before the husband flew back the next morning. Like the school teacher, they were strong buyers and very nice people to deal with, so I didn't mind putting myself out.

We weren't always quite so lucky, and many times we'd show properties beyond our working hours where the viewings would amount to nothing. Sometimes, prospective buyers would be late or wouldn't turn up at all, and we'd be left waiting outside the property.

I remember arranging a viewing appointment for a couple who agreed to meet me at the property at six o'clock in the evening—the time we normally closed. At five past six, a colleague called me to say the couple were running late and would be another fifteen minutes or so. At half past six, they pulled up outside property. They apologised for being late and followed me up the garden path. I opened the front door, and we walked into the house. Just a single step into the hallway, the woman paused, looking rather nervous. "Someone's died here, haven't they?" she asked, with a quiver in her voice.

"The property is a probate sale being sold by the relatives of the deceased, but I honestly don't know if the person passed away in the property," I explained.

Appearing to ignore what I'd just said, the woman looked up; her eyes moved across the ceiling from wall to wall. "No… someone's definitely died here. I'm not living here, Brian. Come on, we have to leave," she said to her husband before turning and walking out. Now I was spooked! After a quick glance in the direction where the woman had looked, I too decided not to stay at the property any longer than necessary. My buyers were thirty minutes late and the actual viewing lasted all of sixty seconds.

A few years into my estate agency career, I became very selective about whom I'd go out of my way to show properties to. Very rarely would I carry out viewings outside of office hours. I remember one particular incident that contributed to my adopting this attitude.

I'd registered a first-time buyer who wanted to view a one-bedroom flat, of which I'd given him the particulars.

We viewed the flat one afternoon, and he asked if it was possible for him to bring his girlfriend back to see it later that day, after she finished work. He said he'd collect her from the station just around the corner from the flat and could meet me outside for around six thirty.

I wasn't busy that evening, so the extra half an hour waiting around and the fifteen minutes or so to show the flat didn't bother me too much. However, I reminded him that it would be dark at the time of the viewing and that there was an area of the flat where the lighting wasn't working.

"Can you bring a torch?" he asked.

"I don't mind bringing one and showing you the flat at that time, but are you sure you want to view what may be your biggest financial commitment to date by torchlight?" I replied. The first-time buyer laughed, agreed with me, but wanted to view nonetheless.

The torch in the office wasn't working, but as I was passing my flat on the way to the viewing, I stopped off there to pick up mine. I showed the young man and his girlfriend the flat. He gave me back the torch, thanked me, and said he'd call me the next day, but he didn't. He also didn't return any of the messages I'd left for him.

For reasons which I'll explain in chapter 9, "Making an Offer," the young man decided to make his offer on the flat through the other agent who was instructed. This meant that if the offer was accepted, and the transaction completed, the other agent would've got the commission and not us. As mentioned, I'll explain more in that chapter but as you can see, incidents such as this made me rather dubious of showing properties on my time.

Aside from scenarios where a negotiator is confident that their buyer will make an offer, conducting viewing appointments outside of normal office hours is not recommended. There are several reasons for this, all of which concern the health and safety of negotiators and members of the public. For example, walking around properties by torchlight after dark because of poor or failed lighting isn't a good idea, especially when that property is in a state of disrepair. Also, in my experience, people viewing houses or flats at night will almost always want to view again in daylight before making an offer.

We had a three-bedroom terraced house come onto our books just after Christmas one year. The property belonged to an elderly lady who'd moved to a care home somewhere in the Home Counties, where she could be closer to her family. The lady's nephew had arranged for the property to be cleared of her belongings, and a set of keys was given to us to carry out viewings.

The house was within two hundred metres of our office, so showing people around could be done at very short notice. Prospective buyers could pop into our office to register with us, and if they wanted to, could view that house a few minutes later. Even though it was winter, and a great number of the viewing appointments were conducted after dark, the lighting inside the house was fully functional. However, another problem soon became apparent.

The first time I went to the property to show a buyer around, I noticed a strong smell of gas in the lounge, which was at the front of the property. As the rest of the house seemed okay, I assumed the gas fire in that front room was faulty. I told my manager about it as soon as I got back to the office, who in turn, phoned the seller's nephew. The nephew's response was that the gas supply to the house had been disconnected shortly after his aunt vacated the property, six weeks before we started marketing.

We continued with our viewing appointments, and each time we opened the lounge door, we were hit by the smell of gas. I went back to my manager and expressed my concerns. Once again, we called the owner's nephew and advised him that we would err on the side of caution and report the suspected gas leak.

We telephoned Transco who, at the time, was the company that dealt with gas emergencies. Engineers arrived within the hour and after carrying out an inspection, put up warning signs and immediately sealed off the front garden and the pavement outside the property. We were told that a mains pipe leading to the property was damaged and leaking, hence the smell in the lounge. Furthermore, each time we turned on the light switch, we risked an explosion. Essentially, every viewing appointment conducted after dark could have been our last!

## Security

I've already mentioned the scenario where a single female selling her property may feel uneasy about showing single males around her home on her own. In such circumstances, the estate agent's presence at the viewing can provide the seller with some reassurance, even if the negotiator is not over six feet tall and ex-Special Forces. In this section; however, we're going to look at security from the estate agent's perspective.

Over the years there have been numerous incidents involving the assault and even kidnap of estate agents at viewing appointments. The most serious of such was the disappearance of estate agent Suzy Lamplugh who, in July 1986, left her office to show a property and was never seen again.

In my first week as an estate agent, a company-wide memo was circulated to remind all staff of the security measures to be taken when showing vacant properties. This communication was prompted by an attack on a male negotiator the week before. The twenty-six-year-old estate agent had arranged to meet a prospective buyer outside the property he was to show them. The house was a repossession, so it was vacant. The negotiator told colleagues he remembered greeting the buyer and walking into the property, then the next he knew, he was face down on the bare floorboards of the lounge. The attacker, posing as a buyer, had provided false contact details and was never caught. The young man recovered from his injuries but did not return to work as an estate agent.

The company where the above incident took place had very clear guidelines on how staff were to conduct viewings on empty properties. Subjects such as health, safety, and personal security were incorporated into new employee induction training, which consisted of a three-day course that ended with an exam. Unfortunately, the negotiator who was assaulted did not follow the correct procedure and made several mistakes.

Firstly, for all accompanied viewing appointments, the prospective buyers had to meet the negotiator in the office and not at the property being viewed. This was especially so with new buyers who'd yet to introduce themselves in person to the estate agency. Once the buyer was known, their contact details verified, and the first viewing conducted, the negotiator could then choose whether to meet them in the office or at the property for subsequent appointments. And where the negotiator was a female, it didn't matter if the parties had met several times before, buyers still had to visit the office prior to the viewing. In fact, I knew of one estate agency that insisted on all prospective buyers going to the office before the viewing, regardless of who would be escorting them on the appointment.

Secondly, the assaulted negotiator failed to verify the contact details of the man requesting the viewing appointment. When the police began their investigation, they were not surprised to find that the address and telephone number provided by the assailant were false. Had the negotiator carried out a quick check, perhaps by asking to call the buyer back to confirm the meeting time, the viewing and assault would never have taken place.

All viewing appointments, including the contact details of buyer and seller involved, must be recorded by negotiators in their personal diaries. Any appointment requiring the negotiator to leave the office must be recorded in the main office diary and include the contact details of any other party attending. An example is: "15.00 Mr and Mrs Jones CTO (coming to office) to view 10 The Crescent 079...020 7..."

Some years ago, a colleague made an appointment to show a repossessed house to a buyer he'd just registered over the phone. Details of the viewing were written in the office diary. Another negotiator was looking at the diary and noticed something strange about the viewing. The name given by the buyer translated into a rather rude word in a language in which the negotiator was fluent. When he pointed this out to his colleague, they decided to call the number provided by the buyer. When they asked for the man, the person at the other end told them that there wasn't anyone there by that name. My colleague decided not to attend the viewing.

Had the buyer been genuine (albeit with an unfortunate-sounding name in Greek), and his telephone number was incorrectly noted by my colleague, then that buyer would have gone to the property for the viewing. After waiting outside for an estate agent to turn up, he would've phoned us to find out why we weren't there at the agreed time. We didn't receive any such call and dismissed the incident as a prank and not something more sinister.

Most estate agencies will use industry-specific software for many of their operational tasks, such as producing property particulars and uploading details to their website. Some firms also use software to record their appointments. This has the benefit of ensuring all information, including telephone numbers, are entered in the correct fields before the event is logged on the system.

Whether an estate agency records their viewings electronically or in a paper diary (most do both), verifying the accuracy of the details falls to the negotiator's discretion.

One small but hugely successful independent estate agency was owned and operated predominantly by females. The director had a policy that all buyers should meet in the office prior to an accompanied viewing. Anyone wanting to arrange a viewing, or to get particulars of a property, had to register their details. Furthermore, in order to register, a prospective buyer had to provide their name, address, and a landline telephone number— a mobile alone was not sufficient. And if you didn't like that, they very politely refused to deal with you.

As mentioned earlier, an estate agency where I worked would incorporate the correct procedure for showing properties into their staff training. When conducting a viewing, negotiators were advised to let buyers enter the property and any subsequent rooms before them. Not only did this appear well-mannered, but it also meant the negotiator wouldn't have their back to the buyer when entering different parts of the building, which is how the young man mentioned earlier was hurt. Also, a negotiator was to ensure a clear line of exit at all times and never allow the person viewing the property to stand between them and the door. And should anything cause the negotiator to feel uneasy, they were to leave the property immediately.

I remember a story of a man who was in the process of buying a repossessed house and asked to go back to the property for another viewing. The offer had just been agreed, and so he wanted to make notes on the renovations he'd planned. At the property, the buyer went from room to room, jotting away with his pad and pencil and commenting on how pleased he was with the proposed purchase.

The negotiator stood in the hallway just outside each room; hanging back slightly, but making himself available for any questions the buyer had. When finished, the buyer returned his notepad to his briefcase. Then he told the negotiator that he was so excited to be buying the house that he needed to "relieve" himself.

The negotiator explained that the toilet wouldn't flush on account of the water supply being disconnected and the system drained down (routine procedure when a property is repossessed). The man's demeanour immediately changed, and he gave what the negotiator described to his colleagues as a creepy smile just before saying, "Oh, I don't need to go to the bathroom. I need to… you know…*relieve myself*!"

The negotiator, realising what the buyer meant, was quite shocked, but calmly replied, "Well, I'll be outside," and left the house to sit in his car, which was parked on the drive. Minutes later the man appeared at the front door, nodded at the negotiator, waved goodbye, and left. The negotiator secured the house and went back to the office, where he told his colleagues of the incident. Apparently, the sale went through, but on the day of completion, the buyer did not collect the keys from the estate agency himself; he had a friend do it for him.

As you can see, showing people around empty properties is not without risk, but luckily, such incidents like those mentioned are quite rare.

## Annoying viewings

Carrying out viewing appointments can be an enjoyable part of estate agency work. It gets you out of the office, meeting new people and seeing different properties. Time passes quickly, and if you come back with an offer—result!

Some viewing appointments, however, can be incredibly frustrating and also a complete waste of time.

There was once a woman who registered with us as a buyer. She really liked to view properties. She didn't want to buy any of them; she just wanted to view them. In fact, we later learned that she was notorious amongst estate agents in a different area who dubbed her the "serial viewer."

Before we were aware of her strange hobby, we showed this woman a couple of one-bedroom flats. She took more than half an hour viewing each one. That's over thirty minutes to look around two rooms, a kitchen, a bathroom, and a landing. I've known surveyors who take less time carrying out valuations of such properties.

We found out that this woman would register with different estate agencies for different types of properties. So she'd view three-bedroom houses with one agent this week, then flats with another the following week. After viewing another flat through us and saying that she really liked it, we asked the woman if she wanted to submit an offer. Strangely, this seemed to make her uneasy. "I'll have to think about it and get back to you," she said, but we never heard from her again.

One particularly stressful viewing was when I arranged to show a house to a young couple who brought their extended family along. The property belonged to an elderly lady whose health had deteriorated to the degree that she could no longer live on her own. She put the house onto the market, and the proceeds of the sale were to help pay for her stay in a residential care home.

I was inside the house chatting to my client when the buyers turned up—husband and wife, the wife's mother, the sister, and her two children. I greeted them and showed them in to the lounge, where I also introduced them to the owner of the property. The elderly lady gave a friendly smile and said, "Please feel free to look around, and if you have any questions, this young man [me] will be able to answer them for me."

The seller barely finished her sentence when the buyers were off in different directions. The husband and his mother-in law were in the garden looking at the exterior of the house. The sister-in-law didn't seem to care that her children were trying to swing from the dining room curtains, while the wife was on her mobile phone, inviting her cousins round to view the property.

We'd advertised the property as needing refurbishment, and I can understand prospective buyers not realising the full extent of required works until they view. However, what I didn't like was that these people were rather indiscreet with their comments on the condition of the house. They could see that the owner was a frail pensioner, and yet they didn't seem to care, but I did. I brought the viewing to a close, saying that I had to leave for another appointment. They should call us if they wanted to see the house again. They never did, and we sold it to another buyer.

During the so-called buy-to-let boom of recent years, I met more than my fair share of wannabe investors. Showing amateur property developers around houses and flats was an interesting pastime. A retired and rather acidic couple had arranged to view a repossessed flat that had just come to the market. The property generated a lot of interest, and so we staggered the viewings for every fifteen minutes on a Saturday. At their viewing, the man was opening and shutting the kitchen cupboards rather aggressively. I remember thinking he'd cause damage, when at that moment one of the doors came off its hinge. He took a very brief look at what he'd done, but he was promptly instructed by his partner to leave it alone, because it was, apparently, "already like that!"

The intercom buzzer signalled the arrival of the next viewing, and I went to answer the door. On my return, I found the man attempting to lift the carpet in the lounge. When I asked him to stop, he voiced dissatisfaction at his viewing crossing with that of another buyer's—fifteen minutes was not enough time to view properly. He and his partner then stormed out, saying that they'd never deal with our estate agency again. I apologised to the other buyer, who made a joke about the couple's outburst and went on to view the property.

On another occasion, a woman requested a viewing for a different flat saying she and her daughter were investors. At the property they pulled up in a high-performance vehicle, heavily made-up and draped in designer wear. I greeted them and showed them into the flat. They spent the duration of the viewing each chatting on their mobile phones. And from what I could gather, the conversations were not about property, although one of them was blatantly talking about me. I waited patiently for them to finish, and when they did, having only seen the entrance hall and lounge, they told me the property wasn't suitable.

Sometimes viewings go perfectly until it comes time to discuss money. I once registered a couple who were both professionals with good careers and a budget that would easily buy them the house they wanted. We seemed to get on very well, and after showing them several properties, I found what I thought was the perfect one for them. It had everything they'd asked for. It was in a very sought-after road, and it was well within their price range.

Inside EA

I explained that a house like that would not be on the market for very long, and they arranged to view it immediately.

We spent thirty minutes walking around the property, during which they told me several times how much they liked it. Then, at the end of the viewing, they made such a ridiculously low offer that, at first, I thought they were joking. The offer amounted to just over half the asking price. I explained that the property would likely be sold in the next day or two; if they really wanted it, they'd have to come up with a figure a lot closer to the asking price.

The man turned to his wife and tilted his head in my direction as if to mock what I'd just said. He told me that he didn't think the property was worth any more than the amount he'd offered. If someone was silly enough to pay more, then they were welcome to it. The property went under offer at the full asking price to a buyer my colleague introduced an hour or so later.

## Selling it

What is the best way to conduct a viewing? Should the estate agent be giving a dynamic sales pitch, or will the property sell itself? If the owner is willing to show the property, should they conduct the viewing, or is it best left to the estate agent?

A broad answer to all of those questions is that it really depends on the situation at hand and the people involved. However, when I first started out as an estate agent, we were trained to follow a general format when conducting viewings. For example, we were

166

told to allow prospective buyers to enter a room before us and that in some cases, we should stand just outside the doorway. As mentioned earlier, this was good practice for personal safety, but it also meant there were fewer people in a room, making the room appear larger and less cluttered, in turn making it easier to view.

As far as what we were to say at viewings, in the main, we were to point out the benefits and potential of the property and answer any questions the prospective buyers may have had. Some estate agents believe such dialogue to be sufficient. People will offer on the property without being "pitched," and the agent's role comes into play when negotiating the sale price. Other agents feel that a bit of salesmanship at the viewing assists in achieving the right price for the property. Personally, I've always thought it to be more of the former than the latter.

The wise women and men who trained us all those years ago said that salesmanship was more listening than talking. "You have two ears and one mouth. Use them in that ratio," we were told.

So as a negotiator, if you asked a buyer the right questions and then actually listened to their answers, you'd have a better idea of their requirements. And when a suitable property became available, and you showed those buyers around, you could highlight the specific features of interest to them without going into a full-blown sales presentation, unlike a former colleague who'd become verbally incontinent at viewings. Accompanied by his manic hand movements, this chap would bombard prospective buyers with reasons (many irrelevant to them) as to why they should make an offer on the property before someone else did. On occasion such high-pressure sales techniques worked for him, but more often than not, people thought he was an idiot. In fact, "moron" is how one woman referred to him.

He once registered a prospective buyer who specified that she wanted a flat located within walking distance of a tube station, as she worked in Central London and didn't drive. And because her job often took her abroad, during which time her flat would be vacant, she preferred it to be on an upper floor, as this was more secure. What did this cloth-eared negotiator do? He took the lady to see a ground-floor flat that was two miles from the nearest station. He then proceeded to sell the benefits of having direct access to a rear garden and off-street parking at the front—several times.

I remember a negotiator at a rival estate agency who operated in a way similar to my moronic colleague. His hard-selling and forceful methods earned him infamy amongst those who dealt with him.

A friend told me that she'd popped into this chap's office to register her details and before she knew it, was out viewing a house. A house, she added, that lacked any of the requirements she'd specified, but which the agent pretty much insisted she view. At the viewing, when she tried to explain why the house wasn't suitable, the agent just continued talking. And without pausing to hear what was being said to him, he told my friend that if she wanted the property, she'd need to offer immediately, because another buyer had already expressed interest. Recounting the story, my friend said that when the agent finally accepted that she didn't like the house, he acted as if she'd wasted *his* time by viewing it.

In contrast, some of the best viewing appointments I ever witnessed were conducted by the property owners themselves. In my opinion, these people did a far better job of showing their homes than many of the estate agents I knew could ever have. One such example was the family selling their Edwardian semi in North London. The wife had set up a business from home that was doing well, and she needed more space for her office and design studio. The couple had found the perfect property to move to and to expedite matters, were proceeding to buy it independent of selling their own. As they would need to sell their house eventually, they gave it to us to put on the market.

When it came to booking viewing appointments, our clients were quite flexible. However, because the woman worked from home and was often busy, we would have to accompany and show prospective buyers around ourselves.

Within minutes of my manager taking the property onto our books, I'd arranged my first viewing. I went along to the property, where I introduced the buyers and myself to the seller. The woman greeted us with a smile, looked at me, and said, "Tell you what, as you've not seen the house either, why don't I show everyone around this time?" and off we went on our guided tour.

While showing us her home, the seller made casual conversation, during which she found out how many children the buyers had, and their ages. Just a few minutes later she knew the occupations, hobbies, and interests of the people viewing her house. She then provided detailed information on local schools and established that Mrs Buyer had the same occupation as one of her neighbours, saying she thought the two women would get on really well. She also mentioned that Mr Buyer had a choice of two very good squash clubs in the area. And because the seller had explored the possibility of extending her home, she was able to share the knowledge she acquired on local planning consent.

Now, some of you may be thinking that this woman sounded like a real busybody, but it was the buyers who did most of the talking. The seller simply asked the right questions and listened to the answers. She was then able to provide information that her prospective buyers found useful. It was all very subtle—just a friendly chat.

That was the only time I went to that property, because after the viewing, my buyers offered the full asking price. And to this day, I don't know if the seller actually knew that she was doing it, or if dealing with people and selling houses was something that just came naturally to her. Nonetheless, it was a viewing that many of the motor-mouthed estate agents I knew could've learned from.

Over the years I met several sellers whose pleasant manner assisted them in selling their property. One man told us, "Just get the buyers round here, and I'll do the rest." Again, the very first person we sent to view bought the house.

In sharp contrast to this story was the man whose sales technique actually put buyers off making an offer on his home. Remember our used-car salesman from earlier on? This was the chap who insisted we accompany all buyers wanting to see his house, even though when we got there, he'd take over and conduct the viewings himself. We'd be pointing out benefits, such as the house being within the catchments of popular schools, when he'd interject to say where the wooden floors were purchased from and at what cost per square metre.

This seller's home was quite well presented, a little person-alised in parts, but on the whole, a nicely maintained house. However, when he launched into super-sales overdrive, this burly car salesman would actually deter people from offering. He'd focus on points like the master tradesman who plastered his bedroom wall, and then he'd get people to acknowledge the quality of the finish. Some people were almost intimidated into agreeing with everything the seller said. Then, at the end of the viewing, he'd attempt to close the deal by asking prospective buyers, bluntly, "When do you think you'll be making an offer, then?"

We didn't sell that man's house, and he withdrew it from our register.

Certain properties, especially those correctly priced, seem to achieve offers with little or no input from the estate agent.

In many cases all we needed to do was let people view the property. Many buyers know exactly what they want and how to go about finding it. And no amount of selling by the agent, whether refined or otherwise, will change their mind.

Equally, any experienced estate agent will tell you that they've seen buyers start their search with one type of property and end up viewing and buying something different. Perhaps that's what the negotiator in our earlier story was counting on when showing my friend that house.

If a buyer likes a property, they'll make an offer regardless of how much talking the agent did or didn't do at the viewing. Some sellers will do a better job of showing their property than their estate agent would, whereas the conduct of other sellers may actually deter an otherwise interested buyer from offering.

If the house being viewed is not suitable for a buyer, then it is unlikely that a smooth-talking negotiator at a viewing will convince him to make an offer. And if they do, will that offer go the distance? With property transactions taking around eight weeks (often longer) to become contractual, and abortive rates as high as 50 per cent, I'll leave you to answer that question.

# 8. Buying

Anyone who has bought, or attempted to buy, a property in recent years will tell you that it was no simple task. Buyers have had a tough time in the last decade or so, and I will personally attest to that. Moving home may be listed as one of life's more stressful events, but I can tell you that for me, organising removals, packing, and unpacking was a doddle, compared to searching for a property and trying to buy one.

## A seller's market

Unfortunately, the laws of supply and demand sent the housing market in a direction that made life rather difficult for buyers. As estate agents, we'd take a property onto the register and have a dozen viewings for it before its particulars were even typed up.

One Friday morning, I took on a two-bedroom garden flat, which was a nice property, but if I'm honest, not particularly special. What's more, the asking price was higher than that of similar properties we'd sold on that road prior. Viewings were to commence that Saturday, and by Friday afternoon we'd confirmed fifteen of them. The task of conducting the viewings was split into shifts and shared between negotiators, one of whom said he was so busy, he didn't have time to visit the bathroom.

Scenarios like this were, and sometimes still are, quite common. A buyer booked in to see a property arrives for the viewing just as the appointment before them is leaving. As they finish viewing the property themselves, they see the people booked in after them arrive for their appointment. Different estate agents are telling the buyer that there's very little coming onto the market, and this is the first suitable property he's viewed in a while. This creates a sense of urgency. No negotiation to be had here. If the buyer wants the property, he's got to go in at the asking price. And if he doesn't, someone else will.

If you think that the above sounds harsh, it's the environment in which I bought my own home and one that I worked in for many years. Don't you think that's a terrible setting for people to make one of the most important financial decisions of their lives?

## Buyer's market

There was a time in the market when a big concern for estate agents during a running sale was hanging on to the buyer. A slight problem with the survey, delays in the chain, or simply a better property around the corner, and we'd lose our buyer.

Back then, banks would report monthly falls in house prices. The cost of borrowing was higher, and mortgages were a little harder to come by. There were properties that remained on the market for months on end, some for over a year. Sellers were more willing to negotiate their asking price, and strong buyers stuck out like sore thumbs.

I remember when I joined a new company. One of my first tasks was to update the register of prospective buyers. This involved calling everyone whose records were more than six weeks old to check if they were still looking for a property and if their requirements had changed. In those days, very few people had mobile phones, and an attribute that defined a strong buyer was if they provided a daytime contact number. Put differently, many prospective buyers at the time did not want to be contacted at work by estate agents offering them properties. As a result, I found myself leaving messages on a lot of answering machines. In fact, when I called one woman, her outgoing message included that she no longer wanted to be bothered by estate agents, or words to that effect.

It's a different story today. Buyers provide estate agents with mobile numbers and email addresses and want to be contacted as soon as a suitable property becomes available. So let's now have a look at how estate agents work with buyers and the dos and don'ts for both parties during the house-buying process.

## Registering

A person looking to buy a property in a particular geographic area will need to register their details with the estate agents that cover that location. They can do this by telephone, by email, or in person by visiting the agent's office. Sometimes, the process of registering starts from an enquiry. A prospective buyer may see a board outside a property they like the look of, call the estate agent for more information, and register their details. The same applies to properties seen online or in the local paper.

When a negotiator registers a prospective buyer, they will need to obtain certain information as a minimum. Other than the obvious, such as name, address, contact details, and what sort of property they're after, the first thing a negotiator should establish is the prospective buyer's position. How serious are they? How urgent is their property purchase? The best way a negotiator can qualify this without an offensive "How serious are you?" is by asking a more subtle open question such as "How soon do you need to move?"

For those of you who don't know, an open question is one that cannot be answered with yes or no and should elicit information from the person to which it is being asked. Posing the above open question to prospective buyers should receive answers such as:

"We need to find something urgently, as we've sold our own property, and we're holding up the chain below us."

"Well, I start my new job in September, so I'd really like to be moved in by August."

"I'm living with my parents. This will be my first property, so whenever the right thing comes up."

"We're just looking at the moment and haven't put our place on the market yet."

The first two answers tell the estate agent that they have a motivated buyer. The third is from a first-time buyer who wants to buy a property and may want to move quickly, but they don't need to. As for the last, this person is just fact-finding at the moment. Their situation may change quickly, and if they live locally to the agent, they will be a prospective client; however, presently they are not the type of buyer you'd send to a property if you were competing with colleagues or other agents. They'd lose to buyers like the first two every time.

Estate agents will place their buyers in one of several categories, which I've listed below. The brackets show the acronyms used by estate agents when defining a buyer's position in their notes.

*First-time buyer (FTB)*—This one is pretty much self-explanatory. Some first-time buyers are more motivated to buy than others. One that is renting a property and whose tenancy will expire shortly may be more pushed than a FTB who's living with parents.

*Nothing to sell (NTS)*—Also classified by some agents as unencumbered, or chain-free, this type of buyer doesn't have a property to sell in order to buy.

They are very similar to first-time buyers, except that someone who is NTS has been through the house-buying process before.

*Sold subject to contract (SSTC)*—This type of buyer has a property to sell that is currently under offer. A buyer that is SSTC has a chain below them and therefore is motivated to find a property in order to keep that chain together.

Some of the most committed buyers I ever worked with were those whose status was SSTC. However, their strength as a buyer will depend on their chain being complete and its other participants proceeding. And it is for this reason that in scenarios where the property being sold is a repossession, offers from SSTC buyers will not be considered by the seller or those acting for them.

*Own to sell (OTS)*—These are prospective buyers who need to sell their own property in order to buy. I'm going to spend a little more time talking about this type of buyer, as their status can be a little more complex than the others.

OTS buyers can be divided into two subcategories. There is the OTS buyer whose property is up for sale but is yet to go under offer, and the OTS whose property isn't on the market at all. Estate agents consider OTS to be the weakest category of buyer, especially the latter of the two.

If either of these two types of buyer made an offer on a property, even if the offer was at the asking price, it would be deemed insignificant, because the sale cannot proceed until the OTS becomes SSTC. And a buyer who hasn't got their property on the market stands no chance of becoming SSTC.

A further subcategory still was the OTS with a property to sell in our catchment. We'd monitor them closely, as they were potential clients, and we would always ask for the opportunity to appraise their home.

The negotiator would also ask the prospective buyer what arrangements they've made for the financing of their purchase. In other words, do they have funds available, will the money come from the proceeds of the sale of their existing home, or do they require a mortgage? This question assists the negotiator in further qualifying the strength of the buyer, but also, where relevant, leads him into offering the company's mortgage services.

An interesting point here is that a buyer does not really have to prove their financial position and ability to purchase until they actually find a property they want to buy. Even then, rarely did we ask a buyer to provide proof of funds, like a bank statement, for example. On the other hand, we always asked for details of who was arranging the mortgage.

What the negotiator is trying to ascertain at this stage of the registering process is how committed the prospective buyer is, and whether they can be passed on to the mortgage consultant as a lead.

## The mortgage appointment

The subject of estate agents providing mortgage services was covered earlier in the book; however, here's a brief recap, along with some notes for buyers.

Nowadays, it's pretty much standard practice for estate agents to offer their mortgage service to buyers when they register. And where I worked, if the buyer didn't agree to an appointment with the consultant when registering, negotiators were trained to try again when the buyer was viewing, and yet again if they offered.

A mortgage consultant working for or with an estate agency will act much in the same way as a broker. They will have access to various lenders offering different home loans. Many consultants I worked with were independent as to which lender they could use for the mortgage, but they were usually affiliated to one company for mortgage-related products like life assurance.

One of the advantages to the buyer for using this service was that the mortgage consultant would look to several lenders to find the most suitable loan. One of the larger estate agency groups would, on occasion, get exclusive deals through some of the high-street lenders. This could be anything from a preferential interest rate to a free mortgage valuation.

Also, the mortgage consultants would gather the documentation required by the lender in order to approve the loan before a property was found. The benefit to the buyer was that as far as they were concerned, the mortgage was pre-approved. All they needed to do was find their new home, and as long as there weren't any problems with the survey or legal work, the formal mortgage offer was issued. The other benefit for the buyer was that the agent, having the potential for two deals (the mortgage and the house sale), would do their very best to find the right property for that buyer.

By getting buyers to sign up to this service, the agent would earn commission from the loan and any associated products taken by the buyer. If the buyer found a property through the estate agency, the agent also got commission for the house sale. If the buyer found a house through a competitor, as often happened, all was not lost, and the agent still got paid for the mortgage.

For the negotiator, he knew that he was dealing with a financially pre-approved buyer who could afford what they said they could. Also, the mortgage appointment and sign-up would count towards the negotiator's monthly performance target, which senior management would watch closely.

During my time in the business, most of the buyers we registered would not want to see the estate agency's mortgage consultant. Many would say that they'd made their own arrangements, or that they wanted to find a property first. Choosing to get a home loan from your own bank, building society, or financial advisor is fine. However, waiting until a property is found before starting the mortgage process isn't a good idea.

As mentioned, one of the unique selling points that we'd use when offering our service was that getting the mortgage pre-approved would put the buyer in a stronger position. After all, it's common sense that a seller who has two buyers offering the same price will favour the one who has arranged finance over the one who hasn't.

So if you're looking to buy a property and need a mortgage to do so, it's a good idea to explore your options before commencing your search for a new home. Speak to your bank, building society, or financial advisor. If the estate agents that you register with offer their mortgage services, as long as there is no cost or obligation involved, see what their consultant has to say.

I remember stories in the press about estate agents operating lists of preferred buyers—also known as hot or special buyers. These were the people whom estate agents would notify first of any new properties to the market, as they were deemed to be in a stronger position than other buyers. Now, as a negotiator, my job was to get my client the best price for their property from the best buyer. In trying to achieve this, I was often up against colleagues and competitors with the same objective. In those circumstances, I was hardly going to send my weakest buyer to the property first.

The problem stories the press were highlighting were like that of the negotiator who told a prospective buyer that in order to get on the "hot buyer" list, he'd have to see the office mortgage consultant. This can be construed as blackmail. Unfortunately for the negotiator and the estate agency he worked for, that particular buyer was a financial services regulator.

Arranging mortgages is big business for estate agents, and they take it very seriously. As a negotiator, booking mortgage appointments was a main part of my monthly performance target. I once agreed five property sales in a week, and yet my area manager was not impressed, because my buyers didn't take mortgages through us. So when you register with some estate agencies, don't be surprised if they really push to get you in front of their mortgage consultant.

## The applicant register

A prospective buyer registered with an estate agency may also be referred to as an applicant. Their contact details and property requirements will be placed on a database known as the applicant register. In the past, this information was usually written on a pre-printed A5 card and filed in a ring binder of the same size. Today the applicant's details will either be logged on a computer database directly, or on the card first and the computer after. Some estate agencies operate a communal register, while at others, the negotiators have their own personal applicant register. I'll explain how this works.

An applicant registers their details with an estate agency. The negotiator lists their requirements and will recommend any suitable properties that are available. The applicant will either arrange to view those properties or request the particulars be sent, which the negotiator will do—either by email or posting hard copy. The negotiator will hold on to the applicant card, making a note to follow up on the property particulars sent for feedback or to arrange a viewing. Whatever the outcome at this point, the negotiator will update the applicant's record accordingly, and if there is a card, it will be filed in the applicant register, usually by order of price.

If the estate agency operates a communal applicant register, all sales negotiators can offer properties and arrange viewings for any of the prospective buyers listed. The responsibility for updating applicant records will be shared by all negotiators.

If the office operates personal applicant registers, then each negotiator will be assigned their own list of prospective buyers. This list will be made up of the people whom the negotiator personally registered. Where applicants are registered by staff in non-selling roles, or the buyer enquiry has come via the company website, those applicants are distributed evenly to negotiators. Servicing that applicant register, offering new properties to buyers, arranging viewing appointments, and updating their records are solely the tasks of the negotiator who owns the register. Should a personal register become neglected, the office manager may reassign some of its applicants to a different negotiator.

Each type of register has its benefits and disadvantages for both the estate agent and the applicant.

The main point of contact for a buyer on a personal applicant register will be the negotiator who owns it. If that negotiator happens to be absent from the office when a property comes to the market, the applicant may not be notified and can miss out. Meanwhile, other negotiators in the office will be contacting their applicants about the property. The same applies if the negotiator isn't particularly good at their job and neglects some of the applicants on the register assigned to him. As mentioned above, it is in such situations where a good office manager proves his or her worth.

With a communal applicant register, there is less chance of buyers not being informed of new instructions, because all office negotiators will be using it. That way the register should be kept up to date, resulting in fewer missed opportunities.

Some buyers (and sellers) like having a single point of contact; preferring to deal with the negotiator they've built a rapport with, rather than several different staff at the estate agency. With a communal register, a buyer might receive three calls in one week, all from different negotiators.

A negotiator may work with a buyer for weeks to find them a new home and establish exactly what that person is looking for in a property. In the negotiator's absence, a colleague picks up the communal register and calls the buyer about a property that's literally just come to the market. The colleague arranges a viewing; the buyer likes the property, and their offer is agreed. The negotiator has just lost a sale to his colleague.

This happened to me more times than I care to remember. The owner of a property we appraised weeks prior would call to say he'd like to put it on the market and gives the go ahead for viewings to commence. I'd be out showing a property or appraising another, and by the time I got back to the office, my best applicants had already been phoned by my colleagues. This is a common occurrence in a competitive office environment. And if the manager isn't on top of things, negotiators will do things like hiding applicant records from their colleagues. We'll discuss the infighting that goes on in chapter 12 of the same name.

Before we move on from the subject of registering with estate agents, there are a couple of points I'd like to mention.

Estate agents know that a great number of the applicants they register will end up being a complete waste of time.

Typical examples are those people who register, ask for property particulars to be sent, and then never return the estate agents' calls when they try to follow up. I've also known applicants who'd request a viewing but fail to respond when the negotiator called back to confirm the appointment time. Some we'd never hear from again, others might email a viewing request for the same property a week later.

There were also people who would email their property requirements but not provide any other contact details. At best, such applicants might get a reply from the agent acknowledging the request, but asking for an address and contact numbers before placing them on the register. Very few of these people would respond.

Anyone can miss an appointment or forget to call someone back. It happens; we're all human. However, if an applicant continues to display some of the behaviour I've just mentioned, it won't be long before their applicant card goes in the bin, and their details are removed from the system.

## The phone out

When an estate agency receives a new instruction, they can instantly bring that property to the attention of their buyers in several ways—email and text alerts being two. However with all the available technology, the phone call still remains the best method of communication, in my experience.

Once the go-ahead has been given to commence marketing a new property, negotiators will immediately begin calling their prospective buyers, which is known as a "phone out." First, they will speak to the people who they know can and want to buy now. These will be buyers whose property requirements the negotiator is fully aware of and generally someone that the negotiator has been in regular contact with.

A negotiator's hottest prospects should be listed in their viewing diary. In other words, these are the people who have been out viewing properties recently. Exceptions to this are buyers who have just registered with the estate agency, and also those who haven't had anything matching their requirements become available of late.

Next, negotiators will begin calling people on the office applicant register. They will go through the A5 cards or database for all the people in the price range relevant to the new instruction. Some negotiators will only speak to applicants whose requirements match closely with the property's specification. Others may speak to as many applicants as they can; updating any changes in the process. This could be an applicant whose property needs have changed, including their budget and area of search. It may be that the person is no longer looking or has found a flat through a competitor. Here, if it's the latter of the two, ideally the negotiator should try to find out which flat and what competitor. Could the property be one the estate agency appraised?

Whatever the outcome of the telephone call, the negotiator will update the applicant's card or record on the database. If a viewing was requested, the negotiator will arrange the appointment and log the details in the relevant diaries. If the applicant is no longer looking, their details will be removed from the system. Should the negotiator not be able to speak to the applicant, has left a message for them, or sent an email, then this too will be noted.

When phoning out on a new property instruction, I came across a first-time buyer who'd registered their requirements as urgent, but had failed to respond to any of our calls. In fact, her applicant card had six entries to say voicemail messages had been left. So, I left a message to ask the applicant if she was still looking for a property and mentioned that we'd tried to contact her numerous occasions without success. I also said that if we didn't hear from her within a week, we'd assume she was no longer looking and remove her details from our database. Some of my colleagues wouldn't have bothered leaving a message and would have either removed the applicant's details automatically, or they'd just skip to calling the next applicant.

A day or so later, the first-time buyer's father visited our office to complain that his daughter and her fiancé had registered for property, but no one was calling them with any! We showed the gentleman the notes logged on his daughter's applicant card, and he verified the number we were leaving messages on as being correct. The man sighed and then explained that he was assisting his daughter and future son in-law with the financing of their house purchase. "I offered to help them with their deposit, but I didn't expect to have to find the house for them, too—typical!" Rolling his eyes and giving a simultaneous tut, the man muttered something under his breath that sounded like "Lazy little sods!" He then asked that going forward, we contact him and not his daughter about new properties. We did as the gentleman requested and found him a house within a week. The young lady and her fiancé were quite fortunate, because her father put up half the purchase price in cash. And yet when we were trying to find them a property, they couldn't be bothered to return our calls.

When I first started working as a sales negotiator, in training we were told to try to match at least four of the prospective buyer's requirements with the property's features. For a house, this could be its price, the number of bedrooms, its location, the condition of the building, what direction the rear garden is facing, the house's proximity to schools, what parking facilities it had, and so on. This part is a lot easier if the negotiator who registered the buyer asked them the right questions, listened to their answers, and logged the information on the system. In my experience, not everyone did, and some applicants were registered for three-bedroom houses at a certain price, and that was it. When I called them at a later date, I found their requirements to be far more specific, like a garage being a necessity, or that they wouldn't consider properties in need of refurbishment.

So let's imagine a buyer calls to register, saying that their move is urgent. They're looking for a ground-floor converted flat that has two bedrooms, period features, direct access to its own rear garden, and off-street parking, and is within walking distance of the tube station. Two days later a property with all of the above features comes onto the market. It's exactly what your buyer has asked for. You rush to dial their number and can't help thinking to yourself that this sale's in the bag. They answer, you tell them about the property, listing the features they requested one by one, and their response is, "Sounds good. Can you send me the details first?" Send the details!? Your colleagues, Great White and Hammerhead, are booking viewings for their buyers as you speak. You tell your buyer that it's a very sought-after property, and they risk losing it if they don't view as soon as possible, but they still want to see the property particulars first.

At this point, a negotiator may no longer consider the buyer to be a serious prospect, either for this property or future instructions. As pointed out earlier, we were trained to match at least four of a property's key features to that of a buyer's requirements. And when we did, if the buyer wouldn't jump to view we'd wonder why.

Before we all started using email, if a buyer wanted to see a property's particulars, we would have to post them to him and follow up with a call the next day. Even then, most people would leave for work before their post arrived, so we'd have to phone them again the next day.

Nowadays, a negotiator can telephone a buyer about a new instruction and either refer them to a website or email the details within seconds. They can then call the buyer for feedback and arrange a viewing if required, all of which can be done within minutes. But as mentioned earlier, talking to buyers remains the best way for an estate agent to communicate new properties to the market. In fact, there are often scenarios where the Internet and email can't be used, and a simple phone call is the only option. Let me explain.

When estate agents receive instructions to sell a property, they will begin contacting their prospective buyers straight away. They will not wait for the property particulars to be printed or uploaded to the website before calling applicants. In fact, any estate agent worth their salt would compile a list of strong buyers before even appraising a property. I've sold many houses and flats by lining up my best buyers prior to the property coming onto the market.

If the office manager came back from an appraisal with instructions to proceed with marketing, or the owner of a previously appraised property called to give us the go-ahead, we'd be on the phones immediately. Any property specifications we'd provide for buyers over the phone were quoted from the manager's handwritten notes. So, when we'd commence a phone out on a new instruction, at that point in time, the property particulars would not yet be available for posting, emailing, or downloading.

Imagine a scenario in a busy estate agency where three or more negotiators are simultaneously phoning out on a new property instruction. If you're one of the people called, and you want to wait for the particulars to be prepared before committing to a viewing, if it's a half-decent property you've probably already lost it. Unfortunately, that's how tough it can be sometimes.

A buyer may have valid reasons for wanting to see a property's full specification prior to viewing it. For example, they may have previously travelled a fair distance to view "the perfect property," only to find that it wasn't at all how the estate agent described it to be. And now their confidence in estate agents has diminished. Some buyers, especially if unfamiliar with an area, may want to see the outside of a property and get a feel for its location before committing to viewing it internally. Such reasons aside, when an estate agent calls about a property whose features match up with at least four of a buyers specified requirements, that buyer should make the effort to view.

## Buying property and the Internet

Imagine the following scenario: a house hunter goes online and registers their details and property requirements with a well-known property website. They've also set up alerts to receive an email or SMS message when a suitable property comes to the market.

At 9.45 on a Monday morning, the buyer receives an automated email alert to say that a house matching their requirements has just come onto the market with an estate agent they've registered with. The buyer has a brief look through the property's specifications and immediately calls the estate agency to request a viewing. At 9.53, the estate agent tells the buyer that the property is under offer and no longer available for viewing. The prospective buyer, quite understandably, is very puzzled. Are they expected to believe that in the eight minutes since the email alert was received, another buyer has been to view the property and made an offer, which the estate agent put forward to the seller and got the sale agreed, and the property has been taken off the market?

I've encountered such scenarios countless times. In fact the one mentioned above relates to a family home that we brought to the market on Saturday lunchtime and agreed its sale before the end of the day. The owner telephoned us that morning to ask if we could fit in an appraisal that same day. They'd found a property they really wanted to buy and so needed to get theirs sold as soon as possible.

Our manager rearranged his lunch break and went along to the property where the owner gave instruction. We began phoning prospective buyers, many of whom weren't available for viewing that day, and some we couldn't reach. Of those people we did speak to, the first one to view the house made an offer, which the owner accepted.

Later that day, our manager, while chewing a chicken Caesar wrap, began preparing the property particulars for the administrator to type up when she was back in the office on Monday. When the office administrator prepared the property particulars on the Monday morning, as soon as she put them into the database, they were automatically uploaded to the websites we advertised with, which in turn triggered the buyer alerts.

Why prepare particulars and advertising if the property is already under offer? Firstly, when a sale is agreed, the estate agent will notify the buyer, seller, and their respective solicitors in writing and will also include a copy of the particulars of sale. As for the advertising, estate agents might not use up a paid slot in the local newspaper for a property already sold, but they will upload its details to their website. This allows whoever it may concern—prospective clients or competitors—to see that the estate agent is active and has gained another success. And while they may not be fully marketing the property, the estate agent will display its details on the website and have particulars ready, just in case the running sale falls through. What they should do, however, is indicate that a sale has been agreed by marking the property as sold subject to contract (SSTC).

In the next chapter, we're going to look at what happens once a buyer has viewed a property that they like enough to make an offer.

# 9. Making an Offer

When a buyer offers on a property, the estate agent will need to obtain certain information before presenting the offer to the seller. At this point, the estate agent should already be aware of their buyer's position in terms of whether or not they have to sell a property. If a related sale exists, then the agent will need to speak to the buyer's selling agent to establish chain details. In certain circumstances, this may involve speaking to more than one estate agency in the chain.

The agent will also need to confirm financial aspects of the proposed purchase. Does the buyer need a mortgage? How much deposit do they have? Who is the loan with, and has it been agreed in principle? Once again, the estate agent may already have this information, but at this stage, they should obtain the contact details of the person arranging the mortgage at the lender or brokerage.

A buyer who does not require a mortgage is referred to as a cash buyer by estate agents. This doesn't mean that the buyer has a suitcase full of money, but rather that they have the funds readily available to make their property purchase. In certain circumstances, when such a buyer makes an offer, the estate agent may ask them for proof of funds—a bank statement or letter from their bank manager.

A point worth mentioning here is that an estate agent is required by law to put all offers forward, regardless of the buyer's status or the level of their offer. So when a buyer's offer is so low that the agent is certain the seller will reject it (maybe even scoff at it), the agent still needs to notify the seller of the offer. The only exception to this is when the seller has authorised their agent, in writing, to automatically reject on their behalf offers below a certain amount. When a buyer has made an offer which is deemed too low, the agent will use their discretion as to whether or not chain and finance details need to be checked at this stage.

When putting forward an offer to a seller, we were taught to follow a specific protocol. Firstly, we'd talk a bit about the buyer's position—their status, chain details and financial arrangements for the purchase. Then after the build-up, we'd tell them the amount offered and pause for their reaction.

## Is that your best offer?

When I started out as an estate agent, my manager assisted me in agreeing my first few sales. I found the buyers, carried out the viewing appointments, and when the offers came in, he did the negotiating. This was part of the on-the-job training given to new negotiators.

A buyer telephoned to say they wanted to make an offer on a property they'd seen through me the day before. I transferred the call to my manager and sat opposite him as he asked the

9. Making an Offer

prospective buyer a few questions and jotted the answers. "And is that your best offer?" he asked the buyer. His question was very politely put and not in any way condescending, as its written context may imply. However, it did make me think that the offer submitted by the buyer was low, but it wasn't—it was a good offer. So why was the buyer asked if that was their best offer? I was soon to learn that there was a lot of psychological manoeuvring in estate agency, especially when negotiating offers. And questions like that asked by my manager served far more than to qualify the spending power of prospective buyers. I'll clarify what I mean with an example.

Let's say a buyer offers £97,000 on a property that's on the market for £100,000. At just 3 per cent off the asking price, that's not a bad offer. The estate agent asks if it is their best, which can convey to the prospective buyer that their offer may not be enough to secure the property. The buyer replies that £97,000 isn't their best offer.

Now, bearing in mind that it is the estate agent's duty to get their client the best price for their property, how do you think the offer will be presented to the seller? The answer is that any half-decent estate agent will immediately tell the seller that a higher offer can be achieved; it is how they do it that is interesting and sometimes where the fun and games begin. Let's now have a look at how that offer may be presented.

The agent phones the seller to put the offer forward. He explains the buyer's status and their ability to proceed. He then presents the figure of £97,000.

"That sounds good, doesn't it?" the seller says in response.

"Yes, I thought so, too, but I had hoped we'd get a bit more for you. They really like the house, and it seems to meet all of their requirements, so I'd like to try to get a higher offer," says the agent.

"Well, it's a good offer, but if you think they might increase, please try. Every little bit helps, especially towards estate agency fees!"

At this point, the estate agent has an offer that his client might accept, but also one that his buyer has indicated they'll improve on. The agent has control of the situation, greatly assisted by asking a simple question: "Is that your best offer?"

Obviously, the next phone call will be to the buyer, but the agent will not be in a rush to dial their number. A slight delay in getting back to either buyer or seller creates the impression that the parties are mulling over the situation. In other words, it's not a foregone conclusion that the sale will be agreed, and the agent's really working hard to close the deal. The reality of the matter is that the agent already knows he'll agree the sale at around £98,500, or he is at least confident of doing so. It's worth mentioning that the agent would not employ any tactical delays if they were up against one or more competitors.

So, the agent calls the buyer to update them on their offer and ask if they're prepared to increase on the £97,000.

"The seller is really pleased that you like the house, and he'd love for you to be its new owners. With regards to the offer, we're close, but he was hoping for a little bit more."

"Okay. Did he say what he'll accept?" replies the buyer.

"He didn't, I'm afraid. More so, he asked me to see what I can get from you."

"Hmm. What do you think?" asks the buyer.

"Well, I'd like to say another two thousand would do it, but I don't want to steer you to £99,000 only for the seller to say he wants nothing short of the asking price," explains the estate agent, lying through his teeth, of course.

"Do you think he'll consider £98,000?"

"I'd be happy to put that forward for you, but before I do, can I make a suggestion? We're three thousand adrift. If we split the difference, that's £1,500, which increases the offer to £98,500, which I'm not sure the seller will accept, but approaching it that way shows a willingness to meet them halfway. What do you think?"

"Yep, that's fine, go for £98,500," confirms the buyer.

About thirty minutes later, the estate agent calls the seller to advise him of the increased offer.

"I've spoken to Mr Buyer and have got an increased offer from him. I'm afraid I couldn't get him to the asking price, but he has asked if you'd consider a meet in the middle at £98,500," said the agent. The seller is happy, and the sale is agreed. Everyone thinks the agent's a good bloke, and he might even get a bottle of Merlot on completion day. All of this was made a bit easier by the agent asking, "Is that your best offer?"

The example was taken from a real-life scenario and, admittedly, it was one of the easier that I've known. In fact since then, there were situations where getting an extra £3,000 on a house worth half a million proved a harder task.

So while the above is a basic scenario, it gives you an insight into how the middleman may operate when it comes to negotiating an offer.

If you're a buyer who is asked whether your offer is the best, do you have to tell the agent that it isn't? After all, we've just said that the agent is acting in the seller's best interests, and if they're given an indication that there's more money to be had, they'll do what they can to get it. Telling an estate agent that your offer is not your best is like telling your opponent in poker that before they raise the stake, you feel that it's only fair to warn them that you're holding a straight flush. You just wouldn't do that.

So using the same example scenario, when the buyer was asked if £97,000 was their best offer, if they replied that it was, they may have saved £1,500. If the seller rejected the £97,000, and the buyer came back with £98,000 or more, the agent could say, "I thought £97,000 was your best offer." But who's to say that the buyer didn't borrow the extra £1,000 from family, or even the bank?

If there are several buyers interested in the same property, and the agent specifically asks for everyone's best offers, this is an entirely different matter. In such situations, holding back your best offer could result in you losing the property. The subject of submitting a best and final offer, and in what circumstances an agent may ask that of a buyer, is covered in another chapter. However, we'll look at a related scenario in a moment.

Sometimes, going straight in with your best offer will save everyone involved a lot of time. It can also prevent you from being drawn into a bidding war, should several people be interested in the same property. If your best offer is rejected by the seller as not being enough, then you just move on to a different property. At least you tried. One of my directors used to advise buyers, "Offer as much as you're prepared to lose the property for." In other words, if your best is not good enough, walk away.

## The law and best practice

Under the Estate Agents Act 1979, an agent must provide their client with written details of all offers received from potential buyers. Exclusions apply where the seller has given their estate agent authorisation (in writing) not to pass on certain offers. Examples of such offers could be those below a certain level or from buyers who are not immediately able to proceed.

Estate agents are also required to keep a written record of all offers made on a property. Quite often, in negotiations a buyer will make more than one offer on the same property—for example, when their first offer has been rejected, they've increased. When this was the case, we would submit the offers orally as and when they came in and then post written copies of all offers at the end of the day.

If an offer was rejected with no increase pending that same day, we'd write to both parties confirming that the offer was unacceptable. This allowed everyone to know where they stood.

When an estate agent knows the amount of offer their seller will accept, they should not divulge that information to prospective buyers unless specifically requested to by their client. Doing so is bad practice because of the potential to lose money for the seller. For example, the agent knows that an offer of £95,000 would be sufficient to agree the sale. If a buyer intended to pay £98,000 and yet was told, prior to offering, that £95,000 would do it, the agent has just cost his client £3,000.

The same principle applies in not telling one buyer what another one has offered. If Buyer B is told that Buyer A offered £95,000, Buyer B may offer £96,000 instead of the £98,000 they originally intended to. Furthermore, if the agent then goes back to Buyer A and tells them there is now an offer of £96,000 from Buyer B, a bidding war may ensue, instigated by the agent's actions.

So when a buyer asks an agent what the seller will accept, the agent's response should be that it is down to the buyer to make an offer. One cheeky colleague would respond to such questions by saying, "My client should accept the asking price!"

Personally, I've always thought it okay to tell a buyer what the seller will not accept. This is especially so if someone makes an offer that is equal to or lower than one previously rejected. This practice was fully supported by every seller that I dealt with to whom it applied, except for one.

I'd arranged a viewing on this seller's property, and when I confirmed the time with the buyer, he asked me if I thought the seller would accept £XXX,000. My reply was that he really should see the property before talking money, but if £XXX,000 was all he could afford, then it wasn't worth viewing the property as the seller rejected an offer £2,000 higher the week before. The buyer told me he could pay more and went along to the property, but tried to negotiate with the seller directly while at the viewing. And in doing so, he mentioned that I'd said £XXX,000 had been rejected.

As I've already said, most sellers would've applauded my action, but not this one. He came into our office to complain, saying his wife was a former estate agent, who found my telling the prospective buyer what figure was rejected totally unethical! Remaining calm, I tried to explain to the seller that my intention was to prevent anyone wasting his time by viewing his property when they couldn't afford it. I then mentioned that some sellers I'd acted for, including banks, solicitors, and property developers, actually insisted that I tell buyers if a higher offer than theirs had already been rejected.

"Well, my wife was an estate agent, and she said what you did was wrong," the seller maintained.

"How long did she work in estate agency?" I asked.

"Three months, but that's not the point!"

## Offer accepted

Once a sale has been agreed, the estate agent will need the details of the respective solicitors acting for the buyer and seller. Once they have this information, the agent will then write to all four parties and confirm the sale.

Should the property be taken off the market once its owners have accepted an offer? This is an interesting question that raises a point that's regularly debated both inside and out of estate agency.

If the property is withdrawn from further viewing, and after two weeks the buyer doesn't proceed, both the seller's and the agent's time has been wasted, and they have to start again.

If the property is left on the market and available to view, is the seller encouraging a higher offer, and in turn gazumping? We'll take a closer look at gazumping in a moment, but for the benefit of anyone reading this who doesn't know what that word means, here's a basic definition. Gazumping is the term used when a seller agrees a sale to one buyer but then accepts a higher offer from another. Sometimes there isn't another buyer involved, but the seller just chooses to raise their price midway or towards the end of the transaction.

For some sellers, it is their policy to leave a property on the market and fully available for viewing right up until contracts are exchanged. This is how mortgage lenders want repossessed properties to be marketed. However, with the countless repossessions we were instructed to sell over the years, I never once saw a bank, building society, or the asset management companies acting for them gazump a buyer. We'll talk more about repossessions in a later chapter.

Developers also tend to leave their properties on the market until contracts have been exchanged. Most investors that I dealt with wouldn't drop their existing buyer for a slightly higher offer, but there were many who would, especially if the buyer delayed the transaction in any way.

Selling a property can be quite an inconvenience, what with having it available for viewing (often at short notice) and estate agents showing strangers around your house. So when an offer is agreed, some sellers are only too pleased to withdraw their property from the market, particularly if they and the buyer like each other.

As you can see, there isn't a rule to say whether or not a property should remain on the market or be withdrawn after a sale has been agreed. My personal opinion is that if both the seller and the agent are happy with the price achieved and the buyer's ability to proceed with the purchase, then there's no need for further viewings. Good communication should be maintained between all parties, so if things do start to go wrong, the agent, buyer, or seller can act accordingly.

Quite often, the property being taken off the market is something that's included in negotiations. For example, a buyer's offer may be just short of what the seller will accept, so the counteroffer could be: "If you increase your offer to £XXX,000, we'll take the house off the market."

A buyer may propose to the seller that if they withdraw the property, they'll ensure the survey is booked within the next week. If the estate agent has direct contact with whoever is arranging the buyer's mortgage and can support the buyer's proposal, this greatly assists.

Conversely, when I bought my house, I was told that the property would only be withdrawn once my survey had been carried out and I was happy with the result. The significance of a property being surveyed is that it is a measure of the transaction moving forward and confirms the buyer's commitment. The survey can also be a hurdle in a property sale. Once the report is back, and it doesn't contain anything ominous, the sale moves forward.

A point worth noting is that even when a sale has been agreed, and the property has been withdrawn from the market, until contracts have been exchanged, anyone can offer on it. And by law, the estate agent must submit all offers, even if the people making them have never seen the property, which is something I found out early in my career.

I'd agreed the sale of semi-detached house to a young family. The property, which required extensive refurbishment, had attracted a lot of interest, and I was very pleased when this couple's offer was accepted. Their parents lived close by, which was to be of considerable help with child-care when the wife returned to work. The sale was agreed at less than 5 per cent below the asking price, and the survey was booked the following week. All was going well.

A few days after the sale was agreed, a man walked into our office and asked to view the property. I explained that an offer had been accepted, and the house had been withdrawn from further viewing, but this rather abrasive character persisted.

"Is the offer at the asking price?" he asked.

"I'm afraid we won't disclose that sort of information. What I can say is that the seller is happy with the current buyer, and the sale is proceeding. I can take your details and let you know immediately if things go wrong, or if a similar property become available," was my reply, which seemed to fall on deaf ears.

"I'm a property investor. How do you know that I won't offer more money?" he went on.

Now, I later learned that this man dabbled in property and wasn't a fully-fledged developer, as he made out to be. Also unknown to me at the time was that he'd earned himself a reputation amongst local estate agents as a tricky person to deal with, often employing the practice of gazundering. Gazundering is where someone buying a property reduces their purchase price, usually towards the end of the transaction when contracts are about to be exchanged. This can sometimes result from a bad survey or a sharp downturn in market conditions. Sadly, some unscrupulous investors set out to buy a property with the full intention of gazundering at a later stage.

Coming back to our scenario, the man asked me to put an offer forward of £500 above the asking price.

"But you haven't seen the property," I told him.

"Well, let me see it, then!" was his reply.

"You can't. It's off the market."

I didn't care too much for this man's attitude, but being an inexperienced estate agent, I allowed myself to be drawn into an argument. To make matters worse, my manager and senior colleagues were out of the office, so I couldn't seek the advice of someone more knowledgeable.

The man left the office, returning moments later to tell me that his solicitor informed him that it is an offence for me not to put forward the man's offer. At that point, one of the senior negotiators walked into the office, saw who I was talking to, and asked if they could assist. I explained the situation. Then my colleague took over and spoke to the man who was sitting at my desk.

"Our manager is dealing with all offers on this property. He's out of the office at the moment, so if you can let me know how much you'd like to offer along with the financial details, my manager will speak to the seller and update you as soon as possible."

The man's offer was put forward, both orally and in writing, and the seller's response was that he preferred to sell his home to a family than an investor. I might add that this was preceded by a "Thanks, but no thanks," from the seller, who said it would be wrong to go back on his word.

Unfortunately, not all sellers displayed the same integrity as the man above, as my next story will illustrate.

We were instructed in the sale of a house that formed part of probate. An elderly lady had passed away and left her home to her niece and nephew. The nephew lived overseas, so our contact was his sister, who asked that we market at a slightly higher figure than we appraised. The three-bedroom end of terrace was located on a popular road, so even though it needed extensive renovation, it attracted a lot of interest. In fact, we had twenty-three viewings in the first week, which resulted in offers at various levels; however, none were near the asking price. My director decided that we needed to bring the matter to a close, so he suggested that we set a deadline for all interested parties to submit their best offers in writing. The seller was updated.

We spoke to everyone who'd made an offer or had viewed the property and expressed interest, and we advised them of what was required. All interested parties were to provide their best and final offer in writing along with details of how the proposed purchase would be financed. We also asked for the contact details of the individual dealing with any mortgage arrangements.

On the day of the deadline, we had seven offers. Two were reasonably close to the asking price, the others were significantly lower. I spoke to the mortgage consultant acting for the man who made the highest offer, and he confirmed that they were ready to proceed.

I updated the seller who accepted the higher offer, and I then called the buyer to let him know that his offer had been agreed. We also phoned the other people who'd made offers to let them know that, unfortunately, they'd been unsuccessful this time.

Coincidentally, the two buyers who made the highest offers were both builders and both of Eastern European origin, although from different nations in the region. The successful buyer had a much stronger command of English than the man who'd narrowly missed out. So when I called the latter to tell him what had happened, I wasn't sure if he'd fully understood me.

The next day, we received a fax from a solicitor's office advising that their client (let's call him Buyer Two) would like to increase his offer to £2,000 above the asking price. So much for best and final offers in writing, I thought. We telephoned the seller, who was delighted with the extra money, which was an increase of £5,000 from Buyer Two's original offer. We mentioned that we'd need to speak to Buyer One to let him know, to which the seller replied, "Oh yes, please. Tell him how much the other man's offered and see if he'll go higher, too. Then I can order my new car."

Well, bully for you, is what I wanted to reply. Instead, I told the seller that I'd give Buyer One the opportunity to increase and call her back. I also explained why disclosing Buyer Two's offer would not be ethical. We didn't want people to get carried away in a bidding war then not be able to pay for the house.

Next, I telephoned Buyer One and gave him the bad news. At first he was confused. "You asked me to give you my best offer, you tell me the house is mine, and now you're asking for more money?" The man's reaction was totally understandable; however, his confusion was quickly turning to anger. I told him that I didn't like the situation either, but as an estate agent, I was bound by law to put all offers forward. I then asked if he was able to increase his offer, too, to which he replied with several threats before slamming the phone down.

A few minutes later I received a call from Buyer One's mortgage consultant. He'd just spoken to his client but wanted to get clarification from us as to what was going on. I explained the situation to the mortgage consultant, who being a former estate agent, understood my position. I also told him that Buyer One wasn't doing himself any favours by making threats, which some people might have thought warranted police involvement.

The mortgage consultant said that his client did have the means to increase his offer if he wanted to; however, what assurance did they have that there wouldn't be a third round of best and final offers? My response was that we'd deal with that issue and provide confirmation before asking them for another offer. The mortgage consultant said he'd have a word with Buyer One about his behaviour.

We called Buyer Two and explained that since he'd increased his offer, it was only fair that we afford the other party the same opportunity. This didn't go down too well either, and now he was also upset, although he said he'd increase his offer, too. Meanwhile, Buyer One had popped into the office to apologise for his previous conduct and said he was still interested in the house.

With matters and tempers seeming to settle a bit, my next call was to the seller. I updated her on the situation, adding that one or two people had become upset, but that both parties were prepared to increase.

"Ooh, isn't this exciting!" she said.

Excitement wasn't what I was feeling. And if I did have an adrenaline rush, it was angst at the prospect of a disgruntled Albanian bricklayer putting a cement mixer through our front window.

It was time to rein in the seller's expectations with a few facts. Firstly, we'd already achieved a higher price than expected for a house that required extensive modernisation. And it didn't matter that the prospective buyer would be a builder and could carry out repairs himself cost effectively. What did matter was whether or not the surveyor carrying out the mortgage valuation agreed with the sale price. The seller understood our concerns. I told her that we'd go back to the two prospective buyers for their last offers making absolutely clear that any increases beyond that would not be entertained. My director suggested that the seller provide us with her written authorisation to reject any offers submitted after the best and final were made. The seller agreed and had her solicitor fax over a letter to that effect.

This time we wrote to the two buyers requesting their best and final offers. We also stipulated that if their offer wasn't successful, there would not be an option to increase. Buyer One offered the asking price, Buyer Two came in at £5,000 above.

As mentioned earlier, we were concerned that the inflated sale price might lead to the property being down-valued. If that happened, and the buyer could not meet the mortgage shortfall with his own funds, the sale would fall through. All of our time, effort, money, and a great deal of stress would've been for nothing. When asked, Buyer Two said he'd cover that eventuality.

So this is how it ended. When Buyer One was informed that the sale was agreed to the other party, he told us to "go away" (although in rather harsher terms), and we never heard from him again. The surveyor down valued the property by £15,000 and

Buyer Two stood true to his word; buying the property at the agreed price by meeting the mortgage shortfall using his own money. So the seller was very lucky to get the money that she did for the house.

The sale took fourteen weeks to get to an exchange of contracts from the point of the offer being accepted. The solicitors involved would not speak to us or return our calls. From start to finish it was one of the most difficult transactions my colleagues and I had ever dealt with.

So, even if best and final offers have been submitted in writing, or a property is off the market and in the final stages of the sale, a buyer can still make an offer. And regardless of whether or not the prospective buyer has even viewed the property, the agent must put that offer forward. Should a seller choose to drop their buyer at the eleventh hour in favour of a higher bid, they're perfectly entitled to do so.

The people mentioned in the above scenarios were in the minority. Most of the buyers that I dealt with over the years would not want to get involved with a property that was already under offer. One man was really keen to view a property, but he quickly lost interest when I told him it had just gone under offer. "I wouldn't want to get involved with that if someone else is proceeding. I've been gazumped before and lost money on the survey and solicitor's fees. I'm not doing that to someone else!" he told me.

## Gazumping

I remember a rather bizarre situation when I was showing a house to two first-time buyers. The young couple really liked the property but were up against another buyer. They asked to see the house again before deciding whether or not to increase their offer, and they brought their parents along for a second opinion.

Quite randomly, one of the parents turned to me and said, "Does this other buyer really exist then, or are you lot just making it up to get my son and daughter-in-law to pay more? Because I know that agents gazump people in order to get more commission!"

Everyone in the room went silent and looked to me for my response. I guessed the family had probably discussed the subject before attending the viewing, and they appeared taken aback but at the same time glad that their mother spoke out. This wasn't a jibe either; the woman was quite serious.

Now, I was in the fortunate position to have introduced both sets of interested buyers to the property, so whichever couple bought it, I'd still get paid. Even so, I decided to set the mother straight on a point or two.

"Yes, estate agents can instigate gazumping, but they can't do it without the seller's agreement, and I doubt it's done to increase commission. And I'll explain why," I said, continuing to talk before anyone could respond. "How much do you think my company is charging the seller of this house?"

"I don't know. One, maybe two per cent," the woman reluctantly replied.

"Okay, let's say it's one and a half per cent. So if your son and daughter-in-law increase their offer by two thousand pounds, my employer gets an extra thirty pounds, right? Now I don't have to tell you this, but we get ten per cent commission of what the seller pays the company. So, if I gazumped your son in order to increase my commission, I'd be doing it for a whole three pounds before tax. Do I look like the sort of person who would upset people and risk investigation by Trading Standards for making up false offers, for the price of twenty Benson and Hedges?"

There were some rather embarrassed faces in that room, and I received one or two humble apologies. The good news was that the couple bought the house and were very happy with it. After that, whenever they passed our office, they'd always smile and say hello.

Ultimately, it is the seller who would be responsible for gazumping a buyer.

As you can see from my rant at the buyer's mum, estate agents would not instigate gazumping in order to inflate their commission; however, they might do it when competing with each other for a sale.

Let's say a property being marketed on a multi-agency basis goes under offer through one of the agents instructed. If the house or flat remains available for viewing, a competitor will advise any buyers they introduce to offer higher than the sale agreed price (assuming they know what that is). They will then encourage the seller to accept the higher offer. Sounds a bit daunting for buyers, but fortunately, more people are aware of the potential to be gazumped in such circumstances and request the property be withdrawn from the market. This does not mean that the competitor will forget about the property. They will go about their business in the normal way but contact the seller from time to time to ask how the sale is progressing. And if they see an opportunity to scupper a rival's sale and win the business from them, they'll take it.

In competitive offices, the infighting amongst colleagues can also lead to gazumping. In such circumstances it is the manager's responsibility to keep control. However, I have known of firms where the bosses positively encouraged competition amongst staff, believing it kept everybody sharp. And gazumping was seen as an unavoidable consequence of that ethos. Those estate agencies were not nice places to buy a home from.

While agents may instigate gazumping, the decision to switch buyers for a higher offer lies with the seller. Even though losing a sale and the commission as a result of gazumping was very disappointing, I'd always ask myself whether I'd do the same if I was the seller involved. In an earlier chapter, I mentioned a sale where the chain was moving so slowly that by the later stages of the transaction, the property's value had increased by almost 15 per cent. A few days before contracts were to be exchanged, one of our competitors knocked on the seller's door and assured them he could get them more money for their house. In fact, it was considerably more—£20,000, to be precise. If you were in that seller's position, would you have turned down that sum of money and stayed with a buyer whose chain caused months of delay?

One final point before we move on to the next chapter. A buyer making an offer should do so via the estate agent they saw the property through. This may sound simple enough, but some buyers will view a house through one agent and then submit their offer through another. I've known some buyers who did this by mistake, while others did it intentionally. Whatever the reason behind it, offering through an agent who didn't show you the property can create problems for everyone involved.

A buyer told me they viewed a house that was being marketed by several estate agents. They short-listed the property as one they might want to see again. A few days later, an estate agent called them to say that the seller had decided to reduce the asking price. For some reason the buyer thought the person calling was from the same estate agency that showed them the house, so they arranged another viewing and made an offer shortly after. Matters then got confused when the original estate agent called to advise on the price reduction and was told by the buyer, "Oh, we've already offered through your colleague Nick and are awaiting the seller's response." The agent, not having a colleague by that name, would've realised what had happened and called the seller, who in turn would confirm receipt of the offer.

Now that both estate agents have shown the property to the buyer, each one may claim their fee. As I have experienced in my career, such scenarios usually end with the agents agreeing to split the fee between them. Another outcome is where the seller rejects the offer—and any subsequent ones from that buyer—and also dismisses both estate agents. I once saw this happen when two estate agents (bitter rivals) refused to cooperate with each other, each insisting that their full fee be paid, as it was they who introduced the buyer to the property. The seller got fed up with the bickering and, not wanting to be liable for two estate agency fees, withdrew the property from the market. A few weeks later, they put the house up for sale again and sold it to a new buyer through a different estate agent altogether.

In a slightly different scenario, we once took a property onto our books that had been up for sale with a competitor a year earlier. For personal reasons, the seller withdrew the property from the market, and then thirteen months later, he decided to have another go at selling and gave the instruction to us. A day or so after advertising the property for the first time, we received a strange call from a prospective buyer. The man told us that he'd already seen the property a year earlier when it was being marketed by our competitor. He wanted to buy the house then, but the seller withdrew it from sale. Furthermore, the prospective buyer said he was happy that the seller hadn't given the property back to the original agent, because he thought them rude, arrogant, and difficult to deal with.

We spoke to the seller, who remembered the buyer and was pleased to hear that he was still interested in buying the house;

however, there were some concerns. If the buyer viewed the house and made an offer through us, could the original agent pursue a fee, having originally introduced the buyer a year earlier? We sought the advice of a solicitor and also spoke to the trade association of which we and our competitor were members. We were told that because more than six months had elapsed since the buyer first saw the property and the seller withdrew it from the market, the other agent could not claim a fee.

We sent the buyer along to the property, he made an offer, and a sale was agreed. When the other estate agency found out, they were very upset, but they knew that there was nothing they could do about it. They tried to intimidate the seller a couple of times by saying they'd take legal action; however, they quickly backed off when he threatened to report them to their association for harassment.

Do you remember the first-time buyer I mentioned in the previous chapter? This was the chap to whom I showed a flat twice (once under torchlight), who then decided to offer on the property through another agent. As mentioned in chapter 7, I'll explain the reasons for his actions below.

The owner of the flat in question instructed two estate agents, us and one other, on a multi-agency basis. Shortly after giving us the flat to sell, she decided to increase the asking price by £3000. We did as the client requested and amended our adverts and the sales particulars. We noticed that the other estate agent, who was of a dubious reputation, I might add, didn't bother changing the price on their advertising materials.

The first-time buyer, having seen the property with me twice, was about to make an offer, until he noticed the other agent advertising it for £3000 less and approached them instead. The young man obviously thought that by going to the competitor to make an offer, he immediately had a £3000 discount on the asking price that we were advertising. And when he walked through the door of that estate agency, the negotiators knew exactly what was going on and how they were to play things out.

So how did I get to know that the first-time buyer went to our competitor? And what happened after I found out?

The seller called to say that she'd accepted an offer through the other agent but asked that we continue showing the flat for the time being. She already had a previous sale fall through, so she didn't want to take the property off the market just yet. Now, because I'd kept the seller up to date on what I was doing to sell the flat, she asked if I'd heard any more from the first-time buyer who'd seen it twice.

"No. I'm afraid Mr X hasn't returned any of my calls. I think it's safe to say he's no longer interested," I told the seller.

"That's a coincidence. The offer I've just agreed is from a Mr X," replied the seller.

"Yes, that is a coincidence. This chap's first name wouldn't happen to be…"

The seller confirmed that it was indeed the same person I'd shown the flat to. She then asked if my findings would jeopardise the sale and told me that she didn't want to get involved in an estate agency war.

I eventually spoke to Mr X after calling him from a number he didn't recognise as ours. I asked him why he approached the other agent and had not submitted his offer through us. He was terribly apologetic, saying that he'd already seen the flat through the other agent but had only realised it was the same property after viewing it through us. The young man then pleaded ignorance saying that as a first-time buyer, he was not aware of the correct procedure for viewing and offering. His response was well rehearsed, and no doubt scripted for him by the other agent. My tone made it clear that I didn't believe him.

"It took you two viewings through us before you realised that you'd already seen the flat through the other agent? What was the problem, then? Didn't they have a torch in their office?" was my sarcastic reply.

Mr X knew that I didn't believe him, and even though I could sense uneasiness in his voice, he stuck to his story of having seen the flat through the other agent first.

Our agency fee for that particular property was so low that my senior managers didn't think it was worth pursuing the matter any further. The other agent was aware of this, so when I challenged him, he casually said, "If you think you can prove it, I'll see you in court!"

There was nothing we could do; however, the sale did not proceed and fell through after the survey was carried out. The building was found to have several structural issues, which we later learned were the cause of the previous sale aborting—something the seller neglected to mention. And who do you think was the estate agent handling that sale? Yes, you guessed it, our dishonest competitor. So not only did he withhold that information from the first-time buyer, but he also encouraged the young man to lie about whom he'd viewed the property with first.

Viewing properties is quite different from looking at other items you'd like to buy. If you're after a new television, and a sales assistant in an electrical store spends fifteen minutes showing you the latest forty-two-inch model, you are still free to purchase that TV elsewhere. However, if an estate agent shows you a property that you're interested in buying, you really should make your offer through that agent, even if you don't like them. Doing otherwise can create problems for all involved.

# 10. A Day in the Office

As the title suggests, in this chapter we're going to look at a typical working day in a busy estate agency office. We're going to go behind the scenes and examine the everyday activities of estate agents and the various systems that they use to take property onto their books and sell it for commission. So let's begin at the very start of the day.

## The morning meeting

The cigarettes would be stubbed out, and the manager and negotiators alike emerge from a smoke-filled staff kitchen clutching mugs of tea and coffee. The team huddle around their manager's desk, some continuing their chats about anything but property, while they wait for a tardy colleague to turn up. The door opens, and the late one walks in. After a quick apology and moan about the M25, he wheels his chair over to join the rest of the gang. Conversations about the referee's bad decision from the previous night's match cease, the secretary is asked to cover the incoming phone calls, and the morning meeting begins. At least, that's how I remember it.

The morning meeting is essential to the start of the day. It brings the team together and is the time where the left hand gets to know what the right hand is doing, if I may use that phrase. When a good office manager conducts the morning meeting, they will set the agenda for the day, delegate tasks, and ensure no opportunities are missed.

Here's what a typical morning meeting in a large estate agency might consist of:

*Daily statistics*—The manager will gather performance figures for the previous day's activity. They will note how many applicants (prospective buyers) were registered, and how many viewing appointments and mortgage introductions were made by each negotiator. Did any of the applicants view a property for a second time? Of those applicants registered, do any have a property to sell in the estate agency's catchment?

Managers will check if any offers were received and ensure they were submitted to the respective sellers both orally and in writing. All details relevant to the offer will be discussed, such as what the buyer's position is. Do they have their mortgage arranged, and is there an opportunity for the office mortgage consultant to assist? Is the buyer in a chain and if so, have details been checked with the relevant estate agent?

The manager will also go over the previous day's market appraisals. The inspecting negotiators will describe to their colleagues the properties they appraised. They will outline the prospective sellers' position and cross-check opinions on the potential asking price with the rest of the team. They'll discuss things like the fee that was quoted, if the seller will accept a FOR SALE board, and whether or not other agents had already been in or were scheduled to visit. Potential buyers for the property would've been noted in the morning meeting prior to the appraisal, but may be mentioned again now.

If the appraisal converted to an instruction, the negotiators will be provided with the seller's contact details, viewing arrangements, and a brief description of the property—asking price and measurements. A temporary specification sheet may be handed out to negotiators for reference until the full sales particulars are produced, printed, and uploaded to the computer system. If the property came onto the market the previous day, then the above process would've been put to action immediately, especially if in a multi-agency scenario. Whatever the case, details of all new instructions are discussed in the morning meeting.

If the seller did not put the property up for sale straight away, the agents will action a follow-up. And many will do this using a diary system known as the "1-31," which I'll explain.

*1-31s*—A drawer in one of our office filing cabinets would contain thirty-one suspension files; each one allocated a number from one to thirty-one to represent the maximum days in a month. There will also be twelve files more files, which are named after the months of the year.

Now, let's say that on 5th March, a negotiator attends a market appraisal. Several other estate agents have also been asked to attend over the next three days, so the seller's decision as to which one (or ones) to instruct will be made after that. The negotiator returns from the property, discusses various details with his manager, and arranges for the appraisal letter to be sent to the seller. He will then place the appraisal form for that property in the number eight suspension file, representing the 8th of March. The negotiator will log the property into the 1-31 register—which is basically an address book—and mark the next action for the 8th March. Each day, the manager or negotiators will take out the contents of the suspension file relevant to that day and distribute it to members of the sales team.

Using our example, one of several things may happen when the negotiator calls the seller on the 8th March. He may be given instructions to sell the property, in which case he'll need to pre-pare the sales particulars. The seller may still be undecided as to when they'll put the property on the market and which agent they'll give it to when they do. Should that be the outcome, the negotiator will put the details back into the 1-31 system, using their discretion as to the date for follow-up.

Lastly, when the negotiator calls the seller, they may be told that sole agency has been given to a competitor. The negotiator will then put the seller's file back into the 1-31 system, perhaps with a follow-up date that's midway through, or towards the end of, the other agent's sole agency term. At that point, if the instructed agent has yet to generate enough interest in the property, the seller may begin considering alternative options, like instructing a new sole agent or going with multiple agents.

So even if an estate agency has missed out on the instruction the first time around, the 1-31s, when correctly used, can give them a second chance at getting a property onto their books. The 1-31 system can also be used as a reminder to action other day-to-day estate agency activities, such as providing an update for an existing seller or chasing up a point on a running sale. Nowadays, more and more estate agencies use computer applications or diary systems to help schedule their 1-31 follow-ups; however, many of them will also use a manual system alongside as a backup.

*Existing instructions*—In the morning meeting, the team will also discuss their existing property register. They will look at a number of instructions (perhaps prompted by the 1-31 system) and assess their marketing efforts to date by gathering certain information. What advertising has been carried out? How many viewings has the property had, and what's been the general feedback from prospective buyers? Have there been any offers? Why has the property not sold? Is it overpriced? Should the seller be advised to reduce the asking price? Are there any other problems that may be hindering the sale? Is the neighbour's loud music putting buyers off making an offer, or does the seller's pet Rottweiler frighten the people coming round to view?

All of the above will be discussed by the manager and negotiators, and a plan of action formulated before they speak to the seller.

*The day's agenda*—The manager will go through the office diary and confirm which members of the team will be carrying out the listed appointments. Where viewings are concerned, the manager may ask what the buyer's position is. Do they have a property to sell and if so, is it within the office's catchment? Are there any opportunities for the mortgage consultant to assist the buyer with finance?

For market appraisals, the manager will go through the MA form, ensuring all relevant information about the property and its owner has been noted. Is the property already on the market? Have other agents already provided appraisals, or are they scheduled to visit? Where is the prospective seller hoping to move to? Have they already found a property or seen something they like? The team will look at comparable properties that have been sold and discuss a recommended asking price.

The manager will delegate such tasks as who will speak to which seller to provide them with an update on the marketing of their property or perhaps to recommend a price reduction. The 1-31s will also be divided amongst the negotiators.

*Any other business*—Here, the negotiators and mortgage consultant are given the opportunity to raise any points they wish to discuss. Other things that may be mentioned are whether any estate agency boards need to be ordered, replaced, or collected. Also, what are the competitors up to? Have any of their boards gone up to signify new instructions? And with that last point in mind, the manager may organise canvassing activities for the team, such as board counting or leaflet drops.

The estate agency morning meetings that I remember would last thirty to forty-five minutes. And as you can see, some can be quite intense affairs, covering many details to ensure there aren't any missed opportunities for the office. The morning meeting also serves to let everyone know what their teammates are doing. So if a seller stops by the office to speak with a negotiator who isn't available, at least a colleague will be able to help with the enquiry. How bad would it look if a client asked a question about the sale of their home which none of the staff could answer, except for the one negotiator who wasn't in the office? Lastly, with some estate agencies, a morning meeting, especially the part where daily figures are gathered, can be a platform for commending staff for their efforts, or naming and shaming them for shortfalls in their performance.

## The rest of the day

After the morning meeting, one of the first tasks the negotiators will undertake is to follow up with the people who viewed properties through them the previous day. Depending on how those viewings went, the negotiators will either be submitting offers to the relevant sellers or providing them with the prospective buyers' feedback. Negotiators will also be speaking to the applicants who registered the previous day, checking to see if any of the properties recommended to them are of interest and if so, arranging viewing appointments for them.

The rest of the day's activities will include carrying out viewings and market appraisals. For new instructions, negotiators will prepare the sales particulars and then bring the new property to the attention of their prospective buyers by phoning or emailing them. Registering new applicants and arranging viewing appointments is something a negotiator may do throughout the working day.

Negotiators may also check progress on their running sales, although in some estate agencies the managers prefer to carry out this task and leave the negotiators to chase new business.

The office manager's day may consist of recording staff performance figures, preparing advertising, progressing sales, and delegating other tasks. Most of the managers with whom I worked would carry out the market appraisals and deal with, or supervise, the sales progressing; however, they'd also answer phones and register applicants if required.

If a negotiator has managed to chase up all his applicants and viewings, spoken to all the relevant sellers and prepared property details, phoned out the new instructions, and checked the running sales, there's still other stuff they can do. I remember ploughing through a heavy workload and feeling rather pleased with myself for completing the day's to-do list by three o'clock. My manager then handed me a bunch of leaflets and a clipboard and said, "Drop these on Old Park Avenue, and on your way back make a note of all the boards on Station Road."

The same manager once told me that in estate agency, there's no such thing as getting all your work done, because it's a job where there's always something to do.

# 11. A Competitive Business

My first estate agency job was with a large corporate, working in a branch located in suburban North London. The catchment in which we operated was set out by our regional office and covered approximately three square miles, touching four different postcodes. There were many different estate agencies working the same area, as you would expect. As more firms began to spring up, I decided to check just how many competitors we had and found at least thirty-two. That's thirty-two estate agents, all of whom were actively dealing with the sale of residential property in the same geographical area. Some of these competitors we came up against all the time, while others we only crossed paths with at properties located in different parts of postcodes we dealt with. And if this sounds like a competitive arena, other areas were far worse.

While travelling through a part of London I'd not visited before, I noticed a cluster of estate agencies on the high street. Three were adjacent to each other, with two more being a couple of shops down and a further three located directly opposite. In fact, there could've been a dozen or more different agents within a hundred-metre stretch of road. They were as abundant as souvenir shops found along the beachfront of a Mediterranean resort.

I'm sure you've heard it said that competition is good for the consumer, right? Companies vying for a share of their industry's marketplace will constantly strive to improve the goods and services they offer, also reducing prices to further attract the end user. Selling people's property is not different in that respect. Strong competition amongst a town's estate agents will provide the seller with more choice, which in turn should result in a quality service at a more competitive fee. However, when conditions in the property market toughen up, some estate agents will resort to sharp practices in order to succeed over their competitors. And the skulduggery is not just reserved for dealing with rival companies, but also extends to colleagues battling amongst themselves for the commission.

Let's now take a look at the various methods, both ethical and underhand, that are employed by competing agents and what their effects are on buyers and sellers.

## Company vs. company

For an estate agency to have any chance of success, it must have a constant stream of properties coming onto its registers. And if those properties are to come from within an area measuring three square miles—in which thirty other agents operate—competition for instructions will be fierce. So what do estate agencies do to ensure they get their share of properties on the market for sale in their catchment?

I knew of several small but well-established estate agencies, where consistent advertising, a good board presence, and the occasional promotion would get them regular instructions. Such an approach might be considered too passive by some companies, and so they'll go after properties that are already on the market with other agents. These agents will identify their competitors' instructions in order to approach the relevant sellers and offer to sell their homes. The intention here is to try to get instructed alongside the other agent(s) or take the business away from them altogether. Estate agents refer to this practice as "canvassing."

Several different activities can constitute canvassing; some are perfectly ethical, whereas others breach industry codes of conduct, because they involve deceit. Let's take a closer look at the different methods of canvassing for instructions.

Firstly, estate agents will need to identify their competitors' instructions. The easiest way to accomplish this is by noting the addresses of all properties displaying For Sale boards. Negotiators will drive around various roads in their catchment, stopping to write down the numbers of those with boards outside.

If we saw a property advertised in the local newspaper or on a website that didn't have a board, we'd check the image for distinctive features that might help to identify it. If a house had a certain type of tree outside it, a unique style of front door, patterned paving, or an alarm box located below the middle of the small bedroom window, we'd find it. With one employer, canvassing was such an integral part of our job that negoti-ators would have to do it on a weekly basis at the very least. We got so good at it that I once identified a house from a small black-and-white newspaper photo, the advert for which didn't even list the property's road—just the area postcode.

The activity of driving around an area trying to identify buildings featured in newspaper adverts isn't in breach of any industry codes of conduct. As long as you're not stalking your competitor or the homeowner, you're okay. Joking aside, I remember pulling up to a house for an appointment and catching a brief glimpse of what looked like a woman ducking down behind a parked Volkswagen Golf. I got out of my car and went about my business, but I was alert to the fact that the woman had yet to appear. As I looked around I saw her peek over the car bonnet and then duck back down very quickly. I walked up the garden path of the house, opened the front door, and walked in. It was a vacant property that we'd previously rented for the owner, and now that the tenants had left, the owner had asked us to put it up for sale. Inside the house, still curious about the woman hiding behind a car, I stood behind the net curtains of the lounge bay window and looked out onto the street. Standing next to the car was a smartly dressed woman in her thirties. She was looking in the direction of the house and writing on the clipboard she was holding. She opened the car door, put her clipboard and a folio case on the front seat, got in, started up the engine, and pulled off, still looking at the house.

A few days later a competitor's For Sale board went up outside a neighbouring house and a letter, from the same estate agent, was sent to the property I'd visited. The lady behind the car was a negotiator at that estate agency who, at the time, was probably appraising the house that went on the market. My guess is that she'd just left the property as I was pulling up, and she hid so that I wouldn't see where she'd been, but she could see where I was going. I thought then, as I do now, that she looked rather silly, but then maybe that's why I'm no longer an estate agent, and she is.

As mentioned, driving around the area making a note of what the competition are up to could be deemed market research and not against the rules. What the authorities and estate agency associations might be interested in is what a company does with the information their research gathers.

After identifying properties listed with a competitor, if you then approach the sellers directly, by putting a business card through their letterbox or knocking on their door, you're now deemed to have targeted the property. And that is frowned on. In fact, I've known cases where the unsolicited approach of an estate agent offering their service was met with accusations of harassment and trespass. One seller took exception to the negotiators of rival firms knocking on his door, and another was fed up with the constant leaflets and business cards being put through his letterbox.

So, if a property is on the market for sale with one estate agency, is it against the rules for a competitor to approach the seller and offer them their services?

As long as the estate agent does not appear to have singled out or targeted a specific property, it is okay for them to write to the owner. However, under those conditions, the only way they can do this ethically is by writing to the owners of other properties on the same road, at the same time using a generic letter.

I remember a canvassing campaign where we wrote to the sellers of several properties that were on the market with other estate agents. One of our competitors got very upset and threatened to report us to various associations. Our mistake was that the opening sentence of our letter was worded: "We have noticed that your property is on the market for sale and have written to you to offer our services."

Our competitor had a valid complaint (probably fuelled by his sellers responding positively to us) as our letter showed clearly that we were targeting his instructions. We immediately amended the wording on our letters, and future ones were sent to all properties on a particular road.

When an estate agent writes to a prospective seller, certain wording should be included in the letter. The agent should state that if the seller is already in a sole agency, they should check the terms of their contract before instructing another agent, so as to avoid the possibility of paying two commissions (or words to that effect).

Estate agents also approach competitors' clients by dropping business cards or compliment slips through the letterbox that usually have written on them: "Please contact me urgently regarding the sale of your property." When I started out in estate agency, our training tutors told us to never do this. Firstly, the warning of the seller exposing themselves to paying two commissions was absent. Secondly, even if a genuine buyer exists; who wants to buy immediately, and will pay a top price, the agent should not build up the seller's expectation via a scribbled note on a piece of paper or card.

I remember being told the story of an elderly widow who put her house up for sale so that she could buy a flat in a residential care home. A buyer was found and an offer agreed. A few days later, a negotiator from a rival firm put a compliment slip through her door saying, "Please call me as a matter of great urgency regarding the sale of your home." On reading the note, the poor old lady, who'd not long ago lost her husband, went into a panic, thinking something had gone wrong with her sale. She immediately phoned her son-in-law, who happened to be a successful barrister specialising in property boundary and landlord tenant disputes. I was told that there were several complaints against the imbecilic negotiator, but his last stunt ensured he didn't work in estate agency in that area again.

The senior management of one company that I worked for insisted that once we identified a competitor's instruction, we were to knock on the door and speak to the owner directly. And our canvassing activities were only deemed successful if we got back to the office with, at the very least, the owner's name and phone number. Our bosses had worked out that this rather aggressive method was the most effective for getting instructed alongside a competitor or taking the property off them altogether. No letters or leaflets were to be posted, and if you rang the doorbell and didn't get an answer, you had to keep going back until you did.

Some area managers wanted each member of staff to engage in such canvassing on a weekly basis, and they even paid bonuses for properties that were taken onto our books this way, once they were sold. I absolutely hated "door knocking," as it was known, and so did most of my colleagues. In fact, just before I left that company, I learned that most of the negotiators would skive off and do something else during their allotted canvassing time. Some would drive to coffee shops in neighbouring towns; one chap would frequent the bookmakers; and another, who'd just become a father, would catch up on lost sleep by having a nap in his car.

One of my more memorable canvassing trips was prompted by my area manager's research. He'd obtained several copies of the local newspapers for our office's catchment, scanned our competitors' adverts, and singled out six properties he wanted someone to door knock. And that someone, whose turn it was to go canvassing on that wet Wednesday morning, was me.

My boss handed me the newspaper clippings, which had the relevant properties circled in blotted blue ink from the expensive fountain pen he only used when at his ivory tower HQ. The adverts listed the roads, so all I had to do was identify the properties when I got there. Now, when your area manager hands you a list of houses and flats to canvass, he or she is conveying several messages. Firstly, they shouldn't have to be doing your job for you, but nonetheless, that's how it's done. Secondly, they're earning every bit of their Five Series BMW, private health care, share options, and £80,000 a year. And lastly, after their pains-taking efforts (all three hundred seconds), you'd better knock on those doors!

So off I went, driving around various roads trying to identify the properties on my list in between my windscreen wipers clearing away the rain. The first doorbell I rang belonged to a ground-floor converted flat. A child answered the intercom, and I asked if I could speak to his mummy or daddy. For the next few minutes, I stood in the rain while the toddler spoke gibberish and called me "bum head" in between bursts of laughter—his, I should add. Eventually, the child's mother came to the intercom and asked me who I was and what I wanted.

"I'm from XXXXXXXXX estate agents, and we noticed that your property is for sale..."

I hadn't finished my sentence when the woman said, "Thank you, but I'm not interested, and I'm very busy. Bye!" And that was that. Number one crossed off the list. A disappointing start.

There wasn't a reply at the next few properties I located, and the woman at the one after that told me they'd just agreed a sale. When I asked if we could help them find a property through our referral system, she said they were relocating to Birmingham.

There was a break in the downpour as I parked up on the road of the last property on the list. The Edwardian house didn't have an estate agency board outside it, but I was able to identify it from the unusual gateposts—on each was mounted a carving of what looked like a Yorkshire terrier. As soon as I opened the gate and stepped onto the garden path, I heard a loud slam against the front door which was accompanied by growling and a deep bark. Whatever dog was behind the door trying to crash through, it was definitely not a Yorkie.

A woman opened the front door, but only slightly, to prevent the dog getting out. She politely asked what I wanted. I was trying to maintain my composure as I explained who I was and why I was on her doorstep, but this proved a task. You see, my eyes kept switching between the woman and the chunky black-and-tan paw of the Rottweiler or Doberman pinscher that was trying to get around the door to eat me. Introducing myself, I tried to hand the woman my business card, but as she was struggling to contain the dog, it was mutually agreed that it wasn't a good time to talk.

Strangely, my area manager never followed up with me on how my canvassing went that dreary morning. However, when I got back to the office and mentioned the fun and games I'd had, a colleague said, "Oh…that house with the funny gate posts. I was gonna go to that one last week, but they've got a fierce dog, so I didn't bother."

A common practice amongst rival estate agents attempting to poach instructions from each other is to register with their competitors as a prospective buyer. An unsuspecting negotiator, thinking their deceitful counterpart to be a genuine buyer, will forward property particulars to them and may even arrange viewing appointments. The agent, masquerading as a buyer, will then have the full name and address of the seller and can approach them to offer their services.

Some of the more unscrupulous agents will take the charade a step further and register with their competitors under the names of several pseudo-buyers.

They will target a property and request viewings for it, which they obviously won't attend. One after the other, the fake buyers do not turn up for their appointment. The seller, who has had to rush home from work each time to prepare for the viewings, is understandably upset at having their time wasted. And after several no shows, any seller can be forgiven for thinking their estate agent's doing something wrong. At this point, the rogue agent, having the seller's full details, will approach them to offer his services.

One agent, posing as a buyer, booked a viewing appointment under a false name and then had the audacity to attend and pitch his company to the seller. His story, apparently, was that he was looking for a similar house for himself, but if he'd registered using his own name, other agents wouldn't deal with him. After a fleeting look around, he told the seller that the property wasn't suitable for him, but as an agent, he could offer a discounted fee and accompany all viewings. And here's the interesting part: the seller instructed him.

Now, whenever I told this story in the past, people always questioned why a seller would give their business to someone so openly deceitful. For years, I wondered the same thing. Losing out to a competitor who employed such underhand tactics was bad enough, but when their actions were so blatant, and the seller still instructed them, it was incredibly frustrating. I was keen to find out why a property owner would instruct an estate agent who they knew had lied to them. Through analysing several real-life scenarios and a conversation with a psychologist at a dinner party, I found several possible answers, but the clearest one came from one such seller. This successful, middle-aged businessman told me that he wanted someone who was prepared to lie in order to sell his house for him. He told me that he knew the agent was lying, but admired his "front," which he thought was an attribute that would help him get the best price for his home.

Similarly, the whole door-knocking exercise was something most people, including estate agents, would detest. After all, who wants to open their front door to a stranger, discuss their home-selling plans on the doorstep, then give out their name and telephone number? However, for every group of sellers who'd shut the door on the estate agent canvassing for business, there'd be one who'd admire that agent's gumption enough to instruct them. The big wigs at our company knew this well and had a standard response to sellers' objections to aggressive canvassing: "The same initiative and determination used to take your property onto the market will be applied to selling it."

As you can see, some sellers would happily overlook an estate agent's dubious reputation if they felt they'd benefit financially from that agent's go-getting qualities. And as long as that mindset exists, the sharp practices will continue to do so, too.

We've already looked at how competition between estate agents can lead to them purposely overpricing a property at the appraisal stage. Recommending an inflated asking price to a prospective seller, and being convincing with it, in many cases is enough to win the instruction over your rivals.

In a tough market, competing agents may be more amenable to negotiating their fees. Some companies may run special promotions offering discounted sole-agency rates as a way of attracting new instructions. As mentioned in an earlier chapter, when I worked for a franchised estate agency, we were a new business in a town that had many well-established agents. We needed a way of kick-starting our company, so for a limited period, we reduced our fees by half. The only condition was that the seller allowed us to display a For Sale board outside their property. Everyone involved benefitted: we beat our competitors and got our business off the ground, and our sellers made a saving on the fees they paid.

Moving on, what happens when an estate agent loses an instruction to a competitor? Do they give up on that property and concentrate on finding the next one, or will they try to sabotage their competitor's sale? The answer really depends on the agent and the property involved. However, in my experience, most agents will focus their efforts on new business but won't give up completely on the lost instruction. Also, they may not go out of their way to scupper a rival's sale, but should the opportunity arise, few will pass it up. I'll explain what I mean.

Let's say an estate agent has lost an instruction to a competitor who appraised at a higher price. Perhaps the asking price suggested by the rival agent is a little too optimistic for that property in the current market. The losing agent will place the seller's details in their 1-31 system for follow-up. They'll contact the seller periodically to see how the marketing of their property is coming along (or not), and it is here where they can have a dig at their competitor.

One of my colleagues would telephone such sellers every other week and always use the same line. "Are you telling me they (the other agent) haven't sold it yet? Oh dear! Why do you think that is? Have they had enough viewings? Do you think they've overpriced it?" And then he'd finish off with: "Remember, if they ask you to reduce the price, give me a call first."

Some sellers got fed up with my colleague's calls, while others admired his persistence and eventually gave him the instruction. By constantly following up that way, he was causing the sellers to doubt whether they'd chosen the right agent. I'm sure that my colleague's stirring led to many of those sellers having a good grumble at their respective estate agents. And as already mentioned, he won many instructions this way, too.

I remember a competitor applying the same tactics in trying to win back an instruction from us. This estate agent didn't succeed; however, his efforts and sheer doggedness deserve commendation. We were in a multi-agency agreement with this one other local estate agent. The property being marketed was a house that had just been converted to two flats by a developer. We received a viewing request from a man claiming to be the financial advisor of an overseas businessman. He told us that he was looking for an investment on behalf of his client, who'd given him authority to make an offer once a suitable property was found. The man looked at both flats—the ground and first floor—and submitted a full-asking-price offer for the whole building on the condition that the freehold was to be included in the sale. Furthermore, his client had funds readily available and did not require a mortgage.

Now, I have to say, my manager, colleagues, and I were very surprised at receiving such an offer, and for several reasons. The flats, whilst newly refurbished, were small and overpriced; yet we had a cash buyer who was prepared to pay the asking price for both, in one go. The seller was delighted, but our cynicism was prevailing—the whole thing sounded a little too good to be true.

When I spoke to the seller, he told me that the other estate agent was quite upset at having lost a sale to us, which was understandable, given that the agency fees were over £7,500. Also, the property had been withdrawn from the market, so our competitor's involvement had effectively ceased, and he wasn't going to be graceful in defeat. Just days after letters confirming the sale went out to the relevant parties, the seller told me that the other agent had telephoned to check in as to how the sale was going. The following week, he called again, this time saying he had buyers wanting to see the property; the seller should never have withdrawn it from further viewing.

Now, whilst the seller took a whimsical view of the other agent's comments, the light-hearted conversation we had about it also served to keep us on our toes. In other words, he was letting us know that our competitor wasn't giving up and was in hot pursuit.

The transaction met with several delays, one being that the buyer's surveyor (also a trusted friend) was away on holiday and couldn't inspect the property until his return to the United Kingdom. And the main holdup to the sale, we were told, was the transferring of the funds from various overseas accounts. During this time, our competitor hounded the seller with calls, asking him to allow his cash buyers to view the property. The agent backed his request by saying there must've been something wrong with the existing buyer for them not to have exchanged contracts by that point.

The seller, an experienced building contractor, had only recently branched out into property development, and the building we were selling for him was his third project. He was aware that the other agent's persistence was all part of the tussle for instructions between estate agencies, and he knew that our competitor's claims were likely overhyped. Nonetheless, the seller confided in me that he was starting to doubt our buyer's intentions. And this uncertainty grew when he called his solicitor for an update and was told they'd not heard from the buyer's side for several days. I needed to provide my client with some reassurance and do so in a way that didn't appear that I was simply holding off the other agent.

The situation as I saw it was that the seller had a fantastic deal on the table, and he knew it, but was worried in case the buyer had had second thoughts. In turn, the buyer knew that he was paying a very good price for the property and did things at his own pace; he wouldn't be pushed. As for the other estate agent, it was highly unlikely that they had a better buyer—someone who was prepared to take both flats at top market value and for cash? This, however, didn't stop them trying to cause our sale to go wrong.

After slightly further delay, contracts were finally exchanged, and the sale was completed. The buyer then assigned our lettings department to find tenants for the two flats, which they did in a week. Our competitor saw the For Sale boards turn to Sold and then the To Let boards quickly turn to Let, which must've upset them a little.

Estate agents may also have a snipe at a competitor's sale when the surveyor, carrying out the mortgage valuation, calls for comparable evidence. I mentioned this procedure briefly in earlier chapters, but here I'll explain in more detail.

When a sale has been agreed on a property, if the buyer requires a mortgage, their lender will want the property valued to ensure it is good lending security. The valuer (usually a chartered surveyor) will be instructed to carry out a valuation of the property for mortgage purposes. This is in no way a detailed survey on the condition of the building, but rather an inspection to ascertain the property's present market value. Should the surveyor suspect the property's structure to be defective, he or she will recommend further inspection by an expert in the relevant field. So if there are worrying cracks in the walls, the surveyor may recommend a structural engineer look at the property. If the roof was in poor condition, a roofer may be asked to inspect, if the electrics were bad, an electrician, and so on.

Once the surveyor has completed the inspection, they will research prices of similar properties sold recently in the vicinity in order to help them with their valuation. Surveyors have different sources for obtaining house price data; these include their own company's database of valuations, land registry figures, various house price websites, and local estate agents.

Surveyors are normally assigned a particular area of operation, so they get to know its property stock and estate agents quite well. A surveyor may call an estate agency for comparable evidence as a result of seeing one of their boards outside a property near the one he or she has just valued. Some surveyors may have a rapport with a local agent and will call on them for research, even if they haven't seen their boards displaying in the relevant area. And here is where estate agents may try to get back at a competitor by "knocking the comparable."

Surveyors are not silly. They know that the rivalry between agents may influence and distort those agents' opinions on the prices of certain properties. For example, let's say Agent A appraised a house at £300,000, but the seller went with Agent B, who recommended an asking price of £330,000. Now, Agent B agrees a sale at £325,000, which is the price the surveyor has to justify at valuation. If the surveyor calls Agent A for comparable evidence, what are the chances that he'll get unbiased assistance with the pricing?

As said, surveyors will use their discretion when applying the comparable evidence supplied to them by estate agents. Sometimes the surveyor is forewarned that a particular estate agent may have motive to knock the valuation because, perhaps like Agent A in our example, they lost out on the instruction to the selling agent. In my experience, most estate agents are generally honest with the comparable evidence, and this can work both ways. If a property has achieved a much higher price than similar ones in the same area, and if the estate agent has no comparables to present, you can be sure the surveyor will be advised so.

In the chapter on estate agency agreements, I explained the difference between sole and multiple agencies and looked at the good and bad points of each type of contract. I also mentioned how competition between rival agents could influence the advice given to clients regarding whether to accept or reject an offer. Here, we're going to look at the point where an estate agent's sole agency is about to expire and the trickery that some agents will apply in an attempt to hold on to the instruction and keep their competitors at bay.

I remember a morning meeting where my manager pointed out that we only had two days sole agency left on a particular house. At this point the owner of the property hadn't confirmed whether he'd keep us on and extend the marketing to other agents (multi-agency), or dismiss us and give sole agency to a competitor. What we did know was that the competing estate agent had been in regular contact with the homeowner.

My manager set us the task of the day and offered a bonus payment to the negotiator who achieved an offer on the above-mentioned property. I delivered. At eleven o'clock that same morning, I showed the property to a buyer, who made an offer that was accepted later that day. That's how it's supposed to be done. No lies, deceit, or underhand tactics. I just got on the phone and called everyone I could. A year later, the same manager, when faced with a similar scenario, did something totally different.

Once again, our sole agency term was due to expire on a property—a three-bedroom semi. The only difference this time was that the seller had told us she was going multi-agency, with us and the same competitor from our previous story. My manager didn't care too much for the other estate agency and swore he wouldn't lose the sale to them. Here's what my boss did to ensure our competitor didn't get a look in.

We had a sale agreed on a very well-presented three-bedroom terraced house. It was slightly smaller than the semi, but in much better condition: new kitchen, bathroom, flooring, and so on. My manager had learned that the woman buying the terraced house had a cousin living on the same road as the semi-detached property we were about to lose the sole agency on. The two relatives were quite close and would've jumped at the chance of living in such proximity of each other. So, my manager swayed the buyer of the terraced house over to the semi-detached house near her cousin, which didn't prove difficult to do. During the transition, we were given strict instructions not to say anything to the sellers of the terraced house about why their buyer had pulled out of the purchase. If anything, we were to say that we too were very surprised, and that we'd left several unanswered messages requesting an explanation from the buyer.

Now because the terraced house was more saleable than the semi-detached one, it didn't take long to find another buyer, albeit for slightly less money this time. So we may have won the battle against our competitor, but not without some cost to the seller of the terraced house.

One particular estate agency, not a direct competitor but someone we'd occasionally cross paths with, always managed to hold onto their instructions by achieving an offer just before the sole agency expired. In going through the 1-31 system and speaking to someone who'd instructed this agent, I noticed a pattern forming. The sellers would tell me that their sole agency agreement was about to expire, and because their agent hadn't had much success, they were going to instruct someone else— possibly us. And then each seller would somehow go under offer days or hours before the contract was due to end. Stranger still was that in each case, the sellers were advised by the agent to keep their property on the market and available for viewing; just in case anything went wrong and the buyers withdrew. I was a little suspicious, and for good reason, too. Some years later, I spoke with a former employee of that estate agency, and he explained what his boss would do when their firm was about to lose a client.

In the first instance, they'd get on the phones and try their damnedest to find someone for the property, regardless of how good or bad that buyer may have been. Sometimes they got lucky, found a decent buyer, and negotiated a sale. Most times, I was told, they'd fabricate the buyer in order to buy themselves more time on their sole agency while they continued searching for a genuine buyer.

Basically, they'd send a willing friend or relative around to the property who, posing as a buyer, would make an offer to purchase the property. The seller, thinking they had a genuine buyer, had no reason to leave their existing agent and ran with the sale. The agent recommended to the seller that they continue to show the property, just in case something went wrong with the existing buyer. The agent appeared to be acting in the seller's best interest; however, what they'd now be doing was frantically looking for a real buyer. Obviously, the pseudo-buyer would not have appointed a solicitor nor instructed a surveyor, so as time passed, the seller would be wondering what the delay was.

If all went to plan and the agent found a genuine buyer, they'd recommend the seller drop the existing (fake) buyer and proceed with the new (genuine) buyer. This recommendation would probably be backed with a story along the lines of the first buyer not being able to raise the mortgage on account of being made redundant. Who's going to know any different?

At a large estate agency where I worked, the underhand activities of two long-serving members of staff were brought to light when the pair, a branch manager and his senior negotiator, were dismissed. It was rumoured that these guys were ensuring that certain properties, having investment potential, went to specific buyers in return for cash incentives, loosely known as "bungs" and "backhanders." That they had received payment was never proved; however, what brought about their demise (amongst many things) was that they were releasing confidential information about clients to property dealers. Below is a typical example of the lengths these two rogues would go to in order to prevent competitors from winning instructions that had development potential.

Let's say a gentleman calls to request an appraisal of his elderly aunt's four-bedroom, Edwardian terraced house. The owner of the property has been moved to a nursing home, and her nephew has been appointed to deal with the sale of her house; the proceeds of which will go towards her care costs. The property requires extensive refurbishment, which the nephew knows will reflect on the asking price. He is also aware that the eventual buyer is likely to be a property developer, or perhaps an end user willing to take on a project of this size. Amongst the estate agents invited to appraise the property, the competition to win this instruction will be fierce.

In such scenarios, if the manager or senior negotiator lost the instruction to another agent, they'd pass on the seller's contact details to a property developer associate of theirs. In turn, that developer would approach the seller directly, offering to buy the property from them. So the seller would have a cash offer from a professional property investor and no estate agency fees to pay. If the deal went through, the developer would refurbish the property and then put it up for sale with the manager and his accomplice. The two would probably have been given a cash bonus by the developer for tipping him off, although this was never proved. As for the other agents, all they'd know was that the property was sold privately.

Apparently, the two scoundrels who engaged in the above activity were caught when a disgruntled colleague alerted an area director. They admitted involvement in three such transactions as outlined in the example scenario, although it was rumoured that they were mixed up in several other dodgy deals.

I've also heard of estate agents posing as buyers or sellers and sending their competitors off to false market appraisal or viewing appointments. Such incidents are the pranks of immature negotiators and unfortunately, they do occur quite frequently. Other shenanigans have included registering as a buyer and giving false details. I fell for one or two of these tricks in my time, calling London Zoo and asking for a prospective buyer named Mr C. Lion. I also remember phoning a number and asking for a first-time buyer named Liz, only to find I'd called Buckingham Palace's press office! I've also been out to market appraisals only to get to the address and find the property didn't exist.

An age-old activity that goes on between bickering rival estate agencies is the removal of each other's boards from outside properties. For the main part, such actions were usually the work of office negotiators; however, there have been cases where the senior management of large estate agencies were fully aware of their staff's doings.

Whether it's just a little white lie or an illicit transaction involving bribery, fierce competition in the property market can lead to unethical behaviour on the part of estate agents. And regardless of which agent gets the upper hand, an innocent buyer or seller may lose out.

In the next chapter, we'll look at the competitive element between colleagues and the infighting of negotiators working for the same company.

# 12. Infighting

In the previous chapter, we looked at how rival estate agencies compete with each other and the skulduggery that sometimes results from their tussle for business. In this section of the book, we're going to cover competition amongst colleagues. We'll look at how tough management and demanding sales targets can instigate the infighting between negotiators working in the same office or for the same company. You'll certainly raise an eyebrow or two at the antics employed by some in order to triumph over their fellow members of staff.

So, as it is commission that all estate agents compete for, let's now examine the different pay structures in place. We briefly touched on commission payments much earlier in the book, but here we'll look at what they mean for the sales negotiators and how they can reflect on the buyer or seller.

## Personal commission

Most estate agencies pay their staff a basic salary, plus commission, which is usually expressed as a percentage of what the company is earning from their client. Let's recap on the example used in chapter 1.

An estate agency sells a property at £300,000, and the fee payable by the client is 1.5 per cent, so the company earns £4,500. If the negotiator credited with the sale is on a personal commission of 10 per cent, they'll earn £450 from the deal, which will be paid in addition to their basic pay.

It is worth mentioning here that the basic pay for a sales negotiator is generally quite low. To give you an example: at the time of writing, I know of several different estate agencies in suburban London who pay basic salaries of up to £15,000. Now this may not sound as low a salary as some jobs may pay, but when you factor in that these people could be contracted to work a forty-five-hour week at minimum; their basic salary is not far off the minimum wage. So, if you're a sales negotiator on the sort of pay package mentioned above, you've got to be selling properties consistently if you want to earn close to a living wage. In fact, in a negotiator's monthly pay, if the commission does not frequently exceed the basic salary, that negotiator should reconsider their career options before their employer does it for them.

In an estate agency office where sales staff are paid a basic salary plus personal commission, a competitive environment will always exist—it's the nature of the business. Problems often occur when the competition amongst negotiators goes from friendly rivalry to cutthroat infighting, as the latter extreme can adversely affect all involved—buyers and sellers included—and I'll explain how shortly. Good management will keep the staff wrangling in check; however, I've known some managers and directors positively encourage their staff to battle it out for sales. One or two even turned a blind eye to their rules being broken, which we'll also discuss in a moment.

The theme of this chapter and the real-life examples mentioned will be based on estate agency offices where a basic salary and personal commission was paid to negotiators. In my experience, this was by far the most common pay structure in estate agency; however, before we move on, let's have a quick look at two others.

## Pooled commission

This is where negotiators are paid a percentage of what the office earns as a whole, regardless of who sold what. Put another way, commission earned by the office goes into a pot, so to speak, and each negotiator is allocated a percentage of that pot. So if a branch office brings in, or contracts on, £30,000 in a month and the negotiator's share of that is 5 per cent, they'll earn £1,500 commission.

The percentage received could be a fixed amount, month in, month out, or it may fluctuate depending on performance. For example, if one member of the team consistently achieves more sales than their colleagues, their share of the pooled commission may be greater. Negotiators may also get an increased percentage as an incentive for exceeding their monthly sales target.

Pooled commission, like the personal type, is usually paid in addition to a basic salary. Such is the typical pay structure of office and area managers working within the larger, multi-branch, estate agencies. In saying that, I have also known of smaller firms that pay a basic salary plus pooled commission to their negotiators. One chap to whom I spoke was asked to run the property sales operation of a small estate agency. The package he was offered was commission only at a rate of 25 per cent of the office pool.

Some estate agency bosses prefer using the pooled-commission pay structure, believing it to promote teamwork amongst their sales staff. When paid this way, negotiators can be impartial as to what buyer gets the property, which in turn leads to less infighting and the mischief that often results from it.

Conversely, there are those who oppose the idea of pooled commission, because they feel it can detract from the competitive, go-getting attitude required of an estate agent. Where a signifi-cant imbalance exists within a sales team, the stronger negotiators may end up carrying the weaker ones. This can result in the latter applying less effort, and the former getting fed up with doing all the work.

## Commission only

This pay structure is more suited to negotiators who possess an entrepreneurial spirit, steely nerves, and a hard-nosed approach to selling property.

If you're working for an established firm in the right area, you can earn a decent wage from a commission-only package. For example, at the time of writing, I know of estate agents working in busy parts of London where the average price of a semi-detached house is around £800,000. The companies that these people work for charge a minimum fee of 1 per cent for sole agency. A sales negotiator working for one of these estate agencies claims to do so for commission only, at a rate of 30 per cent. By these figures, if this guy sells two houses a month, and he's targeted to do three times that amount, he'll earn the company £16,000 and himself, £4,800. He told me that some months he earned much more and others, he went home with considerably less. One January, he received no wages at all.

Can you imagine how competitive an environment this chap works in? Not only are the negotiators fighting off rival estate agencies, they also have to watch their backs from their colleagues, who are all chasing the same property deals. Just how tough the competition between negotiators can be, and exactly what some are prepared to do in order to triumph over their fellow employees, we'll look at in a moment. What I'll say now is that I've known negotiators (male and female) to resign or get dismissed, commit fraud, or start fist-fights over sales being stolen from one another.

The stories below refer to negotiators working for both large and small estate agencies, who were paid a basic salary, plus commission on sales they made personally.

## In-house competition

During my estate agency career, I worked in many different offices and with several sales teams. One of my employers would periodically move staff between branches. Promotions, resignations, and dismissals created opportunities for negotiators to work in different areas. Most of the time people were given the choice as to whether they wanted to move; however, those negotiators whose conduct had blemished their careers were not afforded the option. If a vacancy needed filling in an office at a less than desirable location, these naughty boys and girls would be "asked" to move there—a sort of "last chance saloon," if you like. Luckily for me, all of my office moves were my decision, although some were not my best.

Over the years, when relocating to different branches, I made an interesting observation. In those offices where everyone took it in turn to make the tea, or where the person putting on the kettle always asked who else wanted a beverage, teamwork and good management existed. And in those offices where the rule was that you made your own cuppa, the work ethos was the same—everyone for themselves.

Even after several years of estate agency experience working for the same firm, in a competitive yet fair environment, moving to such an office was a culture shock for me. You'll see exactly what I mean as we now take a look at how ruthless the in-house competition can get.

## Applicants and viewings

The role of an estate agent is to achieve the best price for their client's property and from the best buyer. This whole process begins when a sales negotiator arranges for an applicant to view the relevant house, flat, or maisonette. Who wins the sale may often be determined by which negotiator manages to get the strongest applicant through the door of the property first. So, with that in mind, let's start by examining how negotiators fight for applicants and viewings.

When a prospective buyer registers with an estate agency, their property requirements and contact details are placed on the applicant register. Where a company or branch operates a communal applicant register, any of the sales negotiators are free to go through the register, contact all buyers, offer them properties, and arrange viewings for them. In other words, a buyer's record is not assigned to a specific negotiator, as is the case with a personal applicant register (see chapter 8).

Even where a communal register was in operation, quite often, the negotiator who initially dealt with a buyer remained their first point of contact. This was especially so if the two parties established a rapport and communicated frequently. And in a fair office, such a working relationship was respected by the other staff, who wouldn't cut in on their colleague's applicant. In fact, where an element of camaraderie existed, negotiators would cover appointments for one another; although it must be said, they wouldn't always sell the merits of a property to an applicant who wasn't their own.

In some branches where I worked, if a property came onto the market during my absence, the manager would inform my applicants and arrange viewings for them on my behalf. This ensured that my good buyers were treated impartially, and that I didn't miss out on opportunities.

In those cutthroat estate agencies I mentioned, countless times I'd return from my day off to find that a colleague had sold a property to an applicant I'd registered, spoken to frequently, and got on well with. And in each case, my co-workers knew that I'd built a rapport with that applicant, but this didn't prevent them seizing a sales opportunity. Taking the matter up with the office manager didn't help much; in one branch the only solution offered was to do the same back to your colleague. This approach resulted in negotiators hiding applicant records and not putting them on the system, or purposely listing incorrect telephone numbers so that colleagues couldn't contact them. Such actions would put the applicant at a disadvantage because only one negotiator would know how to get in touch with them regarding properties new to the market. Even the office manager would be powerless to help in such situations.

Every viewing appointment made by a negotiator had to be logged in their personal viewing book. Whenever a sale was agreed, only the negotiator who'd arranged the viewing appointment and written it in their book could claim it.

Viewing books were generally A4 in size and had pre-printed rows and columns forming the fields where information relating to the appointment was entered. Typically, the fields from left to right were the day's date, the applicant's name, their contact numbers, and their status—FTB for first-time buyer, SSTC for sold subject to contract, and so on. Next to that were the property address, the seller's name and contact numbers, and the time and date the viewing was to take place. If a property was empty, and we were to carry out the viewings, the word 'KEY' would be entered instead of the seller's name. Lastly, at the end of the row were two small boxes, signifying the applicant's and seller's confirmation of the viewing appointment. Only when both boxes were ticked would a viewing be counted as such. However, once a negotiator had logged a viewing in their book, even if the buyer, seller, or both had yet to confirm the time and date, the viewing was theirs. No other negotiator could claim it.

Viewing books were often used to resolve disputes over which negotiator should be awarded a property sale; however, they were also the source of many arguments.

I remember an applicant asking me to make an appointment for her to see a three-bedroom semi that we were advertising. I'd written the appointment in my book and left a message for the sellers, who conducted all the viewings. I continued with my work, leaving the office to carry out various duties. In such scenarios, if the seller called back during the negotiator's absence, another member of the team could normally be relied on to deal with the matter, either confirming the appointment or taking a message for their colleague.

On my return to the office, I saw that there were no messages for me and the relevant boxes in my viewing book remained unchecked. Just as I was about to call the seller, one of my colleagues announced that he was in receipt of an asking price offer for the same property. And the buyer was the same woman for whom I'd tried to make an appointment, and whose name was written in my viewing book. My colleague persisted that the appointment belonged to him, claiming that he'd sent the woman along to see the property the day before. He then referred the matter to our manager, who took one look at the negotiator's viewing book and declared the appointment mine.

In his haste to grab the viewing appointment, my colleague had written the wrong dates in his viewing book. He'd entered the present day as the date the viewing was made and the previous day as the date the property was seen. In other words, he'd arranged a viewing today that was to take place in the past. For a brief moment he blamed a typo, but then he admitted his misdemeanour when our manager offered to call the applicant or seller for confirmation of the viewing date. I was awarded the sale, which eventually fell through due to chain problems.

The viewing book of a successful sales negotiator was generally where the serious buyers or applicants were to be found. These were the people who wanted to buy a property and were doing something about it. If a house or flat came to the market, a negotiator could spend an hour going through the applicant register, making dozens of calls in an attempt to arrange viewings. Alternatively, they could look through the most recent pages of their (or their colleagues') viewing books and call those applicants who were actively looking.

One estate agent took the above process a little further, ensuring that each day he arrived for work before the other negotiators, allowing him time to photocopy their viewing books. Also, this chap would purposely leave blank lines below each appointment written in his viewing book. He did this, I suspect, so as to be able to claim other negotiators' appointments as his own, much like the guy I mentioned earlier. However, leaving spaces below each day's viewings allowed him to enter appointments for whatever date he wanted. Allow me to use my earlier story as an example in order to clarify.

Let's say that on 5th May, I tried to book an appointment for a woman to view a house that same day at seven o'clock. My treacherous colleague, being aware of this, logs the appointment in his book, using the space under the 4th May with a viewing time of seven on the following day (5th May). In the event that a manager was asked to adjudicate, it would appear that this slippery chap tried to arrange the appointment before I did, thus making it rightfully his. Several grievances highlighted the motive for leaving blank spaces in viewing books, and the practice was stopped. However, I shudder to think how many sales that parasitical negotiator stole from his colleagues using such dubious methods.

Supposing an applicant telephoned the estate agency to request a viewing of a property, but the negotiator who sent them the details wasn't available to take the call. In such scenarios, if the applicant asked to speak to that specific negotiator, then the other estate agency staff cannot claim the viewing appointment and must pass it on to their colleague. Such was the rule; however, not everyone adhered to it, and policing it was very difficult. For example, let's say an applicant telephoned to speak to a negotiator named Dave, who was out of the office on another viewing. Dave's colleague John answers the call and says, "Sorry, but Dave's away from the office at the moment. Is there anything I can help you with?" The applicant explains that Dave left a message for them regarding a house that has just come onto the market. They like the sound of it and are keen to view immediately, because the buyer on their property is anxious for the chain to get moving. John may now respond with any one of the following actions:

- He will take the applicant's details and pass the message on to Dave.

- He will arrange the appointment on Dave's behalf (rare).

- He may arrange the appointment on Dave's behalf for that particular property but offer the applicant viewings on other properties, which he'll then claim as his own; especially now that he knows the applicant is motivated.

- He will steal the applicant and the appointment, and Dave will only get to know about it if an offer is made, or he looks at his colleague's viewing book.

In those ultracompetitive offices I mentioned, the last of the above actions was the most common. In fact, one chap I worked with would routinely claim any viewing he could as his own. Almost whispering into the phone, he'd tell applicants that the person they'd asked for wasn't available, even when the negotiator in question was sitting two desks away, twiddling his thumbs.

One time, a family friend for whom I was trying to find a property called to speak to me. I was out of the office on another appointment, and my rather sharp colleague, not knowing my relationship with the applicant, politely offered to assist. Unbeknown to my friend, the colleague arranged for her to view the property but claimed the appointment as his. Obviously, my friend called me to provide feedback on the viewing, and that's when I learned of my colleague's antics.

Back in the pre-email days, when an applicant registered their requirements, we would send out property particulars to them by post. Envelopes containing the information required by the applicant would be prepared, and the negotiator would include a business card so the applicant would know who to contact for viewings. Such envelopes would be put in the postal tray. All the mail was franked at the end of the day and then taken to the post office. Within the group that I worked, a story emerged about the negotiator who, towards the end of the day, would open all the envelopes in the postal tray; remove his colleagues' cards and replace them with his own. Effectively, this was as if he'd registered every applicant.

Even where a negotiator's business card was stapled to the property particulars included in the envelope, an alarming number of applicants still did not ask for the relevant negotiator when requesting viewing appointments. To remedy this, one estate agent's innovation was to have a rubber stamp made with the wording: "For more information, or an appointment to view please contact xxx."

I liked the idea, so I also bought a custom-made rubber stamp with similar wording. I couldn't wait to put it to the test and grabbed every incoming phone call, so I could register as many applicants as possible.

One gentleman enquired about a specific flat, and I sent rubber-stamped details out to him. I followed up the next day leaving a voicemail asking that he call me back to let me know what he thought of the flat's written specifications. This man had a very distinctive voice and accent. When he called back, I just happened to be the one to answer the phone and instantly recognised him. He requested a viewing on the flat, so in order to test the effectiveness of my new rubber stamp; I asked if he could tell me who'd sent him the property particulars. Was there a card attached, or a negotiator's contact details written anywhere? I could hear the sound of paper being rustled; then the man returned to the phone and said, "Nope, nothing here, but can I see the flat tomorrow evening at seven?" He viewed the property and eventually bought it. Had I not been the one to answer that call, I'd have lost that sale. So much for my twenty-quid rubber stamp!

How can competition between sales negotiators in the same office affect members of the public—buyers and sellers? When new instructions are scarce, the forces of supply and demand will mean those few properties coming to the market are likely to attract more than one interested buyer. When there's more than one offer on the table, each negotiator will want their buyer to triumph over their colleagues', and they may provide a little less than ethical assistance. Allow me to explain.

An estate agent must always act in the best interests of the client—the seller. When a property attracts multiple offers from numerous buyers, the office manager, being impartial, must ascertain which of those offers best suits the seller's circumstances. In such scenarios, it is of utmost importance that each respective buyer's offer remains confidential from their counterparts. None of the competing buyers should know what the other is offering on the property, or what their position is as a buyer.

When such situations were not dealt with in that manner, the bidding got out of control, and buyers ended up offering more for a property than they intended. Almost always, this resulted in a fiscal U-turn at a later stage of the sale, quite often disrupting the chain, or even aborting it altogether.

In trying to beat their colleagues to the sale, negotiators might advise their respective buyers as to what level of offer they should make. It could be as simple as: "You really need to go to the asking price if you want this property." This may not sound in any way strange, and many people who've been through the house-buying process may well have heard those exact words. However, if a sale has already been agreed to another buyer who's paying slightly under the asking price, such guidance could be deemed unethical.

Even worse is when a negotiator tells a buyer that they need to offer £198,000 on a property, because £196,000 is already on the table. As mentioned in earlier chapters, if the asking price is £200,000, why tell a buyer to pay £198,000 when they may have intended to pay more?

In trying to manipulate a buyer to make a higher offer than they'd set out to, some negotiators would cite the mortgage valuation as a fallback. What I mean by this is that the negotiator would tell the buyer to offer a certain figure, perhaps even the asking price. If the buyer expressed reluctance at paying that much, the negotiator would say something along these lines: "If you offer that amount, you'll secure the property. And don't worry if you think you're paying too much, because if your surveyor thinks you've overpaid, he will down value the property, and you can then use the valuation report as a negotiating tool."

The above is terrible advice because firstly, there's every possibility the property will value correctly, and the buyer would end up paying more than they initially wanted to. Secondly, if the property is down valued, there are no guarantees that the seller will renegotiate the price, regardless of what the survey says. I lost count of how many times I saw a surveyor mark down the agreed sale price of a property, and the seller then rejected out of hand the contents of the valuation report. In many cases, the property went back onto the market and achieved a higher price, which a different surveyor agreed with.

Another way in which negotiators influence their buyers is by creating a sense of urgency. They'll tell the buyer that there's a lot of interest in the property and that they need to act fast before a colleague sells it to another buyer. Once again, there's nothing wrong in telling a buyer this; quite often it's the truth. However, what negotiators will tell the buyer is: "Go to the full asking price and insist that the property be taken off the market and withdrawn from further viewing." And this too is a fair request because, after all, the buyer has given the seller exactly what they're asking for, so why should the property continue to be shown—right? The problem arises when negotiators, in their haste to fend off their colleagues, push forward a less than ideal buyer, or worse still, they lie about the strength of their buyer.

One chap I worked with phoned a couple about a property and insisted they view it within the hour if they wanted half a chance of buying it. The buyers agreed and viewed the property during their lunch break. They offered the full asking price on the condition that the property be immediately withdrawn from further viewings. The other sales staff didn't get a chance to make any viewings, and those who did had to cancel them. What was the outcome? Three weeks into the sale, the survey had yet to be booked. A week after that, the buyers withdrew from the sale, admitting they could not raise the mortgage they required. After wasting four weeks, we started all over again. Not only did the seller lose time, but they moved forward thinking they'd got the asking price once, and they could do it again, but they didn't and had to lower their expectations. We, on the other hand, lost the group of potential buyers we initially had, who went on to find other properties. We nearly lost the instruction, too.

Another memorable scenario was where one sales negotiator was on the phone to a seller, tying up a sale on the woman's flat. A colleague sitting at the adjacent desk asked if the seller would show her flat to the applicant who was sitting in front of him. The negotiator on the phone to the seller, not wanting to jeopardize the sale he'd just agreed, ignored his colleague and brought the telephone conversation to an end. Both negotiators then engaged in an argument that very nearly turned into a fist-fight, and all of this happened in front of the young woman applicant sitting in the office. Needless to say, it was an embarrassing situation.

As you can see, competition between staff working in the same office can sometimes cause all involved to lose out and a lot of stress along the way. However, before we move on, let's have a brief look at scenarios in larger estate agencies where the sales teams of two or more offices battle it out for the same sale.

When I worked for a large corporate estate agency, we were encouraged to cooperate with neighbouring offices and use the branch network to the full advantage of the company and the customer. Each office's catchment of operation was clearly defined by head office. Sometimes, where certain properties fell on the boundary, they were marketed by the two neighbouring offices, providing it was mutually agreed by the two relevant managers. This meant that the instructing office bore the advertising costs, but the staff of the second office could make and carry out viewing appointments for the property. Sometimes all contact with the seller would go via the instructing office, and other times the second office would hold all relevant information allowing them to speak to the seller directly.

When a sale was made by the second office, the commission would be divided equally between the branches, although the negotiator accredited with the sale would get the full personal commission. Who'd be responsible for progressing the sale to an exchange of contracts was the decision of the senior staff at the instructing office.

It was perfectly acceptable that when one of the offices took on a new instruction, the staff there would always have the first run at trying to sell it. Once they were sure they'd exhausted their attempts—advertised the property and sent along all their hot buyers—only then would they pass the property details to colleagues at the neighbouring office. And as mentioned above, this would only happen if both managers agreed in advance. As you would expect, such a system was not infallible, and quite often it gave way to bickering between the negotiators of the two offices involved.

Now with regard to market appraisals and instructions, the rules were very clear indeed. If a prospective seller made an enquiry to the wrong office in error, that lead had to be passed to the office whose catchment dealt with the road the property was located on. Once again, the boundaries were clearly defined and there were no grey areas, which also meant there were no excuses for taking another office's instructions. And it is this point about in-house competition we're going to discuss now.

Early on in my estate agency career, I worked for a large corporate firm that had offices all around the country. The branch where I was based handled the sale of residential property across four different postcodes in North London. We shared three of those postcodes with neighbouring branches. The area where one of those branches was situated was considered to be an affluent part of the capital. Now, the postcode we shared with our snootier colleagues consisted of properties that those guys would term as the lower end of their catchment. They still marketed them, but certainly not with the same vigour as they did the higher-priced housing that was the core of their business.

A colleague transferred from our office to the neighbouring one and soon after made an interesting discovery. When the negotiator searched through some archives for comparable evidence for a market appraisal, he found that our friends at that office had been stealing our instructions for years. The commission we lost to those guys ran into tens of thousands of pounds. Such action not only impacted the salaries of negotiators at our office, but it would've also affected those who sold their properties through the other office. I'll explain how.

When unsure as to which office they should approach to sell their property through, some sellers would, quite naturally, choose the one located in the more prestigious part of town. The rationale for doing this would be that they'd probably achieve a better price for their home if it was marketed to the higher earners whom that office had on their applicant register. Our dishonest colleagues took full advantage of this and cemented the sellers' thinking by incorporating that idea into their sales pitch. What they didn't tell those sellers was that buyers looking in that post-code did so because they couldn't afford the properties in the more expensive one. And what those negotiators also omitted to tell the sellers was that the estate agency fees at that office were higher than those we charged at ours. Furthermore, those people's homes would not be marketed to their full potential, as doing so risked our devious colleagues' actions being exposed. For example, those properties could not have boards outside them, nor could they be advertised in certain publications, as we at the other office would've found out.

So as you can see, the only people likely to have benefitted from the above circumstances were the estate agents themselves. As to how those guys managed to evade the attention of head office and our accounts department for so long remains a mystery to me to this day.

Finally, here's one more story that highlights the lengths to which negotiators would go in order to get one up on their colleagues.

Every so often, our senior management would provide special awards as incentives to aid staff performance. On one occasion, a week's use of a midrange sports car was made available to the sales negotiator who achieved the highest number of viewing appointments that month. One chap, in his quest to win the prize, made false viewings, sending personal friends and members of his extended family along to see properties. It was also uncovered that this negotiator often invented viewings, which he sent colleagues to in order to get them away from the office so that he could pilfer their applicants.

That brings us to the end of our chapter on infighting. Next we're going to look at a subject that has been extremely topical amongst the general public in recent years: investment property.

# 13. Investment Property

Some years ago, I was told a story about a man who swaggered into an estate agency and said, "I'm after a bargain, mate!" The rather confident manager he was talking to responded by pointing the man in the direction of the Woolworths half-price sale farther along the high street.

House prices have always been a topical subject, but in recent years I noticed the dinner party conversations leaning more to the theme of investment property. Ordinary people from all different day jobs became property speculators. At one point, I counted over a dozen daytime and prime-time television programmes featuring topics such as the buy-to-let boom and refurbishing dilapidated properties purchased at auction. As an estate agent working on a busy London high street at the time, it seemed as if every other buyer walking through our door wanted to get in on the action.

Now forgive me for saying, but I saw examples where average members of the public, having no business acumen whatsoever, made tidy profits from houses or flats. Some of these people didn't set out to make money from property but ended up doing so quite by chance and in a way that appeared ridiculously easy.

One buyer, a computer engineer in his late twenties, was labelled as perhaps the slowest buyer with whom we ever dealt. This young man set about purchasing his first flat and caused so much unnecessary delay that the seller twice threatened to pull out of the sale. The buyer's inertia paid dividends for him, because he bought the one-bedroom conversion for £70,000, took three months to paint it and fit new carpets, and then decided to sell the property. He got £90,000 for it.

A few years later, a middle-aged businessman with no former experience in property investment bought a run-down flat for £155,000, did absolutely nothing to it, then sold it for £174,000 just ten weeks later.

I knew several newbie investors who took their speculation a little further. These people bought flats and houses that they initially intended to be long-term rental investments. Months later, when they saw the value of their properties increase, they remortgaged them and used the additional equity as a deposit for their next venture. While the banks were happy to lend them the money, these inexperienced and yet gutsy men and women built sizeable property portfolios. Of these investors, some of the wiser ones even managed to survive the credit crunch, although their dreams of building property empires ground to a halt.

Now, while all of the above was going on, the full-time property developers were complaining about the shortage of deals available to them. Many of these professional speculators told me that they had to pay more for their stock and lower their expectations of profit just to stay in the game. In contrast, one dealer told me that he sold a property at auction for a much higher price than he anticipated—the buyer was a novice investor. Can you see the point I'm trying to make? Everyone jumped onto the property bandwagon.

When I first got into the estate agency business, buy-to-let mortgages were unheard of. When an individual wanted to buy a property to sell or rent, they generally needed a deposit of around 30 per cent of the purchase price and a good relationship with the bank manager, who then granted them a commercial mortgage. In recent years, ordinary people became landlords on properties with 95 per cent mortgages.

One of the very last property sales in which I was instrumental was a one-bedroom flat, which we sold for a record price. On the first day of marketing, we had thirteen viewings, which generated four offers. The buyer was a plucky young woman who paid several thousand pounds above the asking price. We thought the buyer wanted the property as her home but later realised she'd bought it as a rental investment. When we calculated her mortgage repayments against the 5 per cent deposit she had, we found that they exceeded the forecasted rental income by around one hundred pounds a month. And that was based on an interest-only loan.

Like many novice investors at that time, the young woman in the above example was convinced that house prices would continue to rise. Paying above the asking price, then having to top up the rental income from your pocket in order to meet the monthly repayments doesn't sound like a prudent investment, does it? In saying that, at the time there were certain properties in our local market that were rising in value at a rate that blew away the national average. Year-on-year increases of 30 per cent were not uncommon, and so by that standard, is it any wonder that some of the braver buyers were being so bullish? The £220,000 that the young woman had paid could've easily been £240,000 the following year. Also, topping up the rental income with £1,200 a year of her own money would've been a minor inconvenience if she'd seen £20,000 increase during the same time.

Just a few weeks after the young woman completed her purchase, I left the estate agency business to embark on a different career. A couple of months after that, the credit crunch hit. The young lady kept her flat, but I don't expect she saw its equity increase the way she'd hoped.

So, what makes a good property investment, and where and how do you find one? Let's take a look.

Simply put, a savvy property dealer or developer looks to buy a house, flat, building, or land at price at which they could make an instant profit selling it. For example, the market value of a house that's deemed to be in good condition is £200,000. Let's say that the property requires refurbishment, which will cost £30,000. The end user looking for a home, whether they're a builder or just particularly adept at DIY, may pay around £170,000 for the property (other costs such as stamp duty have been excluded). Doing so would allow them to improve the property to their taste, and if they're careful, be left with a refurbished home at market value.

The professional speculator, on the other hand, would be unlikely to pay more than £130,000 for that same house. With the many variants that come into play—market conditions and the type of property involved, to name but two—it's hard to say what profit margins developers look for. If I could give you a general figure, based on my experience, I'd say around 30 per cent is what these guys and girls look for, but once again, that depends on many things. Mind you, I've heard of dealers buying a property at £200,000, then turning it for £220,000, just a 10 per cent gross return. I'll explain what turning (also known as flipping) a property is in a moment, but now, let's have a look at where the pros get their stock from.

## Estate agencies

Of the numerous sources for finding a deal, for the newbie investor I'm afraid an estate agency is not one of them, and for many reasons. Firstly, estate agencies are always battling against each other for instructions. And in their tussle for business, estate agencies are more likely to appraise properties optimistically, rather than for a quick or forced sale. After all, an estate agent's job is to achieve the best possible price for their client and not to scout bargains that will line the pockets of property entrepreneurs, although, sadly the latter does happen.

Secondly, on those rare occasions where a seller is willing to forgo a few thousand pounds in exchange for a quick sale to a cash buyer, why should the estate agent contact you, the novice? I'll tell you now that every seasoned estate agent in the country has a contact on their books who could probably buy any property for cash and exchange contracts within twenty-four to forty-eight hours. On top of that, such contacts are likely to give the agent back the property as an instruction once it's been refurbished or developed. Furthermore, it's no secret that some of these developers may show their gratitude to the agent with an illicit cash gift contained within a brown envelope. We'll talk more on this subject in a moment.

So with the above in mind, if a seller wants to dispose of a property to someone who can complete the sale in a matter of days, why should the agent offer it to a newbie? Why should they give the deal to a buyer who may take a week just to decide what amount to offer?

Experienced property developers know their respective local markets very well; they can't afford not to. These people are used to making quick decisions in order to freeze out their competitors. If offered a property on a particular road, chances are they probably already know the layout of the building, having seen comparable ones previously. At a glance they'll estimate refurbishment costs, usually quite accurately. If an area is known for subsidence, you can bet that the developers will know which roads are worst affected. Where certain flats have particularly ominous leases, the developers may already be aware of this.

The other point to remember is that successful property developers are likely to have a team of professionals behind them—solicitors, surveyors, and architects—whose trusted advice can aid a quick decision to buy. For example, one gentleman snapped up a large two-bedroom, first-floor flat at a price that at first appeared to leave no potential for profit at all. Not only did the property require complete refurbishment, but it also had a low lease. When this savvy developer looked at the property, he saw potential to extend it into two flats using the loft space. The solicitor acting for this man obtained a quote from the freeholder to extend the lease. The end result was two newly refurbished flats, a two-bedroom flat on the first floor and a one-bedroom loft apartment on the second floor, on which he made a tidy profit. While everyone else was viewing the property and getting estimates in order to prepare their offer, he'd already agreed a sale.

I once saw a whistle-blowing documentary on BBC1, where a journalist went under-cover to work as an estate agent. One agent was caught on camera telling a pseudo-developer how much of a "drink" he wanted to ensure the developer got a dilapidated flat at a bargain price. The negotiator also insisted on the property being given back to the estate agency as an instruction once refurbishment was complete. Rather cheeky, don't you think?

So, once again, why would an estate agent offer a novice investor a property deal and get a thank you and maybe a bottle of Chianti in return, when a developer will give them an envelope stuffed with cash? Such illicit deals are unethical and illegal. Here's why. Firstly, an estate agent must act in the interest of the client, the one paying the commission. If both buyer and seller are paying a fee, then who is defined as the estate agent's client?

Next, how likely is the agent to inform HM Revenue and Customs of the cash bonus he's not supposed to have received in the first place?

In every estate agency that I've known, staff engaging in the above activities faced immediate dismissal. Furthermore, many estate agencies would not permit their staff to buy through the firm properties that were intended for investment purposes. If an employee of the company wanted to buy a house or flat for themselves, an area director would have to inspect the property to ensure the correct market value was being offered to the seller. Once this point was established, the seller had to sign a disclaimer confirming their acceptance of the fact that their buyer was an employee of the estate agency marketing the property. In turn, the employee had to confirm in writing that should they wish to put the property back on the market within twelve months of having purchased it, they could only do so with the express permission of an area director. Such measures went a great way to improving the standards within estate agency.

In smaller estate agencies, where the directors or owners of the firm are also investors or landlords, they do buy property themselves from prospective or existing clients. There is nothing wrong with doing this, providing that the property has been correctly appraised, and the seller is fully aware of the agent's intentions. There have been numerous cases documented where agents were purposely appraising at below-market value in order to pass the property on to an associate, who in turn made a profit.

## Repossessions

I'm sure that the majority of people reading this book will know what a repossessed property is, so in this section, I'll be explaining exactly how estate agents market such properties.

Firstly, let me dispel the myth that repossessed houses or flats are bargain buys. They are not meant to be. When a bank or building society (mortgagee) repossesses a property, they have a duty to the defaulting borrower (mortgagor) to obtain the best possible price for that property. They do not simply look to recover the amount of mortgage outstanding and their costs in doing so, but they will attempt to obtain the market value of the property. For example, if a house has a £150,000 loan outstanding on it, but it is worth £200,000, the latter figure is what the lender will aim to achieve.

The misconception that repossessions can be vehicles to huge profits probably resulted from stories of illicit deals done by agents who abused the process to sell such properties for their own financial gain. And I'll talk more about that in a moment.

I remember taking calls from buyers who were enquiring about various repossessed properties on our books. I asked one of those buyers how they came to know that the property they'd enquired about was a repossession. The answer was that it was part of a monthly listing of repossessions that they'd subscribed to at a sum of fifty pounds a year. Interestingly, each of the properties this person enquired about had long since sold, so the information they'd paid for was considerably out of date.

Such was the interest created by the idea that buying and selling repossessions would get you rich quick.

So, with the above in mind, you may be asking why I have included repossessions in this chapter on investment property. Well, unlike other properties on the market for sale, a repossession must be sold. It's a forced sale. An individual putting their property up for sale may do so at an unrealistic price with the attitude that unless they get the inflated price, they won't sell. With a repossessed house or flat, the lender will try to obtain the best price, but if the market dictates different, the asking price will be lowered until a sale is effected. Furthermore, with repossessions, there are no chains involved. Someone wanting to buy such a property must be in a position to do so without having to rely on funds from the sale of another property.

One memorable scenario was the repossessed house that attracted offers from four different buyers. One of the offers stood £20,000 higher than the other three, but it was immediately rejected by the lender, because the buyer had a property to sell.

Once a buyer's offer was agreed, they were given a deadline of twenty-eight days in which to get contracts exchanged. Any delays outside of the buyer's control were always taken into account. Also, throughout all my years of dealing with repossessions, I never saw a lender gazump a buyer who was doing what was requested of them.

Let's now take a look at the estate agent's role in marketing a repossessed property.

Repossession is seen as a lender's last resort for recovering outstanding arrears on mortgage repayments. A court must be satisfied that all attempts to prevent repossession have been exhausted prior to issuing the order to proceed. I will not go into the specific steps involved, but there are a set of rules known as the "pre-action protocol" that must be followed by both mortgagee and mortgagor before a repossession order is granted.

During the above process, the lender will have taken steps to establish the approximate market value of the property in question. Exactly how this is done is by selecting the relevant estate agent from an approved panel and instructing them to carry out a "drive-by appraisal." What this means is that prior to repossession, the manager of the estate agency would, very discreetly, take a look at the exterior of the property and provide the lender with requested data. A form would be submitted, supported by comparable evidence, outlining the estate agent's recommendation on asking price, as well as what they thought the property was likely to sell for. Most of the drive-by appraisals we carried out did not come onto the market; I hope this meant that those people involved kept their properties.

If court proceedings got to the point where a repossession order was granted, we, the estate agents, were requested to attend the property on the day of eviction. The mortgagee would ask that we meet the bailiff fifteen minutes prior to the official time of eviction. During my entire career, I was only called on to complete this task a handful of times, and I detested every one of them.

The mortgagee would also instruct a plumber and locksmith to attend the eviction. The first would turn off the water supply to the property and drain the system down, removing the risk of pipes bursting during the cold winter weather. The locksmith would change the lock and provide us with a set of keys. Both the tradesmen in attendance would only commence their work once the bailiff had carried out the eviction and transferred possession of the property to us.

As you can imagine, an eviction is a horrible event to have to attend. A slight consolation (if we can call it that) was that with the majority of cases, the properties were already vacated, so there wasn't anyone there to evict. When this happened, we just followed the bailiff in to an empty building. Of course, there were some rather more tricky situations. The worst one I heard of was when a colleague went along to a repossession, and he and the other officials present were threatened with a meat cleaver. They didn't see the knife, but were told by a person standing behind the locked front door that they'd be hurt if they entered. Police were called to the property, where they found a frail, reclusive man but no weapons matching the one described in the threat.

The most difficult of evictions that I had to attend ended peacefully, although for one of the parties involved, it wasn't the happiest of endings. One was the repossession of an ex-council flat situated in a rather rough estate in North London. When I arrived at the property, I was greeted by the tradesmen, who assumed I was the bailiff. Minutes later, the bailiff turned up—all five foot six and nine stone of him! When there was no answer at the front door, the bailiff nodded to the locksmith to gesture the go-ahead to enter the building. Within seconds, we were walking around a property that had all the signs of a family that had been rushing to get to school and work that morning.

In the kitchen, the radio was on, and on the table were the remains of breakfast. "Someone wasn't expecting this!" said the six-foot-plus plumber in a nervous tone. Unknown to us at this point was the mob that was starting to gather outside the property. As we came back down the stairs of the maisonette, we were greeted by shouts. "You can't evict them, they've got kids. That's nasty!" It was then that I saw a true negotiator in action.

The bailiff instructed the locksmith to proceed with changing the lock but said the water was not to be drained from the property. The tradesmen were then sent on their way and were very grateful, too. Next, in a very calm yet assertive manner, the bailiff addressed the hostile crowd gathered on the doorstep. Even though I was in what you might call a state of hyper vigilance, I didn't hear exactly what the bailiff was saying; I was too busy scanning the crowd, which was gradually dispersing. The bailiff handed me the keys, and off I went, relieved, to say the least.

Later that day we were told that the mortgagee and mortgagor had reached an agreement, and we were to hand back possession of the property to the latter party. A chap in his thirties turned up at our office, just as we were closing, to collect his keys. Embarrassed by his predicament, this man told me that he had several failed entrepreneurial pursuits that led to him falling into arrears. Rather than worry his wife and children, he chose not to tell them of the eviction and tried his best to reverse the situation, which he eventually did. Talk about taking it to the wire! Wherever this family is today, I sincerely hope that they're happy and well and haven't had to endure the same circumstances again.

Towards the latter part of my career, we were no longer called on to attend evictions. Instead, the mortgagees would instruct specialist asset management companies who'd handle repossessed properties from eviction through to completion of the sale. Such companies would take the dirty work (for want of a better phrase) away from us. We would simply be given the keys to the property and instructions to commence marketing.

One day, I received a call from a very irate letting agent whose office was local to ours. The agent told me his tenants had come home to find that their locks had been changed; they couldn't access their home. Furthermore, there was a notice placed inside the porch window asking the previous occupants to contact our estate agency to arrange collection of their belongings. Unfortunately, while these tenants had been paying their monthly rent on time and in full, their landlord wasn't paying his mortgage. And he didn't tell anyone that he was about to be repossessed. So a working mother returned from collecting her children from school to find that she and her family were homeless. Several calls were made, and we arranged for them to collect their belongings. Sadly, we were given strict instructions not to release the keys to them, so this family had to find a place to sleep that evening. As for the landlord, I was told that he owned numerous properties and lived somewhere in the Mediterranean, having retired several years prior.

Whether possession of a property came directly from the bailiff or through an asset management company, the procedure we had to follow next was the same. Firstly, we had to submit our recommendation on an asking price and also state what we thought the property was likely to achieve in the current market. Once again, where possible, we had to provide comparable evidence to support our appraisals. Next, a chartered surveyor would inspect the property to carry out a valuation. This would result in the surveyor submitting what was known as a "best price certificate," which was their recommendation on the minimum amount the property should be allowed to sell for on the open market. Once this process was complete, the mortgagee would confirm the asking price and give us the go-ahead to commence marketing.

It was very rare that any offers would be accepted in the first two weeks of marketing a repossession, except at the asking price. And even then, the lender or asset management company wanted to ensure that the property had been advertised at least twice before they looked to agree a buyer's offer.

Once an acceptable price was achieved for the property, the offer was usually subject to what was known as a seven-day notice or public notice. I'll explain what these terms mean.

Let's say the lender has agreed to an offer of £100,000 for a flat, subject to either one of the above notices. The estate agent may then be called on to advertise the amount of offer and invite other interested parties to exceed it. To my memory, the wording of a seven-day notice goes something like this:

### Flat A, 123 Avenue Road, Anytown, London

We, (estate agency), acting for mortgagees in possession of the above property, are in receipt of an offer of £100,000. Any interested parties wishing to exceed this amount should do so, in writing, to the above agents within seven days of this notice.

Estate Agency 321 High Road Anytown

Tel: 020 ____ ____

The wording of a public notice would be very similar, except that interested buyers are invited to offer on the property at any time until contracts have been exchanged. Now, this may not seem fair to the person who's offered £100,000, but you must remember that the lender is duty bound to obtain the best possible price for the property. By advertising an offer and inviting other buyers to exceed the amount, they are seen to have fulfilled their responsibility to the defaulting borrower to recover as much money as they can for the house or flat.

Sometimes, when a property attracted numerous good offers within the first fourteen days of marketing, the lender would be satisfied that the agent had generated enough interest in the property, allowing the seven-day notice to be skipped. The next stage in the process would be what was known as "sealed bids."

Any person having expressed interest in the repossessed property will be asked to submit their best and final offer in writing (sealed bid) to the estate agent within a defined deadline. A sealed bid should include the buyer's best offer and a breakdown of how they propose to pay for the property—cash, mortgage, etc. Although not always a requirement, it would aid the buyer's chances if they supplied details such as the contact name of the person arranging the finance and if cash, proof of funds. Some buyers would provide all of that information, plus their solicitor's details for verification. The offer letter would then need to be presented to the estate agent in a sealed envelope.

Let's say that the deadline for submitting a sealed bid was for midday the following Wednesday. On that day, at noon, all the envelopes collected would be opened, and the offers presented to the lender for their consideration. Usually, a couple of hours later, sometimes the next day, the lender would notify the estate agent as to which offer they'd accepted. The estate agent would then contact the successful buyer and inform them that their offer had been agreed. The agent would advise the buyer, orally and in writing, that acceptance of their offer was subject to them exchanging contracts within twenty-eight days of their solicitor receiving the contract from the lender's legal representatives.

While a sale is running on a repossession, the estate agent is required by the client to continue showing the property. The agent can, however, exercise discretion as to the suitability of the buyers to whom they show the property. For example, if a buyer is dependent on the sale of another property, the agent can refuse to show the repossession to them. Any offers made on the property must be submitted to the lender, orally and in writing, the same day.

I must point out that with the dozens of repossessed properties that I dealt with; never did I see a lender switch a buyer for one who made a higher offer. Once the lender had accepted an offer, providing that the buyer was proceeding with their purchase, any other offers (some higher) were held in reserve. I always felt that the repossession departments of banks and asset management companies were firm, but very fair. Everyone knew where they stood with them.

Earlier, I mentioned stories of estate agents who abused their responsibility in handling the sale of repossessions. So, before we move on from this subject, here are a few tales of how certain agents flouted the system for marketing such properties; some were exposed in the press, others within the companies where I worked.

First and foremost is the story of an office manager who'd rented out one of the repossessed flats that he was entrusted to sell. This chap's demise came about when the property went under offer, and the surveyor attempting to carry out the survey stumbled on the tenants.

The manager had given his staff strict instructions that they were to notify him as soon as the survey appointment had been booked on that particular flat, and that's exactly what they did.

The problem arose when the surveyors' office received a cancellation, allowing them to bring the survey date forward a day. With the surveyor aware of the property being vacant, he phoned the estate agency to say he'd be in the area shortly and asked if he could collect the keys. As the manager was out of the office, the negotiator who took the call saw nothing out of the ordinary with the surveyor's request and signed out the keys to him. When the manager returned to the office and realised what had happened, he became very agitated.

An hour or so later, the surveyor called the estate agency to say he wouldn't be proceeding with the survey on account of what he thought were squatters living in the property. The occupants of the flat were not squatters but four builders of Eastern European origin. The rumours were that the estate agency manager offered the men cheap, short-term accommodation in return for their work on a refurbishment project that he was involved in. While this was never proved, the manager admitted to providing the men with access to the property and was immediately dismissed for doing so.

Another estate agency manager was caught giving inside information on sealed bids to his preferred buyer. When a repossessed property went to the sealed bid stage, the manager would open all the envelopes prior to the deadline and know what all parties were prepared to pay. The agent would then telephone his associate and advise him of what the highest offer was. The associate would be parked around the corner from the office with his handwritten letter and the offer amount blank.

As soon as the agent advised of the figure required to win the bid, the associate would fill in the correct amount and deliver the letter to the office precisely on the deadline. This eliminated the risk of other buyers turning up in time to make a higher offer. I never found out quite how this chap got caught, but as a result, a company-wide memo was sent out notifying of changes to the way sealed bids were dealt with. From that point forward, all offers had to remain in sealed envelopes, only to be opened by an area manager after the proposed deadline. In turn, the area manager would be the person putting all offers forward to the lender or asset management company dealing with the repossession.

Our next story is one of a very sly, cunning estate agent who greatly abused his position handling the sale of repossessed properties. While working as a branch manager, this chap also owned one or two other companies that benefitted considerably from the repossessions on the estate agency's books. I'll explain how.

Sometimes, the lender responsible for the repossession would require work done at the property. Such work could be anything from appointing the locksmith and plumber at the time of eviction, clearing the property of unclaimed belongings, or even general building maintenance. For example, where properties required immediate attention after storm damage, either for a damaged roof or a tree that collapsed on a neighbour's fence, the lender would ask us to obtain two separate quotes for repairs. We would contact local tradesmen, who'd inspect the property and provide written quotes, which we'd forward to the lender. The same day, the lender would accept one of the quotes and authorise us to instruct the tradesmen to commence repairs. Now, as the estate agent in our story owned a company that could carry out such work, guess whose quote was always accepted? This chap also dabbled in property development, so whenever a repossession went to sealed bids, he'd open everyone else's envelopes, check their offers, and then submit one of his own, usually the highest. Other buyers didn't get a chance.

No one knows how long this agent's activities went undetected or how much money he made; however, it was rumoured that he'd amassed quite a sizeable property portfolio. So when he was caught, dismissed, fined, and banned from working as an estate agent, he wasn't said to be too bothered.

Some years ago I watched a television documentary in which a team of negotiators working for a large estate agency were exposed for numerous illicit deals involving repossessed properties. These guys were reserving certain houses and flats for select buyers who, it was alleged, returned the agents' favours with cash gifts. I'll explain how they were reported to have done this and also what brought about the negotiators' demise.

The lenders in possession of a property require their approved estate agent to provide them with regular updates on the marketing of repossessed properties. Estate agents have to periodically supply the lenders with information, such as how many people have viewed the property and how many times it's been advertised. And just as with other properties, all offers must be put forward in writing the same day they are received.

The team of negotiators involved did not market the properties at all. They prepared the sales brochures, sent them to the lender for approval, but then kept the files in the back of the cabinets. As far as normal buyers were concerned, the properties didn't exist. The estate agents provided the lenders with falsified information on viewing figures and also created fake newspaper adverts of the properties, which they faxed to the lender. The agents' activities gave the impression that they were hard at work, marketing those properties. The fact that suitable offers were not made appeared to be due to the repossessions being overpriced for current market conditions, not to anything the estate agent did or didn't do. Perhaps this sentiment was aided at the time by press releases from the country's largest mortgage lenders reporting monthly declines in house prices.

As time goes by, if such a property hasn't sold, the lender will examine their position. They will take recommendations from the estate agent, but most important, they will consult the surveyor who provided the valuation. The procedure then would be to reduce the asking price; however, if several price reductions do not yield results, the property would then be disposed of at auction. Now, with our example, just prior to the lender taking the above action and removing the property from the open market, the estate agents would put forward an offer. With the property still hidden from normal buyers, the offer, a low one, would come from one of the agents' property developer associates. Perhaps after some negotiation, the developer would put forward a final offer; the decision whether to accept or reject the offer might go to the surveyor who issued the best price certificate. If the surveyor accepted the offer, the sale was agreed to the developer, often without a seven-day or public notice due to the length of time already elapsed in marketing the property. If the offer was rejected, the lenders might then draw a step closer to putting the property into auction.

The scam worked perfectly for these guys until one of the homeowners saw the property he was evicted from back on the market with the same agent. This time the flat's asking price was much higher than when the lender first instructed it to be marketed. The developers had carried out some minor refurbishment and then put it back up for sale with the agent who handled the sale at repossession. Further investigation by senior management found that the same developer had purchased numerous such properties via that estate agency office. The negotiators based at that office, two of whom were driving prestige cars way beyond the means of their official salaries, admitted to falsifying information, which included fabricating public notices that never went to press.

Much of what I've written about the marketing of repossessed properties has changed over recent years. Nowadays, the lenders and asset management companies that handle such properties tend to instruct two estate agents to sell them. Having more than one firm marketing a repossession greatly reduces the possibility of skulduggery like that mentioned above ever occurring. The agents are competing against each other for their commission, so attempting anything unethical would be futile. They'd lose out. Also worth pointing out is that the housing market is totally different today than it was at the height of repossessions in the early nineties. Gone are the days when a seven-day notice attracted just three sealed bids, certainly in London, anyway.

As I said earlier in this section, repossessions are not bargains; however, once the initial bidding is complete, they can be a straightforward way of buying a long-term investment at market value. The seven-day and public notices advertised in the property supplements of local papers usually relate to repossessions, so keep an eye out for these.

## Auctions

For a newbie investor who has the means, property auctions can be a great source for finding a good investment, if you know what you're doing. What you have to remember is that a property entered in an auction is likely to have a problem of some sort—structural or legal. Having said that, sometimes property owners just want a quick sale, and where that is the case, auction can be their best bet.

Auction rooms tend to be occupied mostly by property investors, many of whom are cash buyers. This doesn't mean that you have to have a huge bank balance in order to compete with these people. It is quite possible to buy at auction using a mortgage; however, there are risks involved.

In my career, the vast majority of properties I dealt with that went to auction were repossessions that didn't sell on the open market. There were a few people I knew who'd inherited dilapidated properties that they wanted to sell quickly, and so they sent them to auction.

Auctioneers have mailing lists to which interested parties can subscribe and receive a catalogue listing the properties featured in the upcoming auctions. The catalogue usually displays an image of the property as well as a brief description, viewing arrangements, and the guide price. The guide price is just that: a guide. In all my years as an estate agent and with all my contacts in the property industry, I only ever knew a handful of properties (in London) to not achieve considerably above their guide price at auction.

Viewing a property listed in a forthcoming auction is usually done via what is known as a "block viewing." A block viewing is a designated time slot where any interested parties can attend the property and have a look around it. As agents conducting block viewings for our auctioneers, we'd be present to show the property between two and three o'clock three days a week in the run-up to the auction. Prospective buyers were asked to attend during those times on any of those days.

I met all sorts of people at block viewings. There were guys who pulled up in open-back vans, looking like they'd just walked off a building site. Then there were the slick, suited, and booted property dealers, and the casually dressed middle-aged couple looking to expand their pension portfolio. Amongst the people present, there'd always be one who felt the need to point out the property's defects—rather loudly and for all to hear. At the block viewing, this person would let it be known that he thought the guide price was far too high and so on. However, on the day of the auction, he'd usually be in the front row, frantically seeking the auctioneer's attention. Look out for that sort on any block viewings you attend.

Every property listed for auction will usually have what's known as a legal pack, which supplies information relating to the property's title. It's quite important for anyone interested in the property to ensure they know the contents of the legal pack. For example, the property may have covenants that could potentially affect its value and if so, the legal pack should list them. Usually, the legal pack is all that the auctioneers will supply. If a prospective buyer wishes to carry out a local authority search, for example, they'll need to do it themselves.

At the auction, buyers register their details in order to bid. Should a buyer's bid be successful, they will enter into a legally binding contract to purchase the property. To do this they'll need to put down a 10 per cent deposit there and then. The buyer will then be required to complete the purchase (pay the balance) no later than twenty-eight days from the day of the auction. And this is why buying at auction with a mortgage is risky. I'll explain why using an example of someone who did just that—and successfully, I might add.

A repossessed flat that we were marketing was sent to auction. A buyer approached us to find out when the block viewing was scheduled for. This man had already obtained the legal pack, which his solicitor had looked over. Searches were applied for as well, at a further cost. The buyer had also got his mortgage in place, agreed in principle and subject to him finding a property. A few weeks prior to the auction date, a surveyor called us, wanting to carry out a mortgage valuation on behalf of the lender that the buyer was using. So on the day of auction, the buyer had already paid out for a mortgage valuation, solicitor's fees, and various searches. When he went to the auction, he took along a 10 per cent deposit of his maximum bid and a mortgage offer for the other 90 per cent. The man's bid was successful, so he put down the 10 per cent, and the mortgage offer meant the lender would provide the balance, through his solicitor, twenty-eight days later, thus completing the purchase.

What if the buyer mentioned above was outbid? Well, he would've been out of pocket to the tune of several hundred pounds. To a degree, the same would apply to a professional property developer paying cash. They too would've paid out in legal fees prior to the auction and may have also enlisted the services of a surveyor to confirm the sound structure of the building. The only difference is that, as mentioned earlier, developers usually have a team of relevant experts whom they retain, who probably charge them less for their services than they would us. Also, if buying with cash, you don't have to rely on the lender issuing the mortgage offer prior to you bidding at auction. One woman rather foolishly did this. Winning her bid at auction, she put down the 10 per cent deposit and then went chasing her lender for the mortgage offer. I never heard what happened to her, but if she failed to complete the purchase, she risked losing her deposit.

As said, auctions can be a great source for finding investment properties and picking up a good deal; maybe even a bargain, if you know what you're doing.

## Probate sales

I am not qualified to discuss the legal aspects behind the sale of a probate property but basically, probate is the process of administering the estate of a deceased person.

The last will and testament of a person who has passed away (if they created one) names the beneficiaries of the estate as well as the person nominated as the executor. An executor carries out the directions of the will, which include the disbursing of the deceased's possessions to the named beneficiaries. A person creating a will can appoint anyone they wish to act as executor. No legal qualifications or experience are required, although sometimes people choose a solicitor to act in the role of executor.

Where a property forms part of an estate, it is the executor's decision as to which agent is instructed to act in the sale. I've known occasions when two agents were involved but also when the property was sold directly to a buyer and not through an estate agent at all. We'll talk about that shortly.

Most of the probate properties that I dealt with once belonged to elderly people before they passed away. Many of those houses and flats required complete refurbishment, and even the well-maintained ones were a little dated. This was always factored into our appraisal. Hence, at first glance, such properties appeared to be competitively priced, which in turn, attracted a lot of interest. Executors would come to us either directly or sometimes via recommendation from a solicitor to whom we were known who was handling probate.

Which estate agents the executor instructs and how he or she goes about it differs with each case. Some executors just want to fulfil their role and get the property sold quickly, while others, perhaps having an emotional attachment to the house, may adopt a different approach. Like other sellers, executors may invite appraisals from a number of estate agents. They may then confer with the will's beneficiaries on the suggested asking price and which agent(s) to instruct. As mentioned, one executor I knew (a solicitor) instructed two agents, us and one other, and we shared the commission. Incidentally, we did all the work in that transaction. The other agency just put their feet up, even giving keys to a buyer to view the property alone, as they couldn't be bothered to escort them.

Anyway, moving along, once the asking price and terms were agreed, we would market probate properties much in the same way as any other instruction. The only difference was whether probate had already been granted before a sale was agreed. Grant of probate can be a lengthy process. I've known situations where people proceeded with the purchase of such a property only to encounter lengthy delay waiting for probate to be granted. In many cases, the buyer's mortgage offer expired and had to be reissued.

Can probate properties make good investments? Sometimes they can, but it varies with each case, and like any other property, it all depends on the price paid. There were times when the executor and beneficiaries insisted on marketing at a higher price, which left the property unsold for nearly a year. In contrast, the beneficiaries of one property hardly knew the elderly aunt that had left it to them. They had no emotional attachment to their relative or her home and were happy to sell it to a cash buyer at a discount in return for a speedy transaction.

I remember selling a maisonette to a man who in turn was selling a large detached house that had been left to him by his elderly parents. When we asked for chain details, we found that he hadn't sold through an estate agent and that the buyer, a property developer, was introduced through the solicitor, who was also the estate's executor. It transpired that the developer had obtained planning permission to demolish the house and build six flats on the site. On the morning when contracts were due to be exchanged, the developer revised his offer by £30,000. The beneficiary of the property, not wanting to disrupt the chain and risk losing the maisonette, agreed to the price reduction, albeit begrudgingly. Remember, that rather unscrupulous property developer was introduced to the beneficiary by the solicitor and executor of his parent's estate.

Sometimes, probates properties attract substantially enough interest to warrant best and final sealed-bid offers. It's worth pointing out, though, that unlike repossessions, the executors may not take the same calculated decisions made by lenders or asset management companies. I've known buyers to make a best and final offer that wasn't enough; only for them to return with an increased best and final offer. Lenders dealing with repossessions will not entertain such antics, whereas executors may do so and create problems in the process.

## The dealer network

Some investment properties, the bargain deals you hear about, may never reach the open market; they are offered around networks of property developers and dealers.

Sources of such properties could be surveyors, solicitors, accountants, liquidators, or even estate agents. As an alternative to putting the property into auction, they offer it out to professional investors, capable of performing a quick cash purchase. In such deals, there may often be a middleman or "runner," as they're also known (not someone wearing Nike shoes). A runner will seek out such properties, which they introduce to their dealer contacts in return for a finder's fee.

One property dealer, after building a decent portfolio of rental properties, stopped buying any more houses or flats himself. Preferring to pass on the deals to his peers at a fee of around £5,000 a time, it was estimated that he averaged two sales a month. A tidy income, wouldn't you say?

A property developer was offered a plot of land that had planning consent to build eight flats. The runner's commission on that transaction was a whopping £100,000, which was paid by cheque in a legitimate deal, not using a suitcase full of fifty-pound notes in an illicit meeting. So as you can see, these guys can make a seriously good living from sourcing land and property bargains then passing them on to cash-ready investors.

Rather than buying a building to refurbish or passing a deal on to another investor for a finder's fee, some dealers will turn a property for profit. I'll explain what the term turning a property means.

Let's say that a property becomes available via one of the above-mentioned sources. It's a three-bedroom house requiring complete refurbishment. In good order, the average market value for this home is £350,000–£360,000. Unfortunately, this property will need at least £30,000 worth of improvements to get it to that level. The property owner wants a quick sale; however, the next auction isn't for a month. Also, the auctioneers have suggested a guide price of £250,000 with the aim of achieving a sale at around £275,000; however, the owner wants more.

An associate introduces the owner to a property developer who may be interested in buying the house for cash in a quick sale. Also, selling the property this way will not incur fees for its owner, as it would if he sold it at auction.

After some negotiation, a sale is agreed at £285,000. On top of that figure, the developer also has to pay the stamp duty at a rate of 3 per cent, which works out to £8,550. Then there are the solicitor's fees and other disbursements, which could be another

£1,000. Finally, the developer may also be paying a finder's fee to the person who introduced him to the seller, so let's factor in another £5,000. In total, the property developer has paid £299,550.

So, the developer has paid just under £300,000 for a property that requires another £30,000 to be spent on it in order to achieve £360,000 on the open market. Put another way, if everything goes according to plan, with no additional refurbishment costs (rarely the case) this developer would have spent £329,550 for a return of less than 10 per cent profit. And this doesn't include resale costs of estate agency and the solicitor's fees.

On the surface, the above may not appear to be a wise investment. However, if the developer risked just under £40,000 of his own money in order to make a gross profit of £30,000, you wouldn't think it such a bad deal after all, would you? For those of you intrigued, I'll explain how professional property speculators pull off such transactions.

When the developer exchanges contracts with the seller, he'll do so using a 10 per cent deposit, which in this case is £28,500. The developer may also request a delayed completion, perhaps sixty days as opposed to the standard twenty-eight days after exchange of contracts. Let's say that at this point, the developer, using his network of contacts, finds a buyer for the property who will pay £330,000. The developer's aim is to exchange contracts with the buyer and complete the sale on the same day when he's due to complete with the owner of the property. In other words, the developer uses his buyer's money to pay for the property and keeps the difference—the profit. This is what's known in the industry as turning a property or a back-to-back transaction.

A solicitor told me that while such deals are not illegal, they are very much frowned on because of the risk they carry. Using our example, if the developer did not find a buyer, or his buyer could not complete within the required timescale, he would have required available funds to complete the sale himself. That being the case, the developer would've been in the position we mentioned earlier, investing £330,000 for a gross profit of less than 10 per cent.

Another possibility in such a deal, one that can also bring disastrous consequences, is if the owner of the property withdraws from the sale after contracts have been exchanged between the other two parties. Imagine the legal mess such an action would cause.

Buying and selling properties in the way I have just described is something best left to seasoned speculators. I have provided a very basic example of how such transactions are carried out, and there may be variations on how such deals are done. I'm not an expert on the subject of turning properties for profit, and I've never done it myself. What I will say is that during my career, I saw it happen countless times, but not by amateur investors or those lacking steely nerves. If this is something that interests you, then seek the advice of a suitably qualified solicitor.

In bringing this chapter to a close, the best advice I can offer to an aspiring property developer looking to get their hands on a good deal is to network. Make contacts. Get on auctioneers' mailing lists, subscribe to their catalogues, attend block viewings, and visit the auctions. Get a feel for how things work. Talk to people. Meet property dealers and developers. Speak to solicitors and surveyors and let them know you're in the market for decent investment deals.

The same applies to local estate agents; try to build a rapport with some of them and maintain regular contact. As mentioned earlier, chances are that you'll not find the right property through the agencies on your high street, but who's to say they don't hear of deals going on in different areas? I left the estate agency business many years ago, and my list of industry contacts has diminished; however, even now, I still get to hear of decent land and property deals going on.

One last point on building a network of estate agent contacts: whatever you do, don't swagger into an office, blurting stuff like, "Find us a deal, and I'll sort you a drink!" Estate agents hear this sort of thing almost on a daily basis. Be a bit more subtle, get to know the managers and sales negotiators of the different companies, and see what happens. I'm not saying you'll like or get on with all of them; chances are you won't. However, just doing that first deal can open the door to many others. And even if you pay a slightly higher price for that property than an experienced developer would, as long you still make a profit, the important thing is that you're in. The next phone call may be for a bigger, better deal, and you may even get to meet the dealers behind such deals. Good luck!

# 14. Naughty Negotiators and the Property Public

This chapter is a collection of stories about some of the funny things that I've seen and heard of during my time in estate agency. Some are tales of the crazy antics of certain negotiators, while others reveal the sometimes zany behaviour of the general public when viewing, buying, or selling property. So, if you're ready to be amused, maybe even shocked, let's move on.

Our first yarn is about a sales negotiator carrying out a viewing appointment of a three-bedroom house. The estate agency where he worked was provided with a set of keys by the owners, so the property could be shown during office hours, when they were at work.

The young man tasked with carrying out the viewing arrived at the property just a few minutes ahead of the prospective buyers. While standing outside the house waiting for his people to turn up, the negotiator broke wind, and in doing so, he got a bit more than he bargained for. "Follow through" I believe is the slang for this chap's predicament.

With soiled underwear, the estate agent greeted the buyers and proceeded to show them around the three-bedroom semi. At the end of the viewing, the two parties agreed to speak again later and bade one another farewell. Once the buyers drove away, the agent returned to the property. The young man went upstairs to the bathroom, where he removed his underpants and began cleaning them in the shower, using shampoo. Moving into the bedroom, he found the property owner's hair-dryer, which he used to dry the now clean garment, which he put back on. Then he left the house to make his way back to the office. The owners were none the wiser of the day's events, and the people who viewed the property ended up buying it.

Our next story is of a high-achieving sales negotiator who was making good progress in his estate agency career. After just a few months of experience in the business, this chap's managers considered him ready to commence appraising people's homes. Training for this role would be conducted by the office manager or a senior colleague, whom the negotiator would accompany to market appraisals. At properties, new recruits would observe the more experienced agents present the company to sellers, and they were also taught how to measure rooms and describe the key features of the building.

One day, a woman popped into the estate agency to say she was thinking of selling her flat and wanted to know how much she could get for it. A senior negotiator took down all the relevant details, and a time and date for the appraisal was agreed.

The prospective seller left a set of keys with the estate agency, as she was rather busy at work and would not be able to attend the appointment. This created a good opportunity for the trainee negotiator to practice measuring the property and writing up its description at his leisure.

At the flat, the negotiator and his senior colleague had a quick look around and then set about taking notes. When the pair attended previous appraisals together, the trainee would be instructed as to how to measure the rooms, while the senior negotiator gave a commentary on the features he was jotting down. On this occasion, because the seller wasn't present, there were no time constraints, so the roles were reversed, allowing the less experienced negotiator to take his time noting the property's features.

In the bedroom, the senior negotiator read the dimensions out to his colleague and then entered the en-suite shower room for a quick browse. As he walked back into the bedroom, he noticed his colleague's furtive movement away from the laundry basket located behind the door. "What are you doing? What's that in your hand?" asked the senior negotiator in quick succession. The trainee, looking very embarrassed, had been caught trying to steal a pair of knickers from the seller's laundry basket. Apparently, the young negotiator had a fetish for worn female undergarments, and his role as an estate agent allowed him to expand his collection by taking such items from the homes of sellers.

Our following tale stays with the theme of lingerie and the training of new negotiators, although this one doesn't expose the weird habits of certain estate agents.

In the mid-nineties, I worked as a senior negotiator in a busy high-street branch of a large corporate estate agency. An easy-going personality, good communication skills, and a great sense of humour made me quite popular with my peers. Younger members of the sales team would look up to me and were comfortable approaching me when they needed assistance. So when it was considered time for a trainee negotiator, whom we'll call Dave, to be shown how to appraise properties, I was the ideal candidate for the job.

Dave was an honourable guy who, prior to becoming an estate agent, had served in the armed forces. After achieving his sales targets consistently for several months, our manager asked me to start taking Dave along to selected market appraisals. One such appointment was for a Miss X, who had a garden flat she wanted to sell. The young woman was not going to be present but told us to go along to the property, where her boyfriend would be available to greet us and show us around, although he did neither.

Dave and I walked up the garden path and rang the doorbell. A man in his thirties, with slicked-back hair and forearms that read "Millwall" answered the door. I introduced myself and presented my business card to him. The man looked us up and down then grunted something which we took to mean we could go in.

Another grunt signalled that we could show ourselves around the property. Miss X's boyfriend rolled a cigarette and went off to the kitchen to put the kettle on. Unsurprisingly, he didn't offer us a cup of tea.

Working our way around the property, we moved into the bedroom and began noting its key features. When taking down the dimensions of a room, we'd measure from wall to wall. So where a fitted wardrobe covered most of a wall, we'd measure to the inside of it, but before opening its door to do so, we would always request the seller's permission. We did this out of courtesy, because people keep all sorts of things in their wardrobes that they may want to remain private. However, on this occasion, since the seller's boyfriend was quite hostile, we didn't ask. Also, as there were two of us, measuring into the wardrobe would've taken seconds. We took a chance.

I held one end of the steel measuring tape against one wall, while Dave fed the other into the back of the wardrobe. I noted the width of the room, and as the tape retracted, it snagged a satin lace item, which flew across the room and landed on the floor. We both stared at what looked like a suspender belt lying in the middle of the room and then looked up at each other and simultaneously said, "Oh shit!" Do we pick it up and put it back, risking the boyfriend walking in and finding Dave clutching his girlfriend's undies, or do we leave it lying on the floor on display? The decision to act was over in a second, as Dave kicked the item under the bed and out of sight. We completed our appraisal and left the flat. To this day, I wonder what Miss X thought when she found her suspender belt under the bed. Did she think we put it there, or that her boyfriend was a cross-dresser?

Early on in my career, I was introduced to a negotiator who worked for the same company as myself but was based at a different branch. My fellow employee was an attractive young woman who excelled at her job and was considered by everyone to be a rising star. The only concern amongst management was that her choice of business attire was a little too provocative. On two occasions, her manager (another female) had to have a quiet chat about the low-cut tops and skirts worn high above the knee. The company's dress code for male and female negotiators was conservative. Personal security was paramount for any negotiator when showing strangers around empty properties; however, when the negotiator was a pretty young woman wearing a skimpy and revealing outfit, this was more worrying.

So, when our colleague was two hours late coming back from a viewing appointment, her manager decided to call the police. Just as she lifted the handset to dial, in walked the negotiator, wearing her signature super-mini and a huge grin; totally oblivious to her colleagues' concerns. The manager took the negotiator into a private office and asked her to explain why she took over two hours to show a flat that was less than a mile away. Below is the story she was told.

The young lady had got herself involved in a rather complicated love triangle. Both she and her flatmate were having an affair with the same man—a married man. My wayward colleague could not see that man at his home, nor could she meet with him at her flat. So the little minx would ask her male friend to pose as a property buyer, enabling them to conduct their illicit meetings in sellers' flats. Apparently, she was let off with a stern but unofficial warning, and the matter did not go beyond her manager.

Over the years, I heard many other stories of estate agents abusing their responsibility with empty properties. As mentioned in a previous chapter, one estate agency manager rented out a property that didn't belong to him. In another incident, a negotiator gave the keys to an empty flat to a friend who was organising a Saturday night poker game. There was also the story of an agent who had the audacity to host a stag party—strippers and all—in a seller's property.

Fortunately, the above are isolated incidents, and the vast majority of estate agents treat their clients' properties with respect. Next, let's take a look at how some members of the public behave when buying, selling, and viewing property.

An elderly lady, carrying several shopping bags, walked into an estate agency and asked to view one of the houses advertised for sale in the front window. The negotiator who greeted her provided the sales particulars and asked the lady about her specific requirements and whether she had to sell a property in order to buy this one. The woman wasn't very forthcoming with information. She told the negotiator that she really wasn't sure if she would indeed move home, and at present she only wanted to view that one property. The negotiator took the keys for the house, and although he was still unsure as to how serious a buyer the elderly woman was, he led her to his car and drove to the property.

At the house, the negotiator opened the front door for the woman, who walked in, still carrying her shopping bags. After taking a quick glimpse of the lounge and kitchen, she shook her head, turned to the negotiator, and said, "No. It's not for me. I won't bother looking at the upstairs." With that, she made her way out of the property and walked past the negotiator's car.

"Don't you want a lift back to the office?" asked the negotiator.

"No, it's all right, love, that's my house there!" replied the elderly woman, pointing to a property across the road.

The negotiator involved is still convinced that the old woman wasn't remotely interested in the house, not even to have a nose around, and that her motive for viewing was a free lift home.

On the subject of people nosing around at property viewings, one of my pet hates was buyers opening cupboards and wardrobes. Some people would ask permission before doing so, but even then, I wondered what they hoped to achieve by looking into a kitchen cupboard. The man in our next story got a little more than he bargained for.

We were marketing a repossession that was in very poor condition. The five-bedroom house was rented room by room, and it became evident to us that the landlord didn't inform his tenants that he was being repossessed. On several occasions, we turned up to show the property only to find that someone had broken in. It was the tenants, wanting to collect their belongings, and they couldn't be bothered to follow the correct procedure. Perhaps they were angry, maybe they worked long hours and weren't able to meet us there during our office hours, I don't know. Nonetheless, they took matters into their own hands.

Anyway, we now had an empty property to try to sell. On my very first viewing there, I noticed a very pungent smell coming from the kitchen. As soon as I opened the door to that room, the stench would hit me. It was a gaseous smell that would reach right into my stomach, making me feel really nauseated. At first, I thought it might have been the decomposing carcass of a rat, but I didn't see any flies, and it was summer. In the end I found out that someone had left what looked like a curry in the fridge. And the fridge had been inactive since the electricity was cut weeks prior to visiting the house.

When showing the property, just before opening the kitchen door, I'd warn prospective buyers and prepare them for the odour. My warning also served to excuse me from entering the kitchen or explaining why I'd walk straight through and out into the garden where people could see me and ask any questions. The smell was so bad that most people would heave. In fact it got to the point that each time a negotiator returned to the office after showing the property, we'd all ask if anyone had thrown up. One colleague even suggested we run bets on it.

One day I was showing the house to a scruffy-looking couple who just stood in the middle of the kitchen talking and asking me questions, seemingly oblivious to the unpleasant smell. I remember thinking, "My God. What's wrong with you? Can't you smell it?" In the end I just came out with it. "Sorry, do you mind if we talk in the garden? This smell is really bothering me." To my further surprise, they gave each other a puzzled look, shrugged their shoulders, and followed me to the garden.

On another occasion, I'd just shown the house to a buyer when a colleague phoned my mobile to ask if he could send along someone else to view. I agreed and waited outside for the person to arrive. A Mercedes pulled up, and two large men got out, wearing leather coats, looking like stereotypical KGB agents. They gave me a nod and walked straight past me and into the property. As was becoming protocol, I tried to warn them about the smell, but they seemed to ignore me. In fact, I found one of them to be very condescending. Whenever he asked me a question, he'd appear dismissive of my answer; turning his back to me when I replied.

Starting at one end of the kitchen, the more flippant of the two buyers began opening and shutting the fitted cupboards. Side-stepping from right to left, he made his way towards the fridge. As his hand grabbed the handle of the appliance, I was about to call, "No, don't do that!" Instead, I thought, "No, why should I spoil the surprise? Carry on, mate!" After all, I was now standing just outside the patio door to the garden.

The man opened the fridge and pow! It hit him. It was then that I learnt that just as people's sneezing is unique to them, so is their retching! This six-foot-plus, twenty-stone chap was now outside in the garden leaning against the wall making noises like a sea lion. I tried to warn him.

We didn't sell the property; the other agent involved did. As for the first person to lose their lunch due to the smell, it was one of our competitors.

Over the years, I showed properties to a couple of people who displayed kleptomania. One of these people was an actor, who, on his way out the front door at the end of a viewing, swiped a utility bill from a shelf. We were standing outside the house talking, and just as he bade me farewell and was about to walk off, I said, "I'm afraid I'm going to need that gas bill back." The thespian went bright red, smiled nervously, and handed the envelope back to me. The only motive I could think of for him taking it was that he wanted to write to the seller and offer him a private deal.

I was showing a rather large house to a family, when out of the corner of my eye, I saw one of the children put a silver ornament into his pocket. The father apologised profusely, and after that, we never heard from them again.

On another viewing, a prospective buyer took it on himself to browse the seller's record collection. On seeing something he liked, the man had the gall to ask me if the homeowner would mind him taking the item. In more extreme cases, we had central heating boilers go missing from repossessed properties. They were expertly removed and obviously not on the viewings when we were present.

Moving on to a different subject now—the private sale.

I went along to a market appraisal where the homeowner hoped to move out of the area to be closer to his preferred choice of secondary school for his son. As this is such a common motivation for people to move home, I felt we had a serious seller, and I was right, but not in the way I thought.

At the property, the gentleman greeted me and asked me to show myself around and take measurements and photos as required. This was yet another sign that the man was keen to sell. When I finished what I was doing, I had a brief chat with him on what I thought we could achieve for his property, marketing, and our general terms of business and fees. The prospective seller thanked me, and we agreed to speak again after two of my competitors had carried out their appraisals the next day. I went back to the office, routinely asked for an appraisal letter to be sent to the seller, and made a note to follow up with him in a couple of days.

As scheduled in my diary, I telephoned the seller to ask if he'd reached a decision as to which agent he was going to instruct. "Oh, I'm not selling through an estate agent. I'm going to sell it privately through one of the free newspapers. Would you be able to provide me with the photos and measurements you took?" Unbelievable! Obviously, I declined.

We were marketing a lovely, five-bedroom, Edwardian detached house that belonged to an elderly couple who were hoping to downsize home. The property had lots of original features but had fallen in to a state of disrepair. I arranged for a couple to see the property, and as the sellers would show the house, I sent the prospective buyers along at the agreed time that evening. The following day, I called them to see how they got on and what they thought of the property. I met with a very curt, "No, not our thing!" and never heard from them again. The following week, the owner of the house called to say that due to her husband's ill health, they'd decided a home move would be too stressful, so we could take the property off the market. We wished them well and did exactly as they requested.

Several months later, both couples were featured on the front page of a local newspaper in a story about how planned development works in the area had caused the sale of the property to collapse. The text below the photo of the very sad-looking elderly couple described how they'd lost their dream bungalow by not being able to sell their house. The photo of the younger couple I'd sent to the property months earlier told of how they'd lost over £1,000 in solicitors and surveyors fees trying to buy the house. A private deal, not so private after all.

Every now and then, we'd get a member of the public who felt they knew enough about selling houses to tell us how to do our job. One such example was the woman selling a three-bedroom semi located on a very sought-after road. We introduced a very polite couple to the property who were chain-free and had agreed to pay the asking price for it. We were given details of the solicitors handling the transaction, and we sent letters to all parties confirming the sale. Everything looked good.

The next day, the seller called to ask if we'd heard from the buyers' surveyor. I explained that it was a bit early, and we'd chase up on that in a few days. "Well, please do, as I don't want any unnecessary delay," said the seller in a polite yet assertive manner. At least the seller was really motivated, I thought.

Two days later, I telephoned the buyers, and they told me that they were meeting with their bank the next day to finalise their mortgage application and submit the survey/valuation fee. I eagerly called the seller to update her, and her response was: "Hmm, yes, they're dragging their heels, aren't they?"

"I wouldn't worry too much about it, Mrs X, your buyers are very keen to proceed, and these things can take a week or so to sort out," I replied. It was as if I'd thrown fuel on a flickering flame.

"When I bought my last property (she owned others), I arranged for the survey to be carried out the very next day. If you really want something, you'll get it done sooner!" she snapped.

"I'll express your concerns to Mr and Mrs Y," I said to my client. Of course I didn't do that, because she was being unreasonable, and I didn't want to upset good buyers.

The seller continued to telephone, almost on a daily basis, even speaking to my manager and telling him that she felt I wasn't acting in her best interests. My manager told me about the conversation, but he was fully aware of my efforts.

A week after the sale was agreed and confirmation letters went out, we received a call from the surveyor's office asking if they could inspect the property three days later. You can guess that this didn't sit well with the seller, who still complained as to why the surveyor couldn't visit sooner.

The survey was carried out, and the buyers called to say that they were in receipt of the report and were happy with its contents. The buyers also asked if it was possible to visit the property with their builder in order to get some estimates for the improvements they planned. Once again, I telephoned the seller, keen to tell her everything was moving along well. The lady answered the phone, and before I could finish my sentence, she said, "I'm sorry, but I've decided not to sell. Please pass on my apologies to what's their name!" And just like that, she put the phone down, and Mr and Mrs Y were several hundred pounds out of pocket and as bemused as we were.

Over the years I've seen lots of weird and wacky incidents, as I'm sure other estate agents have, too. I've been to properties where nude photos of its owners were displayed on the bedroom walls for all to see. In a different property, when asking the woman seller's permission to open her wardrobe to measure into it, she quite happily told me, "No problem, please excuse the toys!" And she wasn't talking about Lego.

One seller came across as a decent sort of chap, until he decided to clean his shotguns when we were showing a family around his house. Bad timing! Another man asked me to appraise his Victorian terraced house, which I thought was a little untidy until I entered the second bedroom which had several mounds of dog faeces around the carpet. "Sorry, we haven't had a chance to clear up after the baby," I was told. The baby was a two-year-old springer spaniel.

During my career as an estate agent, I got to meet many people from both sides of my desk. Whether they were buyers or sellers, colleagues or competitors, we were all involved in one of life's more stressful events, and I got to see first-hand how the weird and wacky, nasty and nice characters dealt with the stress. Most of the people I worked with were decent and honourable, others were downright devious, but to my knowledge, very few wanted to remain estate agents until they retired. It's a tough game.

And that, ladies and gentlemen, brings us to the end of this chapter and the end of the book. I hope that I've given you an insight into how estate agents operate, including the woes that working in the industry can bring. I also hope that you've enjoyed reading and that it may assist you with your first, next, or last home move. Remember, not all estate agents are the same. Just before we end, here's one last story to highlight that point.

Across the road from our office I saw two young men sitting on the flat roof of an apartment above one of our competitors' offices. Both were perched with their legs dangling over the side of the building, openly smoking a large joint, their stereo system facing out of the window blasting music. Next to them was a LET BY board that belonged to the estate agent, who was of dubious reputation, and which related to the tenancy these chaps had just taken out. Two weeks prior to this scene, the same tenants walked into our office, reeking of cannabis, and expressed interest in renting a similar flat we had on our books. Our director, who saw them walk in, quickly interjected to tell the young men that the flat was no longer available. When they left the office, the negotiator who greeted them looked at our boss, puzzled as to why he'd turn down potential business.

"I'm not putting that rabble into one of my clients' properties!"

It seems that the other agent didn't have the same dilemma.

Good luck with your property ventures.

Thanks for reading.

5507211R00193

Printed in Great Britain
by Amazon.co.uk, Ltd.,
Marston Gate.